"*God's Good World* is a very important bo
doctrine of creation has been missing—fror
from society at large—Jonathan Wilson sh
with our world is so feeble. He then lays the foundation for a much richer life
through showing the necessary connections between redemption and creation.
Most important, he shows how we can build on that trinitarian foundation—
in our attitudes towards the body, 'consuming,' the internet, business, and
much more—all in the light of transformed worship. All Christians should
read this book."

—**Loren Wilkinson**, Regent College,
Vancouver, British Columbia

"In the current discussions concerning the biblical doctrine of creation, we
often bypass what is most important to us as Christians as we debate issues
like the age of the earth or the length of the creation days. Jonathan Wilson
corrects this oversight as he masterfully guides us to a rich appreciation of God
as our Creator and Redeemer. Here we have a theologian who is committed to
Scripture, who is highly skilled as a biblical interpreter, and who knows that
theology must be connected to our lives. He enriches our knowledge of God
as well as ourselves and moves us to fresh wonder and worship."

—**Tremper Longman III**, Westmont College

"In the many years that I have taught a theology of creation course to undergraduate students, I have searched in vain for a substantial and accessible text
that would address the whole range of ingredient topics: God the Creator;
the world as creation; the human creature; creation-care; the New Creation;
biblical interpretation; theology and science; and so on. My search is over. This
beautifully organized and winsomely written book by Jonathan Wilson far
exceeds my hopes. From the opening chapters on how the doctrine of creation
has gone 'missing' in church, through the bracing central chapters on doctrine
and Scripture, all the way to the moving meditation on bodies near the end,
this volume captivates, instructs, challenges, and delights. It will become the
standard text on creation for years to come."

—**Douglas Harink**, King's University College, Edmonton; author,
1 & 2 Peter in the Brazos Theological Commentary on the Bible

"Wilson is right; the modern church has been 'missing basic research on the
doctrine of creation.' As a result, we modern Christians have very often fallen
prey to or even been cheerleaders for many of the most self-destructive habits
of our age. This book should be mandatory reading for pastors, theological

students, and believers who care about the burning moral issues of our day and want to rethink them theologically."

—**Brian Brock**, King's College, University of Aberdeen

"In *God's Good World: Reclaiming the Doctrine of Creation*, Jonathan Wilson weaves together the stories of creation and redemption. By letting trinitarian creation and redemption in Jesus Christ cast mutual light on each other, Wilson piercingly diagnoses the brokenness of contemporary church, academy, and society. He then offers a beautiful corrective—in which Jesus Christ is the *telos*, the ultimate purpose, for person and community. Consistently addressing creation through Christ's redemption, *God's Good World* is a mature, robust work with the added gift of some profound moments of autobiography."

—**Philip Rolnick**, University of St. Thomas

"Jonathan Wilson's scholarly and comprehensive work insists that the goal of creation can only be understood in Christ and that redemption reaches all things. His careful research has established significant and original connections to a wide variety of related topics but also provides a vital commentary on numerous other authors as well as on scripture itself. *God's Good World* is a major contribution to the growing literature on a doctrine that has been sadly neglected until recently, but it is charged with hope. Anyone who wants to discover the rich resource that Christian theology provides both the church and our world as we face acute environmental challenges will be grateful for this timely book."

—**Peter Harris**, founder, A Rocha

GOD'S GOOD WORLD

RECLAIMING THE DOCTRINE OF CREATION

Jonathan R. Wilson

Baker Academic
a division of Baker Publishing Group
Grand Rapids, Michigan

Published by Baker Academic
a division of Baker Publishing Group
P.O. Box 6287, Grand Rapids, MI 49516-6287
www.bakeracademic.com

Printed in the United States of America

Library of Congress Cataloging-in-Publication Data is on file at the Library of Congress, Washington, DC.

ISBN 978-0-8010-3881-5

13   14   15   16   17   18   19   7   6   5   4   3   2   1

Contents

Introduction

Climate change. Economics. Sexuality. Justice. Gene therapy. Bioethics. Famine. Energy use. Diminishing oil supplies. Alternative energy. Violence. Evolution. Torture. Incarceration. Ecology. And so much more.

All of these are urgent concerns for those of us alive in the early decades of the twenty-first century, not only for ourselves but also for those who will come after us. Books on these topics pour out from publishers, articles on these issues appear on the front pages of newspapers, and conversations fill the blogosphere. For Christians, all these concerns relate to our beliefs about "creation." But when we look for guidance from our doctrine of creation, we find relatively few resources. Yes, we have a lot of books on these urgent issues. But we are missing "basic research" on the doctrine of creation. Our situation is like that of a medical team trying to treat a patient who is experiencing multiple organ failure without knowing what is causing the failures. Or perhaps the team knows that something called a "virus" is attacking the patient, but the team does not know which virus is attacking, much less how it works.

In our circumstances, we are not helped by the familiar debates over "creation." It does not help us make our way through this world and the urgent issues of our times to know how long ago "this world" was made. Or how long God took to make it. Or precisely what means God used to bring the world into being. These questions may be fascinating puzzles for some people, but answers to them do not constitute a doctrine of creation that articulates our convictions about God's world, who this God is, how we find life, and the purpose of creation that teaches us the way of life.

We are poor in resources for a doctrine of creation that could guide our life today because Christian theology began to abandon the doctrine of creation about 250 years ago. We have not totally neglected the doctrine—there have been some bright spots in the last three centuries. Nevertheless, compared to other doctrines, the doctrine of creation has been neglected; the result is an atrophied doctrine. This is what happened: as the sciences developed in the age of modernity, theologians began to think that they could not compete with the explanatory power and "control of nature" exhibited and promised by the sciences. Instead of rethinking the doctrine of creation, most theologians recast Christian convictions in terms of the inner life of humans or of salvation history (Ger., *Heilsgeschichte*). These defensive moves insulated Christian faith and belief from the realm of the sciences by locating Christian teaching within the heart or in a special strand of history that was not subject to "critical history."

The actual history of the development (or lack of development) of a doctrine of creation is more complex than I have presented it here. But the central point is that with the rise of the sciences, theology largely abandoned the doctrine of creation and left the field to the sciences. We need a thorough historical account of this abandonment of the doctrine and its consequences.[1] However, I do not have the temperament or training to provide such an account. Instead I will presume the rightness of my general claim about the neglect of the doctrine of creation, consider the consequences of that neglect, and offer an account that seeks to correct this neglect and contribute to its recovery.

A mature, robust understanding of creation is essential to growth in Christian discipleship and witness to the gospel. We have seldom had an account of creation integrated with the gospel. For many strands within the Christian tradition, the good news of Jesus Christ is the good news of redemption. "Creation" names the setting in which the work of redemption takes place, but "creation" itself is not part of that redemptive action. Some may talk about "soul-winning" and going to heaven when we die. For others, "redemption" is the work going on in the world to make peoples' lives better. In this

---

1. I am imagining someone with the theological acumen, tenacity, and attention to detail who will do for the doctrine of creation what Michael Buckley does for the doctrine of God in his book, *At the Origins of Modern Atheism*. A. Funkenstein tells part of the story in *Theology and the Scientific Imagination from the Middle Ages to the Seventeenth Century*, which focuses on outcomes in the sciences more than in theology. Two recent authors tell this story in ways that illuminate the loss of the doctrine of creation, though they do not cast their work in such terms. See MacIntyre, *After Virtue* and *Whose Justice? Which Rationality?*; Taylor, *Sources of the Self* and esp. his *Secular Age*. See also the older work of Blumenberg, *Legitimacy of the Modern Age*. For a descriptive history from the classical period to Vatican I with a focus on the Catholic tradition, see Scheffczyk, *Creation and Providence*. For a detailed study of a critical period, see Cashdollar, *Transformation of Theology*. For a brief and insightful survey, see Marlow, *Biblical Prophets and Contemporary Environmental Ethics*, 11–51, and with a slightly different focus, 52–80. In the latter chapter, Marlow examines the divide between "nature" and "history," which has had such deleterious effects, and argues for the recovery of "creational theology."

understanding, there is no reference to the world as God's creation, and very little is done to link the person and work of Jesus Christ to this "redemption," which is supposed to be accomplished by political, economic, and social power.

In light of the urgent need for a robust, mature Christian doctrine of creation, I offer this book as a contribution. It does not conform neatly to a familiar, agreed-upon consensus about which topics or scheme should be followed by a doctrine of creation. One reason is that there really is no agreed-upon scheme such as we have with other doctrines. For example, a presentation of the doctrine of God typically covers a familiar set of topics, such as the existence of God, the attributes of God, the trinity, and so on; some theologians may rearrange these topics or drop some altogether, but if they do so they will also usually explain their decisions.

No such consensus about topics and their arrangement exists for the doctrine of creation. Some topics regularly occur in treatments of the doctrine of creation—such as creation out of nothing, time, space, humankind—but we have so few recent treatments and have so neglected older treatments that we have no firm consensus. In my presentation, I follow a set of topics and an order that I judge to be most significant for recovering the doctrine of creation today.

In particular, I emphasize the necessity of always keeping creation and redemption together in our thinking, teaching, and living. To state briefly the necessity of holding creation and redemption together: without creation, there is nothing to redeem; the work of redemption is empty of content. Without redemption, there is no creation; there is only chaos, emptiness, meaninglessness.

This may strike some readers as overblown and even mistaken. After all, do not Genesis 1 and other Scripture passages give us a basis for a doctrine of creation apart from redemption? And if not these Scriptures, then surely the existence of the world itself provides us with material for a doctrine of creation, even if that doctrine might be tentative and incomplete? We have instances of attempts to build a doctrine of creation on these bases. However, neither the biblical passages nor the world as we have it provides a solid basis for these attempts.

The attempt to build a doctrine of creation from select Scripture passages without reference to redemption fails to recognize that all these passages arise from a people who are being redeemed. As I argue at length in later chapters, the story of creation in Genesis 1–3 is a story revealed to and canonized by the people of Israel as they are being redeemed by God. In other words, they did not first have a doctrine of creation to which was added a doctrine of redemption. Nor did they first have a doctrine of creation that was then supplanted by a doctrine (or the reality of) redemption. Rather, the people who became Israel were caught up in God's redemptive work and then came to realize that the very act of redemption revealed to them that this Redeemer-God is also Creator-God. Their doctrine of creation (taught in story form) is what must be true of this world given the God who reveals Godself in the particular way of redemption that makes them a people. In the New Testament, this together-ness of creation and redemption is revealed climactically in the many confes-sions about creation and redemption in Jesus Christ (John 1; Eph. 1; Col. 1; Heb. 1; Rev. 1). Thus, another way of saying that we must hold creation and redemption together in our thinking, teaching, and living is to say that our doctrine of creation must be christological.[2] This same christological focus for creation marks the doctrinal heritage of the early church. For example, at the beginning of his classic text *On The Incarnation*, Athanasius announces:

> We will begin, then, with the creation of the world and with God its Maker, for the first fact you must grasp is this: *the renewal of creation has been wrought by the Self-same Word who made it in the beginning.* There is thus no incon-sistency between creation and salvation; for the One Father has employed the same Agent for both works, effecting the salvation of the world through the same Word Who made it at the first.[3]

Many of us may be made uncomfortable by the recognition that the doctrine of creation does not provide Christians with a place where we and followers of other ways of "life" and "truth" can find a common, neutral meeting ground. At the same time that it does not provide us with neutral public space, this recognition of the christological claims on creation does require us to bear witness to the good news of the kingdom of God in Christ in public, in the places where we share common concerns with others who do not know that "all things have been created through him and for him" (Col. 1:16). The dif-ficulty of observing both of these truths has often caused us to slide one way or the other. On the one hand, we may seek to participate in public witness on the basis of creation disconnected from Christ. In so doing, we fail in our mission to bear witness to Christ. On the other hand, we may disconnect our understanding of Christ from creation in such a way that our witness to Christ does not lay claim to the world but retreats to soul-winning or drawing "believers" into a protected enclave that hides from the world.

In addition to holding creation and redemption together, we must also be thoroughly and thoughtfully trinitarian in our doctrine of creation. The twentieth century brought a resurgence of the doctrine of the trinity, and

---

2. My teacher and friend Loren Wilkinson is completing a book on Christ and creation that will contribute greatly to this necessity.

3. Athanasius, *On the Incarnation*, chap. 1, §1. Emphasis added.

recognition that this doctrine is the "basic grammar" of Christian faith and life. We fall into all kinds of errors if we cease to be trinitarian in our doctrine of creation. On a few occasions in modern times when a Christian doctrine of creation has been proposed, those proposals have been weak and unsustainable because they have not been sufficiently trinitarian. This failure leaves gaps in our doctrine of the trinity that may lead Christians to turn elsewhere in their search for a satisfactory doctrine of creation. Many unpersuasive and heretical doctrines of creation have slipped into our thinking and living by our failure to be vigilantly trinitarian.

These two necessities—the togetherness of creation and redemption, and the trinitarian grammar of creation—set the context for the rest of a doctrine of creation. Regardless of where we place other topics and how we discuss them, they must always be considered in light of these two necessities.

The doctrine of creation, therefore, is primarily about not the nature of creation but the God who creates. And the God who creates cannot be known apart from knowing God as the one who redeems. Moreover, the doctrine of creation is primarily not about origin but end. By *end* of creation, I mean not its cessation or eradication but its purpose, aim, or, as I will later explain at length, the telos of creation. We could also describe this end as the *eschaton* of creation if we carefully rescue the language of eschatology from date-setting and fear-mongering and locate it properly in the *eschaton*, who is Jesus Christ. (Remember that the book of Revelation, which is the source of so much tragically misleading and heretical eschatology, begins with the vision of the risen Lord Jesus, who is "the First and the Last," the one in whom is found the meaning of all history and thus also all creation.)

On the basis of what I have written so far, you should be prepared for the relative neglect and even absence of some topics that have come to occupy our arguments and even wars over "creation," both those internal to Christianity and those external. As my argument and exposition unfolds, I inevitably address some of the concerns that drive our talk about "creation." But this is not a book about "creation and evolution," "science and faith," "science and theology," or "science and religion." Nor is this a book about Christianity and the environment or care for creation. Finally, this book devotes very little space to controversies over the age of the earth, the days of Genesis 1, or the processes by which God creates.

Some of these *are* topics that I address briefly or provide a basis for addressing. In fact, I have written this book because so many issues that challenge us to be faithful in our witness to the gospel depend on a robust, mature doctrine of creation. But I also think that because we have neglected the doctrine of creation, we get lured into arguing about the wrong issues, or arguing about them in the wrong ways, or arguing about them in ways that betray the good news of Jesus Christ.

This book is about the God who is life, who gives life, and who redeems life. This God of life is the one God who is Father, Son, and Spirit. Out of the inexhaustible life of the Father, the Son, and the Spirit, this one God gives life to that which is not God. This continuing work of God, from its origin to its fulfillment, is God's work of creation. The doctrine of creation, then, bears witness to Life, to the God who is Life, and to the joyous, hopeful, loving way of Christ, which is the life of the world.[4]

Reading This Book

This book opens with three chapters that seek to diagnose the deficiencies in church, academy, and society resulting from our neglect of the doctrine of creation. The deficiencies that I identify in these chapters are nearly interchangeable. That is, the life of church, academy, and society are sufficiently intertwined such that a deficiency in one of them is a deficiency affecting all of them. Nevertheless, I have tried to organize my diagnoses so that they make sense and build on one another.

As I investigate church, academy, and society and make my diagnoses, I am already anticipating the doctrine of creation that comprises the four chapters of part 2. This anticipation reflects two judgments. First, any process of diagnosis is already the work of theology. One cannot engage in diagnosis—or "cultural critique," to use another description—without already doing the work of theology. Second, my anticipation of a doctrine of creation in these first chapters reflects my judgment that we need to rethink what a doctrine of creation calls us to in life and witness. Our arguments about "creation" have become so ensnared in issues and ways of arguing that actually obscure a *doctrine* of creation that we need a radical change in our thinking; that is, we need to go back to the roots of the doctrine of creation.

In part 1, therefore, I seek to reset our thinking about the doctrine of creation and our expectations of what the doctrine provides us for thinking, living, and witnessing as followers of Jesus Christ.

In part 2, I develop a doctrine of creation. This development is not a linear, progressive building of the doctrine; instead, the development is an interweaving of themes throughout the four chapters. When I began writing this book, I described the work in these chapters as a mosaic. I imagined the various

---

4. I long—and pray—for E .O. Wilson to believe that his "biophilia" grows from the roots of the life of the world in the God who is Life. See Wilson, *Biophilia* and *Creation*.

chapters providing tiles that would eventually all fit together into a relatively coherent portrait of a doctrine of creation. That description may still be helpful, but it does not quite convey the way in which each chapter covers some of the same ground as other chapters but from a different perspective. Or better yet, each chapter tells the same story but adds different details and different perspectives that make the story fuller and more persuasive.

The first two chapters of this section tell the story of creation in its fullest reality and provide the narrative setting for the next two chapters. In these first two chapters, the focus is on God: the story of God's work of redeeming creation and the story of this work as the work of the one God—Father, Son, and Spirit. It is essential to begin with God because throughout much of the modern history of the doctrine of creation we have begun with creation and tried to work our way to God. (The exceptions to this observation are important teachers from whom we have much to learn, as I will note in the following chapters.)

In the last two chapters of part 2, I turn to creation and Scripture to test the doctrine that I have developed in the previous chapters. This "assaying" of the truth of the previous chapters also provides an opportunity to tell the story of creation three more times, as we test the veracity of the earlier narratives and discover more about God's work of creation. That is, just as we may uncover new insights with each retelling of a significant period of our lives, so with the "retelling" of the doctrine of creation in these two chapters we will deepen our doctrine of creation as we retell the story of the redemption of creation by the one God—Father, Son, and Spirit—as the story of creation itself, as well as the story of Scripture.

In the eight chapters of part 3, I offer short reflections that plant this doctrine of creation in the soil of our lives. In these chapters, I seek to show how the doctrine of creation developed in part 2 may correct the deficiencies identified in part 1. The chapters in part 3 do not correspond neatly to the diagnosis in part 1 or to the development in part 2, but they do add another layer of exploration and persuasion to the earlier chapters.

Although these short chapters may be less specific than some readers will expect, faithful life and witness grow out of the work of the Holy Spirit in actual communities of discipleship to Jesus Christ. Such communities grow in maturity as they bring the gifts of community members together under the guidance of the Holy Spirit around specific questions of faithfulness for their community in their context. Or to return to my gardening analogy, we have to take into consideration local soil conditions, elevation, climate, water, sunshine, and more to successfully grow the same plants in different settings.

As you read this book, you may notice that I refer to other works for additional guidance. I do not agree with all these authors, nor do they agree with one another. It is sometimes popular in academe to label thinkers "lumpers" and "splitters," to refer to those who emphasize the similarities in thinkers and those who emphasize the differences, respectively. It may appear that I am a lumper, and something of a careless and unperceptive lumper at that, because I throw together thinkers who clearly differ greatly from one another. My reasoning about these matters, however, follows a different line. I refer to a wide and disparate range of thinkers not because I think that we can lump them all together but because the good news of the redemption of creation is so great and awesome that no one thinker or way of thinking can capture it. Our task is to enter into the revealed mystery of the good news of Jesus Christ and bear witness to it. This good news is cosmic in scope and utterly unimaginable apart from the story of Israel and the coming of Jesus Christ. This does not mean that anything goes; there are boundaries. But within those boundaries, we need the discernment of one another under the guidance of the Holy Spirit. Our task is not to capture this reality in our words, sentences, concepts, propositions, expositions, and arguments, but rather to bear witness to the reality of the redemption of creation that captures us by God's grace.

As you read this book, you will note some peculiarities in my terminology. In most instances when I quote Scripture that includes the Hebrew "Tetragrammaton" (Heb., *YHWH*), which has often been represented in our English Bibles by Lord, I translate the Hebrew as "I AM." At the appropriate time, I explain this practice. I have adopted it under the influence of Bruce Waltke as a faithful rendering of the Hebrew that conveys the power of the name and the life of God. In reference to the part of Christian Scripture that we normally refer to as the "Old Testament," I will often use the term "Tanak." "Tanak" is an acronym that takes the first Hebrew letter for the three divisions of Torah, Prophets (*nebi'im*), and Writings (*kethubim*). Using this term reduces the mistaken inference that "Old" Testament denotes something that is outmoded or passé. The oft-used alternative, "Hebrew Bible," is too neutral and descriptive a term for a body of writings that is canonical for followers of Christ. Finally, as you read some parts of this book, you will find regular cross-references to other parts of the book. This risks becoming annoying, but I have followed this practice to indicate that the argument and exposition circles itself in different ways.

As readers engage with this book on their own and in communities of discipleship, Bible study groups, and classrooms, they may draw on study resources and guides that can be found linked to my website: www.jona thanrwilson.com/godsworld. The topic of this book and its argument invite us to join together to explore God's work of creation in light of God's work of redemption. Since we cannot all meet in one physical space to do so, the exchange of "letters" by electronic means can supplement the conversations that we may have in our local communities.

Writing This Book

I have been working on this book ever since my grade 10 biology class with Mr. Cox at Glencliff High School, in Nashville, Tennessee. Prior to that class, I had been an indifferent student. Mr. Cox woke me from my intellectual slumbers to the joy of the flora and fauna of this planet. Somewhere in the midst of this awakening, I discovered the, then relatively new, field of ecology. I was enchanted. Since Mr. Cox had been educated many years earlier, he sent me across the hall to a younger biology teacher, Mr. Beasley, who simply directed me to a few books. That was all I needed. Over the next two and a half years, I filled several spiral-bound notebooks with a study of "The Ecology of Mill Creek." (Sometime after I left home, these notebooks disappeared during one of my parents' many moves.) At the same time, I decided that I wanted to be a "big-game biologist." I wrote to the Universities of Montana and Wyoming for their catalogs. My teachers sent home information about summer science camps.

However, in the fundamentalist southern culture in which we lived and through which we knew the gospel, the quickest way to lose one's faith was to study the sciences. My parents resisted my interest in studying science at a "secular" university. We were part of the movement that saw Bible colleges as the only proper place to pursue higher education. I was given many books that grew out of the Creation Research Society and the Institute for Creation Research. All of this eventually wore me down, and I submitted to my parents and my community and attended our denominational Bible college.

During this time, "creation" turned into a *theological* problem for me. I began to try to understand the controversies and conflicts in theological terms rather than simply cultural or even scientific terms. Along the way I began to encounter creative thinking about creation, especially at Regent College and Duke University. At Regent, W. J. Martin, D. J. Wiseman, Bruce Waltke, and especially James Houston began to demonstrate faithful alternatives to the well-established positions and arguments that seemed to dominate. Loren Wilkinson led the way in introducing "earthkeeping" to the evangelical tradition. At Duke, Tom Langford led a lively seminar in which we read Jürgen Moltmann's *God in Creation* and Richard Rorty's *Consequences of*

Pragmatism.[5] Then, once I began to pay attention, the doctrine of creation or, more accurately, hints of the doctrine and longings for the doctrine, seemed to be everywhere. I did not realize it at the time, but my Duke dissertation on Julian Hartt lodged in my thinking a considerable amount of material for a doctrine of creation.

For a brief time after I began teaching undergraduates at Westmont College, my attention was diverted from the doctrine of creation by more tyrannical urgent matters, like trying to captivate first-year college students with the joy of Christian doctrine in a required class and meeting the publishing expectations of the college and the department. I knew that the doctrine of creation was a long-term project. The project claimed my attention once again as I developed faculty friendships at Westmont and began to realize that my students had been taught no effective doctrine of creation in their churches. As a consequence, they were at the mercy of every ideology that sought to control them and suck life from them. This ideological vulnerability is apparent in political and economic realms as well as in my students' submission of their bodies to the deadly, life-destroying stories of our society.

Gradually, the outline of this book began to come into focus. I began working on little pieces of it and wrote many unpublished pages as I sought to bring clarity to my intuitions. When I moved from Westmont to Acadia Divinity College at Acadia University in Nova Scotia, I was given more opportunity to develop my thinking through my service on the Executive Committee of the Arthur Irving Academy for the Environment and many conversations there. When I moved from Acadia to Carey Theological College at the University of British Columbia, I continued with that development in occasional conversations with other faculty at UBC and Regent College. I was especially helped by regular conversations with Jeremy Kidwell and Matt Humphrey, both of whom have made significant contributions to this book.

As the book developed in my thinking and teaching, the audience for the book began to come into focus. I had initially thought of the book as a "university press" book that would enter into conversation primarily with other theologians. However, over time, through the counsel of friends and my own reflection, I came to see the book's audience as leaders and teachers of congregations. These leaders and potential leaders of the church are the people to reach if I hope to reintroduce and reinvigorate theological work so that we can recover a robust, mature doctrine of creation. The way that I present a doctrine of creation represents a change from the familiar debates and

5. See Langford, *Reflections on Grace*, 63–80, for Langford's moving account of "Grace and Creation," which my own account echoes and amplifies in many ways.

conflicts. Therefore, it presents a bit of a challenge to readers, who will need to be patient and ready to engage less familiar topics and ways of teaching a doctrine of creation.

As I wrote this book, I kept in mind the enormous amount of reading that I have done over the years as my thinking took shape. However, this is not a book about books. Readers who are expecting to read my analysis of other doctrines of creation will be disappointed. There are many instructive treatments of the doctrine in the premodern period and a few in the modern period. The Eastern Orthodox tradition represents another significant resource. And the multitude of recent books on the issues that touch on the doctrine of creation provide a wealth of resources for a book about these books. I have read widely and persistently in these sources. However, the audience for this book and the style of book that I have chosen to write have led me to severely curtail my interaction with these other books. Even so, the footnoting is fairly extensive at times.

In addition to footnoting sources, influences, and resources for further reading, I want to note four books that were constant companions, though I do not always agree with them in details: J. Houston, *The Creator*; T. Fretheim, *God and World in the Old Testament*; N. T. Wright, *Surprised by Hope*; and N. Wirzba, *The Paradise of God*. For the most part, these books confirmed for me the thinking about creation that I have been engaged in for many years. They could serve as collateral reading for this book.[6]

Finally, this book has profited from the gifts of many friends. Chapters 1 and 2 were first presented as the Grenz Lectures in 2007. I am grateful for the remarks of the respondents to those lectures, Tama Ward-Balisky and Loren Wilkinson. Those lectures also spurred friendships with Jeremy Kidwell and Matt Humphrey, who met with me for many conversations that improved my argument and exposition. I have been encouraged by many others who have seen outlines and heard brief expositions of the book or portions of it. I have

---

6. I have also been stimulated by Alister McGrath's *Scientific Theology* (3 vols.), and though I have been critical of them, they still represent a monumental achievement. Moreover, I am eager to see his promised *Scientific Dogmatics*, given the preview of that work in *The Order of Things*, chapter 10. Two large and significant works were published in time for me to take them into account, though I have not fully absorbed them into this book: Kelsey, *Eccentric Existence* (2 vols.) and Conor Cunningham, *Darwin's Pious Idea*. As far as I can tell from Kelsey's volumes, his Warfield lectures, and interviews, his doctrine of creation is quite similar to mine in substance and concern, though he distinguishes the stories of creation, consummation, and reconciliation. Cunningham's book is a massive display of erudition and theological acumen but is also, I suspect, more valuable to the specialist than to the audience for which I am writing. I should also note that in the process of writing this book, I rediscovered Francis Schaeffer's 1970 book, *Pollution and the Death of Man*. I know that I read this book in the 1970s, but I do not recall it as I do my reading of other Schaeffer books.

been helped by several people who have read and commented on portions of the manuscript: Matt Humphrey, Marianne Meye Thompson, Marcus Tso, Jonathan Wilson-Hartgrove, and Bruce Hindmarsh. Several friends have read the entire manuscript and contributed significantly to its improvement: Jeremy Kidwell, Scott Kohler, Myrnal and Dave Hawes, Ian Campbell, and Tremper Longman. I am indebted to Philip Rolnick for his extraordinarily careful and insightful comments on the manuscript. I cannot overstate the significance of Phil's friendship, which began with many late-night theological walks around Holly Hill Apartments during our graduate-school days at Duke. It was a delight to "gopenize" this manuscript with him. In the later stages of editing this book I discovered the art of Joy Banks, which often "says" what I am trying to say more perceptively and pungently. I am grateful for her contribution.

To everyone at Baker Academic who contributed to the life of this book, thank you. I am especially indebted to the copy editors at Baker for pressing me to rethink several passages. I am deeply grateful for friendships that arise in the context of doing good work together. To my colleagues at Carey Theological College—faculty, staff, students—thank you for the life that we share together. I am grateful also for the flexibility of Carey's Board of Governors, President Brian Stelck, and Vice President Academic Barbara Mutch in rescheduling my sabbatical leave.

As I noted above, this book began to take shape many years ago. The completion of it has taken place in the twenty-two months following my wife Marti's death on September 16, 2010. Marti was—and is—my muse. I am so grateful for our rich life together. It has been wonderful to love and be loved by Marti in the love of God. I am filled with gratitude by the ways in which I know God's presence and love, as well as Marti's, even in her physical absence.

Part 1

Imagine a group of adventurers who have decided to abandon their experienced guide and find their own way through territory unknown to them. They are so confident and occupied with their journey that they do not realize that they are lost and doomed. Some of them, however, begin to suspect that something is not right. Their guide does not abandon them but continues to plead with them to listen to her instruction and follow her path. The first thing that this group of believers must do is learn from their guide where they are and what dangers they are facing because they have strayed from the path that has already been marked for them and for which the guide has all resources that are necessary.

"Waiting"

1

Missing Creation in the Church

If people are missing an essential ingredient in their diet, we see signs of that deficiency in their bodies.[1] A deficiency of vitamin C results in scurvy; a deficiency of protein may result in kwashiorkor; a deficiency of iron results in anemia. People suffering from one of these deficiencies and consequent conditions may even appear to be generally healthy for a while. But there may be times when physical stress brings on subtle indications of underlying poor health, which may also make them susceptible to other diseases that affect their health and lead to death, not from the underlying condition, but from another medical problem to which their poor health makes them unusually vulnerable. In every case, the underlying deficiency and consequent condition prevents flourishing and shortens lives.

What diseases can we identify in the church that result from a theological deficiency in the doctrine of creation? The remainder of this chapter is devoted to answering that question. If you are still not persuaded by my brief argument in the previous chapter that theology has neglected the doctrine of creation, the present chapter is further indirect evidence in support of that claim. I aim

1. An earlier version of this chapter was delivered as part 1 of the Grenz Lectures, First Baptist Church, Vancouver, BC, March 11, 2007. For comments and conversation that have improved this chapter, I am grateful to Tama Ward Balisky, who responded to the lecture that evening, and to Jeremy Kidwell and Matt Humphrey, who have continued the conversation over several years.

to increase the credibility of my claim by an account of the weaknesses and diseases that the church suffers as a result of this deficiency.

Note that from this point onward, I refer more simply to "creation" rather than the "doctrine of creation." This abbreviated terminology may cause some momentary confusion because "creation" may be used to refer both to the created order and also to the doctrine.

Church Pathologies

Gnosticism

The most common way of identifying the pathology that results from this neglect of creation is to use the term "gnosticism," which describes an ancient way of thinking and living that the church has identified as heresy. In recent years, this term has entered into the public stream and muddied the waters considerably. To discuss gnosticism in relation to creation, I must first clear up some of those muddy waters.

Gnosticism refers to an ancient school of thought that seems to have had a significant presence among some communities that claimed to be followers of Jesus Christ. These gnostic communities were sufficiently developed to produce their own accounts of who Jesus is and what he taught in such documents as the Gospel of Thomas. These texts have become well known through the work of the Jesus Seminar and Elaine Pagels, among others. These scholars often portray the gnostics as an oppressed minority in the church who were the victims of party politics and the orthodox corruption of Scripture, to use Bart Ehrman's deliriously market-driven title.[2]

But the vision of the world and life that undergirds gnosticism is seldom addressed in the media coverage of these scholars and their texts. In gnosticism the world is divided into good and evil. Spirit is good; matter is evil. Matter is not fallen from a good state and therefore capable of redemption. Matter is evil from the beginning; it always has been and always will be. Redemption is not possible for matter because matter never was and never can be good. You and I suffer as we do because we are good spirits trapped in evil matter. Our salvation depends on the escape of our spirits from the trap of matter. (This belief is quite different from "materialism," which values matter and the

2. See Funk and Hoover, *Five Gospels*, a product of the Jesus Seminar that places the gnostic Gospel of Thomas alongside the four canonical gospels; Pagels, *Gnostic Gospels*; and Ehrman, *Orthodox Corruption of Scripture*. Among many excellent refutations of these attempts to rehabilitate gnosticism, see Evans, *Fabricating Jesus*. Also of great help theologically is Allison, *Cruelty of Heresy*. On the gnostic impulse throughout history, see Jonas, *Gnostic Religion*.

material world above "spirit.") Gnosticism denigrates the material creation and exalts the eternal "spirit."[3]

Disembodiment

In neglecting the doctrine of creation, theology has contributed to the church's development of a low-grade gnostic infection that weakens many parts of the church's life. One of the first areas of weakness that I discovered is our theology of the body: not our theology of the church as the body of Christ, but our theology of the *human* body. My undergraduate students at Westmont College taught me this. As I tried to help them through extremely difficult questions of body image often manifested in anorexia, bulimia, steroid use, obsessive exercising, immodest dress, sexual promiscuity, self-mutilation, and more, I realized that they had no way of connecting their bodies to their faith.

I at least grew up with rules about my body. I knew not to drink, smoke, or have intercourse before marriage. But even my tradition had no theology that explained or made sense of these rules. It was simply a matter of identity. If I was a Christian, I didn't do these things. Why not? Because I was a Christian. Why doesn't a Christian do these things? If the conversation got this far, the answer was, "Because your body is the temple of the Holy Spirit." So even here, there is no theology of the body. That is, the rules aren't really about my body and its worth; rather, the rules are about the presence of the Holy Spirit in my body. It is not that these things are bad for my body, but that they are offensive to the Holy Spirit. If the Holy Spirit did not reside in my body, I would have no reason to avoid these "pleasures." The primary function of the Holy Spirit, it appeared, was to narrow the list of pleasures that I was allowed.[4]

We need more. Without a theology of the body, my students—and the rest of us—are weakened and vulnerable to anyone who has a corrupt theology of the body. Those who want to sell us all manner of things to improve our bodies are teaching us a theology of the body; those who tell us that our bodies are beyond improvement are teaching us a theology of the body; those who tell us that extending our bodily lives is the priority for personal and social planning have a theology of the body; those who ask us to use our bodies to serve the corporation, the state, or the cause of democracy have a theology of the body.[5]

The Christian church desperately needs a robust theology of the body. God made our bodies and declared them good. God created them for sexual

---

3. As a complement to this discussion, see Peterson, *Christ Plays in Ten Thousand Places*, 59–62.

4. Thomas Howard tells a story similar to mine in *Christ the Tiger*.

5. See the profound explorations of this dynamic in Cavanaugh, *Torture and Eucharist*.

reproduction and for work. The pain and toil that we experience today, the burden of Brother Ass in the colorful phrase of Saint Francis, is not original or essential to our bodies; it is the consequence of our fall. Our bodies are being redeemed by the power of the incarnation—God in the flesh. And one day we will have imperishable, sinless bodies in a new creation. This is the merest sketch of an outline of a theology of the body.[6]

Ironically, the church's neglect to develop a theology of the body has led not to a neglect of our bodies but to an almost obsessive concern for them. Much more needs to be done—both constructively, in articulating a theology of the body, and polemically, in attacking the devastating errors in the church and society. The absence of a theology of the body indicates an area of disease in the church resulting from the neglect of the doctrine of creation and cries out for nourishment.

Truncated Salvation

Closely related to this pathological condition of the church's theology of the body is the church's doctrine of salvation. Do we need to be saved? Absolutely. Is God in Christ our only hope of salvation? Yes, without qualification. But in our time, two further questions press hard upon us. One is most pertinent to my theme—what is salvation? As I noted earlier, gnostics believe that salvation is the release of our spirits from their imprisonment in these evil bodies. That belief is very close and often identical to the doctrine of salvation taught in churches that would otherwise abjure heresy in themselves and abhor it in others. In other words, in many of our churches we have become functionally and practically gnostic.

With the glamorization of gnosticism, some traditions toward the liberal end of the theological spectrum have begun to drift toward this heresy. But historically, traditions toward the conservative end of the spectrum have inadvertently taught a doctrine of salvation that promises freedom from our bodies and escape from the world. There is biblical precedent for this language, but in the Scripture this language comes within the context of a larger celebration of the goodness of God's creative work. So at the same time that Paul warns about "sins of the flesh" (Col. 2:11 KJV), he also celebrates the goodness of all food and the freedom of marital sex. At the same time that John warns us

6. See chap. 14, and esp. footnote 2, for more on these issues that are swirling around us today. My concern is not to resolve or even enter into these debates but to provide a narrative account of embodiment that participates in the redemption of creation. In this way, "the redemption of our bodies" is an integral part of our salvation. This is one of the points where we need a more robust doctrine of creation.

to "love not the world, neither the things that are in the world" (1 John 2:15 KJV), he expects us to do good with the worldly goods that we have. Since we lack a robust doctrine of creation, we have fallen into error by interpreting "flesh" in Paul to refer simply to our bodies. We have also missed the nuances of John's references to the world.

Sarx

To make clear Paul's use of the word "flesh" in a number of troubling passages, it is helpful to return to the Greek word *sarx*, which is usually translated "flesh."[7] In many passages in Paul's letters, *sarx* is not the body but a power that stands over against God's work for the flourishing of creation to which we mistakenly submit our bodies and other aspects of our humanity.[8] *Sarx* is the anti-God, anti-human power that distorts our body image, seduces us with counterfeit pleasures, promises us life, and then crushes us in death. When we understand "flesh" as *sarx*, then we can see that "the flesh" is not our bodily life from which we need to break free into a contrasting "spiritual" life. Rather "the spiritual life" is our bodily life now under the guidance and power of the Holy Spirit rather than under the guidance of *sarx*.

With this understanding, we can now locate properly the language of salvation, especially its propositions. It is proper to say that we are saved from sin and death and Satan. It is also proper to say that we are saved from *sarx*. But it is a grave theological error to equate any of these with creation or our bodies. Sin, death, Satan, and *sarx* corrupt creation—including our bodies and our spirits—but they are not necessary, essential, eternal characteristics of creation. So salvation is salvation *from*—salvation from sin, death, and Satan. God in Christ has taken our very bodies back from sin, death, and Satan.[9]

Salvation is also salvation *for*—salvation for life. And the form of life for us is creation. Therefore, to have a real doctrine of salvation we need a real doctrine of creation and vice versa. Julian Hartt, from whom I have learned so much, calls this necessity the dialectic of the kingdom: the doctrines of creation and redemption in mutual illumination, correction, and witness. Without this (non-Hegelian!) dialectic, he says, these two realms dissolve into unreality in our understanding.[10]

7. English translations of the NT vary in how they translate *sarx*.

8. This way of understanding *sarx* crystallized for me as I read J. Martyn, "Epistemology at the Turn of the Ages," in his *Theological Issues in the Letters of Paul*, 89–110.

9. This need for correction is helpfully identified in several essays in Stackhouse, *What Does It Mean to Be Saved?*

10. Hartt, *Christian Critique of American Culture*, pp. 75–98. See my elaboration of this in chap. 4.

Alternative Creation Stories

At this point, I must bring into focus a very different consequence of the theological neglect of creation on our doctrine of salvation. For some parts of the church, the absence of a robust doctrine of creation results in a doctrine of the redemption of creation that draws its meaning and sensibilities from accounts of creation outside the Christian tradition. In these parts of the church, there is a profoundly appropriate sense that this world is the realm of salvation. But because theology does not provide a doctrine of creation dialectically related to redemption, these parts of the church turn elsewhere for a doctrine of the redemption of creation. They find it variously in particular accounts of evolution, in *techne* (supposed human mastery of the world), in Gaia, and in other doctrines of salvation.

There is another layer to this corruption of the doctrine of salvation as a consequence of the neglect of creation. This layer is manifested in the seemingly endless debate over evangelism and social action. In some parts of the church, this debate has been decided, and energy has been directed toward one of the options. In other parts, the debate and tension can be debilitating. In still others, there is a balance in practice that lacks a foundation in vision. In very few is there a robust vision and practice guided and energized by a cogent dialectic of creation and redemption.

Church Health

Integral Mission

Such a dialectic is immediately before us. If God's work in Christ is the salvation of this creation, then the church's witness to this work in Christ must be whole. It is not a matter of evangelism as saving people for eternity and social action as caring for their bodies until they die. It is rather a matter of witnessing to God's whole work in Christ for the salvation of the cosmos. So caring for the whole person is the work of the church in witness to Christ.[11]

Justice and Care for Creation

If we locate our understanding of the church's witness in a robust doctrine of creation, then we will find inescapable the conviction that the church's mission

---

11. See my brief treatment of this issue in *Why Church Matters*, chap. 6. See also Stearns, *Hole in Our Gospel*, which is a passionate call to correct this deficiency in practice. In the present book, I hope to provide a doctrinal corrective to this same deficiency.

is to work for justice as our witness to and participation in God's redemption of creation. When people are oppressed, marginalized, impoverished, mocked, treated unjustly, or debilitated by illness or injury, creation is not right. We must avoid "justice without eschatology"—that is, the belief that we can achieve God's justice apart from God's acting to consummate creation in redemption. But at the same time, we must bear witness to and participate in that coming work of God as people called to bring this good news to all creation. To bear witness and participate faithfully, we must abandon the dichotomy between so-called evangelism and so-called social action. We must instead bear witness to God's redemption of creation in word and deed—by caring for all creation, the whole person and the whole world.

This leads us naturally to the church's care for creation. One of the greatest tragedies of theology's neglect of creation has been the church's complicity in the destruction of the natural world and thus also of conditions that contribute to the flourishing of life. An even greater tragedy—let's use the church's language—an even greater *sin* has been the voices in the church that have resisted and mocked the passion for life that leads to care for creation. How far have we, the church, moved from the biblical prophets and the Christian tradition, that many of our leaders could mock God, who creates and who redeems that creation? *Nostra culpa.*

There have been voices crying out on behalf of creation along the way. And today more voices have joined them. But the need for repentance—a change of mind and life—is still great among us. Often Christians seem to be committed to good environmental practices for pragmatic or self-serving reasons. We may cautiously support this commitment if it brings people into right practices that may lead them into more mature convictions and character and deeper practices. A more robust doctrine of creation may provide just such a maturing and deepening influence.

With a more robust doctrine of creation as the ground of our care for creation, we will learn first to recognize that we do not have "an environment"; rather we are a part of creation. When we recognize that we are part of creation, we will also be carried beyond our relationship to the rest of creation. To be "creation" is to be related to the Creator. Care for creation, then, is an act of obedience and praise for our Creator God—Father, Son, and Spirit—in relation to whom we have life. We may be tempted to say that it is more terrifying to think of answering to the Creator for what we have done with creation than it is to face the natural consequences of what we have done and persist in doing. But it would be a mistake to make that distinction. In the prophetic tradition of the Bible, these disasters themselves are God's judgment on our greed, rapacity, and violence (Isa. 17–19; 24; Jer. 4:19–34).

If we had a more robust doctrine of creation, we would also recognize that the God who is Creator favors justice because justice is the world rightly aligned with God's love for life. The prophets of Israel consistently proclaimed God's judgment upon Israel because the people of God fell into the false belief that God had chosen them simply to bless them. But that is not the purpose of God's call; rather it is to gather a people who bear witness to God's passion for life, which is sustained by justice.[12] If we had this understanding of justice rooted in a robust doctrine of creation, we would be deeply and repentantly committed to living generously and mercifully rather than "living" fearfully, anxiously, and vengefully.[13]

Spiritual Conflict

All these weaknesses and errors are seriously debilitating to the life and witness of the church as well as damaging to God's world. But today there is a greater danger that we need to expose, confess, and turn from, without diminishing these threats that I have already identified. I suspect that this danger is always with us, but we are especially vulnerable to it when our doctrine of creation is weakened.

Here is my deepest concern briefly put: without a robust doctrine of creation, the church has little understanding of and grounding for our life in this world. When this condition prevails, the life of the church is directed toward "otherworldliness" and a tepid form of gnosticism takes hold. And it is just tepid enough for us not to realize that it has taken hold. It bathes us in a lukewarm Christianity that leaves us relatively comfortable.

This otherworldliness manifests itself in an understanding of the "spiritual life" that has many reassuring and comforting dimensions. It can offer practices of prayer, Bible study, Christian scholarship, and witness that seem quite impressive in their widespread acceptance and practice. But none of this is grounded in God's redemption of creation. We are called to participate in the redemption of creation in this world, not to escape into another world.

---

12. In the following chapter, I add shalom to this account.

13. A corollary to the scarcity of theological disputation on the doctrine of creation is the paucity of theological disputation on the biblical and theological doctrine of justice. Given the importance of justice in Scripture, we should expect an ongoing, lively debate about the biblical teaching. What we have instead is a fairly lively interaction with philosophical conceptions of justice by Christian philosophers and theological ethicists, but very little properly *theological* disputation—that is, argument that takes the character, work, and will of God as determinative. We need a theological equivalent to Wolterstorff, *Justice*. The debates among Bible scholars over "justification" in Paul may ultimately lead to a larger engagement with the question of justice for all creation.

When we lack this teleological perspective on the redemption of creation, we become vulnerable to other ideologies and claims on our lives in this world. We are creatures of this world, and we have to live in this world. When our life in Christ is not grounded in this world—to which he came and to which he will return, I remind you—then our life in this world becomes terrifyingly vulnerable to other powers. As an illustration, think of the church in Germany and the terrible willingness of the German Christian movement to endorse a theology of blood and soil—an alternative doctrine of creation that is deeply implicated in the Holocaust.[14]

Then think today of the church and its lack of a robust doctrine of creation. What ideologies are seeking to co-opt our life in this world? What ideologies have already co-opted our this-worldly life? Today we may see this demonstrated especially among conservative Christians in the United States. This is partly because they have a bit more cohesiveness and political connections than other Christians. So they may be easily co-opted for this-worldly programs that are not rooted in Christian convictions. But we may also identify in the recent past an occasion of similar co-optation in the ideological support that mainline Christianity gave to the eugenics movement of the early twentieth century. We are all vulnerable to other claims on our this-worldly existence when we are not grounded in a robust Christian doctrine of creation.[15]

Church as Culture

In order to bring our existence in this world under the discipline of God's love in Christ, which is the life of the world, the church must understand itself as culture.[16] The way that we use the stuff of creation for our life as church is training us in this-worldly existence. And most of that existence seems so natural and commonplace that we take it for granted.

The ways that we use the stuff of creation in architecture, music, paintings, food, money, books, cars, water, and more reflect our convictions about creation and teach us convictions for thinking about and living in creation.

14. This I think is the place to locate Dietrich Bonhoeffer's call for religionless Christianity and a worldly Christianity. Bonhoeffer's call for a religionless Christianity is directed toward the "religious Christianity" in both conservative and liberal forms. Conservative "religious Christianity" falls into piety that seeks to escape this world. Liberal "religious Christianity" assimilates to the world. In contrast, "religionless Christianity" is a "worldly Christianity" immersed in the redemption of creation and thus also fully immersed in the world that God is redeeming as creation. See chaps. 8 and 9.

15. For a theologically and liturgically grounded exposé of this vulnerability, see Cavanaugh, *Theopolitical Imagination*.

16. See Clapp, *Peculiar People*; Harvey, *Can These Bones Live?*

If we see the things of this world merely as instrumental to the salvation of spirit or saving souls, then we have truncated the good news of Jesus Christ. That is, if we see music or banners or other visual presentations merely as a means to move people more effectively to faith in Christ, then we are unfaithful to the gospel. There is a fine balance to observe here. Since creation is fallen from the good, it has become the world that must be and is being redeemed. Therefore, we must not be naive or undisciplined in our cultivation of church culture. At the same time, however, creation is not *instrumental* to salvation in Christ; it is the very *substance* of salvation in Christ. It is not enough that we have the arts in the life of the church; we must have them in the life of the church in the right way: as our celebration of and participation in the reconciliation of all things visible and invisible to God through Christ. The stuff of creation is what God the Son redeems through his becoming flesh, bearing our sin, enduring death, and rising to life. When we have a truncated doctrine of creation, we have a truncated understanding of salvation. With a more robust doctrine of creation, we may enter more fully into the life of the redeemed as witnesses to and servants of the only hope of all creation.

One implication of my argument is that we need to work harder at recovering the createdness of life and our faith. This means adopting, recovering, and deepening practices in the church that will reshape our thinking and living into a fuller recognition of the redemption of creation. There are far-reaching actions that most of our churches must take both to develop practices and to ground them in a trinitarian, redemptive doctrine of creation.

Two Practices

Two crucial practices are immediately among us in the central sacraments of the church. In baptism and the Eucharist, the stuff of creation bears witness to God's grace in life because God's redemption of creation makes the stuff of creation sacramental. In baptism, the water necessary to our bodily life and to creation witnesses to the washing of our sin, the outpouring of the Spirit, and, for this convinced Baptist, the raising of this body to new life in Christ. Note that it is what we do to *our bodies* that identifies and unites us with the Messiah here and now. "Therefore . . . present your bodies as a living sacrifice" (Rom. 12:1 NRSV). In order to develop a more robust doctrine of creation, we need to think from this practice into creational life.

In the Eucharist, the stuff of creation—bread and wine—becomes for us a witness to our participation in the redemption of creation. This bread and wine, as signs of the body and blood of Christ, remember the incarnation, life, death, and resurrection of Christ as our salvation. And the Eucharist makes that salvation material; it is located in the redemption of creation. In the Eucharist, the Word who is Creator and who became flesh, the Word who is the life of the world, is our life. We learn here in the bread and the wine that our very life is his gift to us, that our coherence is his gift to us, that our redemption from sin and our life beyond death is his gift to us.

But baptism and the Eucharist must not be merely activities of the church. We have been doing these things for a long time, and they have not led us to recognize or correct our teaching and practices. Our neglect of the doctrine of creation and of the redemption of creation has sadly but easily coincided with our continuing celebration of baptism and the Eucharist. What we must recover is the *practice* of baptism and the Eucharist. By practice I mean that these must be firmly, intentionally, and continually rooted in the story of God's redemption of creation. They must be welcomed and acknowledged as part of our participation now in the telos of new creation. As we *practice* baptism and the Eucharist, we are led more deeply into the story of the redemption of creation, we learn more fully the meaning of the telos of new creation, and we more fully participate in Christ. Learning this, we continue on to our mission in the world.[17]

---

17. This last paragraph is my inadequate way of restating the brilliant teaching of Schmemann, *For the Life of the World*, esp. chap. 2, "The Eucharist."

2

Missing Creation in the Academy

As we continue our exploration of the deleterious effects of the theological neglect of the doctrine of creation, we turn from the dis-ease of the church to the dis-ease of the academy.[1] Although I focus on the relative neglect of the doctrine of creation and the consequences of neglect, this negligence has not been total. There have been a few exceptions. Karl Barth, of course, wrote expansively on creation.[2] T. F. Torrance also provides some guidance, and on the evangelical side, James Houston, the Oxford geographer who is the founding principal of Regent College, wrote *I Believe in the Creator*, which is still a helpful statement. Other works on creation have also played minor roles in theological conversation. Today Colin Gunton's work provides one voice in a developing conversation on creation, along with Alister McGrath's project and a few others.

But in the midst of much theological ferment, the presence of the doctrine of creation has been remarkably marginal. We do not have the kind of mature debates and positions on the doctrine of creation that mark doctrines like

---

1. An earlier version of this chapter was delivered as part 2 of the Grenz Lectures, Carey Theological College, March 12, 2007. For comments and conversation that improved this chapter, I am grateful to Loren Wilkinson, the respondent on that occasion; to Matt Humphrey and Jeremy Kidwell for continuing conversation; and to Telford Work for perceptive comments on the text. After writing this, I discovered (rediscovered, really, since I had previously read the work) this same point briefly argued in Gunton, *Triune Creator*, 125–45.

2. Barth, *Church Dogmatics III*.

those of the trinity, the incarnation, the atonement, pneumatology, bibliology, ecclesiology, and eschatology. Recently, many Christian thinkers have been working on the relationship between "science and religion," Christian care for creation, evolution and Christian faith, intelligent design, and other pressing concerns in our time. But all these thinkers address these necessary issues without a mature theological history in the doctrine of creation.

Even the liveliest arguments that come close to the doctrine of creation—the battle over "evolution"—do not reflect the presence or development of a mature conversation about the doctrine of creation. Rather, they illustrate my concern that we have not had a lengthy theological debate on the doctrine of creation to draw from when we find ourselves addressing the pressing issues of our time.

So my concern here is not with the culture conflict between creationism and Darwinism or other forms of evolutionary thinking, nor is my concern with the relationship between science and religion. I have been a participant in science-religion conversations and received grants for my work in that arena. My experience in those conversations is one of the reasons for the work that I am now doing and for the way that I am doing it. From my early and tentative participation in the conversations on science and religion, I came to realize that theology has not done the basic research necessary to participate with full integrity in that conversation. By integrity I mean that theology, because of our lack of a mature research program in the doctrine of creation, has often lost its way *as theology* in the conversation. Therefore, this book is about theology and the work that we need to do, more than it is about direct engagement with familiar public issues.

As I address this concern, I am aware that the academy is not the only place where a doctrine of creation has been missing. The doctrine of creation is also missing in church and society, to use a rough differentiation. The topics that I address here could, with a slight change in perspective, be appropriately applied to church or society as well. So although the theological neglect of creation has widespread effects, I will narrow my concern here to the academy and make some artful judgments about what is most important without attempting to be exhaustive in my argument.

My precise aim in this chapter is to identify what theology has not contributed to the academy as a consequence of our neglect of the doctrine of creation: a practice of wisdom, a celebration of superabundance, an account of culture, an embrace of participation, or a vision of the peace of creation. I am not arguing that these things are entirely missing from the academy. Other academic disciplines have often contributed the things that theology would have contributed if it had been more robustly engaged with the doctrine of creation. I argue not that the academy is entirely bereft of these topics but rather that theology should have been contributing these things to the academy for the past three hundred years. It is also my intuition, not argued directly here, that if theology had been contributing in these areas, the landscape of the academy would look very different.[3]

The most significant consequence in the academy of the theological neglect of the doctrine of creation is the marginalization or absence of theology itself. Many other factors are involved in this; some have been identified by recent historical accounts, such as George Marsden's *The Soul of the American University*, though Marsden's focus is not theology itself but religion and more specifically Christianity. One factor in this marginalization that has not received sufficient attention is theology's neglect of the doctrine of creation. To avoid having this one topic consume this chapter, I sketch the logic of my argument but leave the details for another occasion. In essence I make a suggestion rather than an argument for this first point.

Theological Retreat

My suggestion is that neglect of the doctrine of creation is woven together with theology's retreat from the very areas of life and thought that would directly challenge and participate in the academy. Even if theology had pursued more vigorously the doctrine of creation, the marginalization and exclusion of theology might have occurred anyway. We cannot know. We can know, however, how theology contributed to its own academic demise. It did so by retreating from creation to interiority and, alternatively, to salvation history.[4] These moves made theology immune to the critical apparatus of modernity and preserved a simulacrum of theology. But in doing so, the retreat also surrendered the center of the field to other academic disciplines.

Both of these moves could have developed differently, but because they arose as strategies of retreat, they marginalized theology in the academy. That is, "salvation history" could have challenged other philosophies of history, but instead it created an alternative game, or an alternative field within which theology labored. Salvation history becomes the exclusive domain

3. This intuition is reinforced from an evangelical perspective by Noll, *Scandal of the Evangelical Mind*, and Marsden, *Outrageous Idea of Christian Scholarship*.

4. For the impact of "salvation history," see Marlow, *Biblical Prophets and Contemporary Environmental Ethics*, 57–74. Marlow accurately identifies the problem with salvation history and its impact. She then moves on to the question of creational theology and environmental ethics. My account of the dialectic of creation and redemption and the trinitarian grammar of creation strengthens her concerns but also approaches the issues in a different way.

of the church, and "general history" is surrendered to the academy. In this arrangement, any theological entry into the academy's claim on history has to be according to the ground rules of the academy. Likewise, the turn to the interior life could have provided an opportunity not for retreat but for engagement with the academy. But it did not. Instead, the interior life became another realm in which theology claimed immunity from modernity. As a result, theology created the conditions for its own marginalization in the academy.

Commenting directly on the early (1935) work of Gerhard von Rad, Karl Löning notes:

> Today, after the passing of more than fifty years, we see clearly that this decisive relativization of biblical creation theology signified at the same time its weakening—and the loss of the universal dimension of the biblical message. That God's history with God's people Israel and with the church stands in the service of the fulfillment of creation, has been relegated to the background in the face of the narrowing of the biblical witness. In contrast to this we can and must today emphasize that the world is desired and loved by God for its own sake and precisely as God's creation. . . . The theology of creation outlined in Genesis 1–9 is not simply a prelude to salvation history, but sustains, pervades, and embraces the entire biblical witness to God.[5]

We do not overcome this marginalization by developing theological accounts of the world that merely use religious language and symbols to say in translation the same thing that is said in other disciplines. No, to return theology to the academy, theology must return to its sources and develop once again, under the conditions of modernity and postmodernity, a wide and deep discourse on the doctrine of creation. If theology does so with humility before God and boldness before the world, it may contribute significantly to the academy.[6]

Theological Recovery

Superabundance

Perhaps the most fundamental contribution that theology will make is an account of the superabundance of creation.[7] If creation is rooted in the life

---

5. Löning, *To Begin with, God Created*.

6. My work here could be seen as a much less ambitious and exhaustive complement to Milbank, *Theology and Social Theory*.

7. See chap. 5, where I develop a fuller account of the trinitarian superabundance of life.

of God and sustained by God, then creation, though finite and dependent, participates in the superabundance of God's life. Here it is necessary to make the point that for Christians, belief in the superabundance of God's life arises from God's trinitarian life. In this triune life of the Father, the Son, and the Spirit, who are eternally giving fullness of life and identity to one another, we know the superabundance of the Living One, the I AM, whose livingness cannot be exhausted by creation.

These awkward phrases reflect the difficulty of properly referring to God in this context. It is not right to say here that God *has* life, as if life were a possession of God. Nor is it quite right to say that God *is* life, since creation is not God, but it does have life. And so we do well carefully and with fear and trembling to name the I AM. We also do well to remind ourselves of the Mystery by regularly practicing greater reticence about naming God (Rom. 11:33–36).

Dialectic of Creation and Redemption

This invocation of the superabundance of creation in the Triune God brings us to a second theological necessity, the necessary dialectic of creation and redemption.[8] In the context of this chapter, this means that we must resist the temptation to see the doctrine of creation as a way to evade the scandal of particularity that simply is faith in Jesus of Nazareth. To believe that this person—born in the line of David, in this place and time, of this woman—to believe that this person is God incarnate is to submit to a scandalous particularity. And any fully Christian doctrine of creation must also embrace the scandal of this particularity—that this Jesus, this Messiah of Israel, is the one through whom "all things in heaven and on earth were created, things visible and invisible, whether thrones or dominions or rulers or powers—all things have been created through him and for him . . . and through him God was pleased to reconcile to himself all things, whether on earth or in heaven, by making peace through the blood of his cross" (Col. 1:15–20 NRSV). Any Christian theology is defective if it seeks to find in the doctrine of creation an escape from the scandal of particularity and an escape to a realm that does not require the fullness of knowledge that comes by faith and the hope that looks to the eschaton. This may be a particularly academic temptation.

When we add this dialectic of creation and redemption to the superabundance of trinitarian life, we are approaching a vision of God's world that

---

8. See chap. 4, which develops a fuller account of this dialectic of the kingdom.

generates many wonderful possibilities. What follows is a partial and suggestive account of the possibilities latent in a Christian doctrine of creation.

Culture of Creation

Out of a Christian doctrine of creation, theology could provide us with an account of culture as the human celebration of the goodness of creation in its superabundance and redemption.[9] If resources are scarce and life is a zero-sum game, then why do we create apparently superfluous artifacts? One partial answer is that some of us simply have more than others, and we use that more for our own selfish security, comfort, and pleasure. But from a doctrine of creation, we can also provide an alternative account: in spite of human misuse of creation and contingent scarcity generated by our practice, creation is superabundant. Our celebration of that superabundance is human culture, and that culture will be welcomed into the new creation.

A Christian doctrine of creation in dialectical relationship with redemption also generates an understanding of culture as an expression of an inchoate longing for that redemption. Culture, in this perspective, is what we humans do with the stuff of creation. Culture expresses our implicit and sometimes explicit belief that redemption is our work, and our anxiety that we cannot in the end accomplish our redemption.[10] A Christian doctrine of creation discerns the goodness in culture that expresses this longing and finds its telos in the new creation, where the glory of the kings and the wealth of the nations have their place (Rev. 21:24–26).[11]

Wisdom or *Techne*?

When the Christian doctrine of creation recognizes trinitarian superabundance and the dialectic of the kingdom and then generates an account of culture, it leads us to recognize that we know creation properly by means of wisdom, not *techne*.[12]

These two terms require explanation. First, *wisdom*. The tie between wisdom and creation is pervasive in Scripture. Several Tanak (or Old Testament) Wisdom texts personify wisdom as the craftsperson who shapes creation. In

---

9. See Wirzba, *Paradise of God*, 149–90; Peterson, *Christ Plays in Ten Thousand Places*, 49–129.

10. Since it is inchoate, this longing must be brought to clarity by the lives of those who have come to know its source in the One who creates and redeems.

11. See the marvelous book by Mouw, *When the Kings Come Marching In*.

12. Houston, *The Creator*, 179–203.

the New Testament, several texts may be understood as announcing that Jesus Christ is wisdom incarnate—not only the Colossians text already quoted but also later passages in Colossians as well as other passages where the connection is less direct but still present.[13] In this connection, wisdom becomes the way to know creation and to know how to make our way in the world as God's creation. The "rainbow of wisdom" (D. Kidner) in Proverbs 1:2–6 portrays a full range of knowledge, insight, understanding, good judgment, shrewdness, erudition, and administration that reflect the character and skill that enable us to navigate life according to the Creator's intentions.[14] This wisdom knows that the world belongs to God, that it can be understood properly only in light of that relationship, that life is found only in this way, and that a love for God and for creation rightly aligned with God's purposes is the only way to life.[15] Proverbs puts it this way: "The fear of I AM is the beginning of wisdom" (Prov. 1:7, my translation).

Now *techne*. By *techne* I mean the power that Jacques Ellul exposes and analyzes in his great work *The Technological Society*. This *techne* seduces us into thinking that it is something that we can control and by which we can also control our world. In the English translation of Ellul's work, the word is translated as "technique," but that translation has been widely criticized as misleading. *Techne*, in Ellul's prophetic unveiling, is a false god that drains life from us by weaving a lie about the world and life. Without being named in quite this way, *techne* is also the target of Alasdair MacIntyre's critique in *After Virtue* and of Charles Taylor's collection of essays on the social sciences.[16] *Techne*, by virtue of its practical atheism, requires that humans master their world. There is no God to trust with that which we cannot understand or, understanding, that which we cannot control or predict. And so we are driven to eradicate mystery, and by doing so we embrace a withered portrayal of life.

Here it is helpful to recall one of my preliminary warnings. I am not arguing that wisdom is missing from the academy or that the academy is under the totalitarian rule of *techne*. Rather, I am arguing that theology would contribute a powerful account of the call to wisdom if it developed a more robust doctrine of creation. This contrast between wisdom and *techne* is an important narrative strand throughout C. S. Lewis's novel *That Hideous Strength*. Wendell Berry, the great poet, theologian, and farmer of creation, expresses it this way:

---

13. See my discussion of the connection between creation and wisdom in Scripture in chap. 7.
14. Kidner, *Proverbs*, 36–37.
15. See chap. 7.
16. MacIntyre, *After Virtue*, chap. 8; Taylor, *Philosophy and the Human Sciences*.

Give your approval to all you cannot
understand. Praise ignorance, for what man
has not encountered he has not destroyed.[17]

Creation Care

If we listen closely to Berry, we will hear that a recovery of the doctrine of
creation (as I have outlined it so far) will also lead to a theological contribution to our care for creation. In some practices of theology this concern is
well established. It filters into and through most of contemporary life. The
church desperately needs continuing voices to sound the warning that life is
desperately ill on this planet and that we who claim to worship the Creator
must change our thinking and our way of living. The wide variety of voices
and arguments in support of creation care displays both our need for a more
mature discourse on the doctrine of creation and a model for how our discourse
on this doctrine can mature through such difference and debate.

As we move to this concern, I must first explain why care for creation is so
important if creation is superabundant and being redeemed. Does not superabundance mean that we can use up the resources of the planet as fast as we
choose and depend on God to provide an endless supply? Do you recognize
the form of this question? Romans 6:1–2 (NRSV): "What then are we to say?
Should we continue in sin in order that grace may abound? By no means!"
What then are we to do? Shall we use this planet more quickly so that God's
provision may be all the more evident? By no means! "By no means" translates
the Greek phrase *mē genoito*. In his Cotton Patch version of the New Testament, Clarence Jordan quite appropriately translates *mē genoito* as "Hell,
no!" because such reasoning participates in the hell that is contrary to life.

"Shall we consume more, so that God's superabundance may be more evident to all?" By no means! (Hell, no! because this way is to submit to the hell
of selfishness that ends up consuming us.) To argue for more consumption
of the earth in order to demonstrate God's superabundance is to mistake the
character and purpose of the Living One who gives. God's superabundance is
not an endless supply for our addictions to pleasure and consumption. Rather,
God's superabundance provides for good ends, not evil. When we seek to use
it for evil ends, we bring judgment upon ourselves, and the lies to which we
succumb lead us to destruction.

---

17. Berry, "Manifesto: The Mad Farmer Liberation Front," in *New Collected Poems,* 173–74.
Originally published in Wendell Berry, *The Country of Marriage.* See my discussion of this
poem in chap. 13.

The foolish woman is loud;
  she is ignorant and knows nothing.
She sits at the door of her house
  on a seat at the high places of the town,
calling to those who pass by, who are going straight on their way,
"You who are simple, turn in here!"
And to those without sense she says,
"Stolen water is sweet,
  and bread eaten in secret is pleasant."
But they do not know that the dead are there,
that her guests are in the depths of Sheol.

Proverbs 9:13–18 NRSV

When we foolishly steal from the poor and powerless of the world and enjoy sweet water and pleasant bread, we desperately need the eyes and ears to come to the fear of the Living One. Therefore, a theology with a robust doctrine of creation would help us see that our environmental crisis is not rooted in our struggle to manage scarcity or to allocate resources properly in a zero-sum game; it would help us to see rather that our environmental crisis is rooted in our misuse and abuse of the superabundance provided by God. Such an account would not reduce the depth of our crisis; it should deepen it by calling us to account before the Living One who sustains the cosmos.

Changing Language and Vision

One result of such vision could be the proper relocation of fear in discussions about "the environment." As I reflect on the debates, I hear many who believe that we do face scarcity, and I hear policy debates that are more about how to secure the future for me and those close to me than about how to honor the One who provides for life abundant. Policies and practices rooted in fear of scarcity are very different from policies and practices rooted in the fear of the superabundant I AM.[18]

Another result of a robust doctrine of creation would be a challenge to change our language, our vision, and our lives to talk of creation rather than the environment. First, to talk of "creation" helps us picture conditions for the flourishing of life. On the other hand, to speak of "the world around us" or of "the environment" tends to make us picture our condition as that of someone living in a house that is falling down: if it falls, we'll just move to

18. See chaps. 10–13 for further elucidation.

another house. But the world is not something in which we live. We are a part of the world, and the world is a part of us. But even that way of speaking is not quite right. We must learn the language of creation. Wendell Berry, once again:

> The idea that we live in something called "the environment," for instance, is utterly preposterous. This word came into use because of the pretentiousness of learned experts who were embarrassed by the religious associations of "Creation" and who thought "world" too mundane. But "environment" means that which surrounds or encircles us; it means a world separated from ourselves, outside us. The real state of things, of course, is far more complex and intimate and interesting than that. The world that environs us, that is around us, is also within us. We are made of it; we eat, drink, and breathe it; it is bone of our bone and flesh of our flesh. It is also Creation, a holy mystery.[19]

Berry properly orients the human to "creation." A robust theology also properly orients creation to Creator.

At this point, by equating creation with a Creator, I have made missing creation in the academy quite a bit more uncomfortable. Even if there is a trinitarian and redemptive shape to superabundance, culture, wisdom, and care for creation, those theologically scandalous elements may be suppressed and we may translate them into terms or transfer them into conceptual systems more amenable to the academy. But the Creator? The Triune Creator? The Living One who redeems? Creation as the medium by which the Living God makes known God's loving? These concepts are difficult to translate or transfer. That is precisely one of the points that needs to be made. If the Christian doctrine of creation and theology generally are merely one way to say things that may be said and known in other ways, then theology and the doctrine of creation are superfluous.

However, the Christian doctrine of creation asserts a claim to knowledge that is not otherwise identifiable—or at least not clearly identifiable. At present, no matter how we characterize the cultural conditions in which we live, two things are clear: particularity is no longer the scandal that it once was, and the demand for universality no longer has veto or exclusionary power over public discourse.[20] Although exclusionary habits linger in some pockets of academe, in most academies there is a growing recognition that Christianity, along with all other particularities of knowledge (which is to say knowledge), may participate in "the university as a place of constrained disagreement, of

19. Berry, *Sex, Economy, Freedom & Community*, 34.
20. However, it seems that "global" is being strongly promoted as a new "universality," driven by the market.

imposed participation in conflict, in which a central responsibility of higher education would be to initiate students into conflict."[21]

Participation

In this educational process, a robust doctrine of creation would also provide a vision and a direction for understanding life and knowledge as participatory.[22] In much of the modern academy, knowledge has been grounded in distance and alienation from the object of one's knowing. But that misconstrues the circumstances that simply are the condition of life. We cannot know apart from our participation in the very processes that we are seeking to know, and we cannot know apart from our participation in the traditions that teach us what knowledge is according to those traditions. Every way of knowing, then, is necessarily traditional.

A doctrine of creation, grounded in Christian convictions, teaches us to understand more fully this participatory necessity of living and knowing. We are part of creation; to live is to participate in creation. The more fully we participate in creation appropriate to our humanity, the more human we become. This assertion must be underwritten by a Christian doctrine of creation to guard it from two dangers. One danger is the tendency to think that we lose personal identity by participation; if our understanding of participation is grounded in a trinitarian redemptive doctrine of creation, then we can offer an account of participation in which we find ourselves by losing ourselves. The second danger that may also produce some understandable anxiety about my proposal is that the particularity of our participation in a particular nation, language, class, race, gender, and so on can provide a basis for horrendous evil and catastrophic violence. The danger is tempting and the worry well grounded, but it is not the particularity of our participation that funds such evil and violence. Rather, such evil and violence result from mistaking as universal that which is really particular. That is, when I think that my participation in creation is the "universalizable" requirement for all who are truly human, then those who do not participate in creation as I (or we) do have rejected their humanity and committed a capital crime.[23] At least that is the way the logic of the false universal works in far too many places today. I

21. MacIntyre, *Three Rival Versions of Moral Enquiry*, 230–31.
22. See a complementary account of this in Milbank, "The Conflict of the Faculties: Theology and the Economy of the Sciences," in *Future of Love*, 301–15.
23. As with many things in these first three chapters, the preceding assertions will be developed and addressed in later chapters. One reader of an early draft recoiled from the barbarity of "universalizable," which confirmed for me that it is precisely appropriate for this context.

recognize your particularity but I deny my own, and in doing so I make you an "other" who has no claim on me.

However, if we understand our particularity as the form of our participation in creation, then we will grant others the freedom of their particularity. If we understand this particularity to be grounded in our participation in creation, then we will also urge others noncoercively and nonviolently to find the means by which they become fully human in God's redemption of creation. This is difficult to grasp and even more difficult to communicate.

The longing for something more in our lives and in creation is either illusory or true. Christians believe that it is true and find its fulfillment in God's acting to redeem creation. As each one of us participates more in that redemption, each one becomes more fully what he or she is created to be until eventually all who participate in this redemption of creation become all that they are meant to be. The African, the Asian, the Australian, the South American, the European, the woman, the youth, and I—to gesture with frustrating inadequacy at the human richness of creation—all become fully ourselves by participation.[24] And since this becoming is grounded in our participation in creation, becoming fully me in all my particularity does not increase the separation between me and others in their particularity; rather, it unites us with one another in a fullness appropriate to our humanity, so that creation is whole. We believe that this will happen in the superabundant, redeeming activity of the Triune God.[25]

Peace

The Hebrew word for this wholeness is *shalom*—peace. To understand this peace and to offer it to the academy would be one of the greatest contributions of a robust doctrine of creation. Creation cannot be rightly understood

24. In the next chapter I will consider the challenges of "participation" for those whom others have excluded on the basis of some particularity—race, class, gender, disability, and so on. Briefly, I will say that such exclusion works against God's creation and redemption and thus brings judgment on those who exclude. This judgment of God is God's work for the peace and justice of creation. Thus, my assertions about particularity and participation are not a basis for exclusion of others but a witness to God's justice, which will fall heavily on those who work against God.

25. Telford Work offered this comment on an earlier version of this chapter: "I like to think about this in terms of speaking in tongues at Pentecost vs. speaking a universal language at Babel. Speaking and hearing the particular language of another is very different from the pragmatic efficiency of a lingua franca. Different in that it's shalom (the gift of God) as opposed to universal peace (the Kantian hope of ending violence by achieving some superhuman culture, beyond our particularity)."

apart from peace. The story of God's creative work and the story of God's consummation of that work is one that can only be understood as shalom.

Peace is the telos of creation—not an immediately obvious description at this point; perhaps a fond longing, a dream surrendered in the harsh light of contemporary experience. And yet, if the Christian doctrine of creation means anything, it is that the telos of creation is peace. This peace is anticipated in the first stories of creation, in the visions of the prophets, in the poetry of the psalmists, in the life of Jesus, in the teaching and practices of the letters of Paul and John, and in the Apocalypse. Certainly there is violence along the way, but that violence must be placed within a teleology of the peace of creation.

When we locate peace as the telos of creation, we do two important things. First, we locate the history of violence in the right narrative. Violence is a *surd* in creation that requires redemption, not explanation.[26] Creation will be made whole only through the redemption, which brings it to its proper end in peace. Second, we locate the practice of peace in the telos of creation, not in the people of God. Certainly the people of God are called to make peace, but we make a mistake when we think that peace is to be located in the people of God. That is, this witness to the peace of creation is not an achievement. Rather, peace is characteristic of the kingdom of God, to which the people of God bear witness by their living.

The knowledge that peace is the telos of creation provides enormous interpretive power for our condition. If violence is the telos of creation, then where does creation come from? That is, if violence has ontological priority, where does anything come from? How do we conceive of violence as that which originates life? We can think of violence as the cycle of living or as that which consumes life. But if violence is all that there ever has been and ever will be, then how is there anything at all? Why is there something rather than nothing?

At this point, a description of *violence* is required. In a Christian doctrine of creation, violence should be understood as acting contrary to the telos of a created entity. So when humans act contrary to their own telos in God, they do violence to themselves. When they act toward other humans contrary to the others' telos in God, they do violence to others. When humans act toward the rest of creation contrary to its telos, they do violence to the rest of creation. If

26. Up to this point, my account has paralleled Milbank, *Theology and Social Theory*, 278–325. I am now arguing that we need to go beyond that account to a "redemptive ontology of the peace of creation." Milbank has made an advance toward that account in Milbank, *Being Reconciled*. My use of the uncommon word "surd" requires some explanation. I have searched for another, more familiar word, but nothing else fits as well. Every other word that I have thought of using actually places violence within a familiar category and thus begins to domesticate it, begins to make violence a natural part of the universe. The strong claim that I am making is that violence has no place in creation.

God were to act toward humans contrary to their telos, God would do violence to them. Our telos is not to be "saved" or "condemned" either individually or corporately. Rather, our telos is to participate in the peace of creation; some of us will do so through salvation, others through condemnation. In right judgment, God will make creation whole.

But that wholeness lies ahead of us. Today, creation anticipates its peace, but its actual life is cruciform. That is, the violence that we see exposed on the cross of Christ is the story of creation today. So the various *agonistic* accounts of the world, such as some accounts of evolution or a Nietzschean will to power, rightly describe the contingent nature of creation.[27] That is why they have such explanatory and experimental power. But they do not go deep enough. Creation is contingently marked by agony, but it is eschatologically marked by peace (to finally adduce the doctrinal specificity for telos). This peace is the redemption of creation.

If we develop this claim in a robust doctrine of creation, then we may give a more persuasive account of the world than these agonistic accounts. Such a robust doctrine would provide a way of reframing all the disciplines that have developed in the academy. The agonistic foundations that shape them are real but provisional. In Christ, we know that peace is the eschaton of creation. Thus, peace is the teleological and ontological reality of creation. This dialectic of provisional agony and fundamental peace witnesses to the story of God in Christ, whose truth provides enormous interpretive power for our day. In telling this story, we may bear witness in the academy to the redemption of the peace of creation in Jesus Christ and offer an account of the longings of those who are now working for "restorative justice," "conflict resolution," and peace.

Sabbath

Finally, I offer a brief account of a practice in which we could engage to participate more fully in the doctrine of creation: keeping the Sabbath. On the one hand, this may seem to be a strange suggestion for recovering the doctrine of creation in the academy. But the Sabbath works wondrously against the pretensions and pride of the academy. On the other hand, keeping the Sabbath may seem a rather mundane and obvious suggestion; it is not. The Sabbath teaches us that wisdom, not *techne*, guides us into life abundant as we reorient our lives toward God. The Sabbath teaches us that the superabundance of

27. An "agonistic" account of the universe construes conflict as a natural and essential characteristic of the universe.

creation comes as a gift, not an achievement, as we give thanks for and give away what we have received. Proper Sabbath keeping turns us toward God as Father, Son, and Holy Spirit in worship. In the two accounts of the Decalogue (Exod. 20:8; Deut. 5:12), Sabbath keeping is located in relation to the dialectic of creation and redemption. On the Sabbath, we set aside competitive, agonistic labor for one day and enter into the Sabbath rest of the peace of creation. We participate more fully in the life of God and of others, so that we come to know more of that telos. We enjoy the good things that we make of the stuff of creation in our places of worship. The Sabbath is for the enjoyment of culture and the contemplation of the good. The Sabbath inculcates wisdom. The Sabbath is, of course, much more than this, as is creation. Creation has been missing for far too long in the academy; it is time for theology to direct significant energy to a lively, maturing discourse on the doctrine of creation.

3

Missing Creation in Society

As we move from missing creation in the church and academy to missing creation in society, we move into a much more amorphous setting. Although "church" and "academy" may be somewhat amorphous, we can nevertheless point to boundaries, institutions, artifacts, and representative characters that help us identify church and academy. In the case of society, however, the task is more difficult. Manifold questions and complications threaten to occupy us before we can analyze and reflect on the effects of the neglect of the doctrine of creation in "society." Therefore, rather than try to give an analytical or deductive account of society before we begin, I will simply let an understanding of society unfold as I make my observations and arguments. My argument is not meant to prove that missing creation has had *this* specific effect on *that* particular culture. Rather, its purpose is to identify ways that recovering a doctrine of creation may heal some of the pathologies manifested in a society.[1]

1. I could have titled this chapter "Missing Creation in Culture," but that requires an account of a particular culture. I intend for my account to be more fluid and adaptable than an account of one particular culture. I could also possibly have titled my account "Missing Creation in the World," but that title would run afoul of my intent to use "world" as a counterpoint to "creation." Yes, the Bible uses "world" in different ways, but for my account, I use it in a very specific way that will become apparent in part 3 of this book, esp. chaps. 8 and 9.

Situatedness

One observation must be made immediately. When we consider church and academy, we are examining settings that do not surround us entirely. It is possible and relatively easy for us to gain some critical perspective on church and academy. However, when we consider society as I am using the term, we are trying to look at the very thing that makes it possible for us to look at things. It is sometimes suggested that when we try to examine our "culture," we are like a fish trying to understand and explain "water." It is an impossible task because we are simply immersed in our culture. We see, think, and act within the formation of our lives. Our "situatedness" cannot be overcome. We can understand our situation only through the means that our situation provides us.[2]

When we seek to examine "society," we may find ourselves in a similar place. That is, society is the (nearly?) all-encompassing context within which we seek to imagine how things could have been and still could be different. To put it most trenchantly: If "creation" is missing from society, how would we know that it is missing? More significant, how would we know what that absence has meant?[3] Yet throughout history there have always been communities and people who somehow are able to imagine something new, something else, something not simply contained in a culture or society. When I begin to move directly into considering the effects of missing creation in society, I will also identify how it is that we might be able to imagine what it has meant for something to be missing. This in itself is a bit of a challenge.

Finally, let me note that this chapter is not meant as a full-scale critique of a society or culture, but throughout this chapter, I refer to numerous critiques that have given shape to my exposition and provoked my thinking about the ways that theological neglect of the doctrine of creation has contributed to some of the pathologies of our age. My reflections will not be exhaustive; rather they will illustrate the significance of the doctrine of creation and introduce

2. This is true even when our situation includes experiences of other cultures. Then our "multicultural" identity simply becomes part of our situation, whether on a personal scale or on larger scales of community, nation, and so on.

3. See the comment by MacIntyre on his "initial hypothesis" in *After Virtue*, 2nd ed.: "If the hypothesis is true, it will necessarily appear implausible, since one way of stating the hypothesis is precisely to assert that we are in a condition which almost nobody recognizes and which perhaps nobody can at all recognize fully" (4). I do not have the historical instincts and erudition to offer a narrative account of the career of the doctrine of creation analogous to MacIntyre's account of "moral theory." Moreover, my intent here is slightly different from MacIntyre's in that I write from within an actual, existing community. In so doing, I also write for that community, the church, which exists not to serve and perpetuate itself but to serve God and the world in trust that God will sustain us.

the kinds of questions and explorations that we should be engaging in light of the doctrine of creation. I do not imagine that my arguments here will turn the tide or calm the waters of society, but I hope that they will induce others to do this work better. And I hope that "better work" is increasing faithfulness to the good news of God's redemption of creation.

Teleological Amnesia

If Christian theologians were to develop a robust, mature discourse about the doctrine of creation that actually challenged the shape of society, one of the primary challenges would be Christian witness to a particular teleology. Simply the introduction of teleological argument and controversy would be an accomplishment, since much of our society has such a deeply ingrained and well-fortified aversion to teleology. In most cases, that aversion is so well developed that society cannot even identify "telos" as something it has rejected. We suffer from "teleological amnesia." That is, our habits of thinking and living are so nonteleological that it would be a healthy accomplishment merely to raise the possibility of teleology in such a way that we actually find the suggestion worth considering.[4] To develop this assertion, I will first attend to the particularity of teleology I will be expositing throughout this book. Then I will distinguish this teleology from other ways of life that are often mistaken for teleology.

For Christians, the telos of the cosmos is Jesus Christ. In later chapters, we will be engaged by this conviction at length. Here we may note that for the Christian doctrine of creation, "teleology" is not a feature or possession of the world simply as the world. Rather, for Christians teleology is a description of the relationship between the cosmos and Jesus Christ. Paul asserts of Christ that "in him all things were created: things in heaven and on earth, visible and invisible, whether thrones or powers or rulers or authorities; all things have been created through him and for him. He is before all things, and in him all things hold together" (Col. 1: 16–17). When Paul makes this confession, he is articulating a telos that requires us to revise our understanding of teleology.[5]

Some may argue that this is not a teleology at all since it is not a feature or possession of the cosmos, but rather a declaration of the relationship of the cosmos to Christ. That is, teleology is usually regarded as a possession or

4. I direct the interested reader once again to the work of Alasdair MacIntyre and Charles Taylor.

5. See Polkinghorne and Welker, *End of the World*, esp. pt. 4. I am especially instructed by Kathryn Tanner, "Eschatology without a Future?," 222–37.

characteristic of the thing itself. But "the world" does not possess a teleology in itself. It has a telos only in its relationship to Christ. This is why a nonteleological account of the world is so persuasive: if we assume that only "the world" exists, then we cannot give a teleological account of it. Only as God acts to redeem the world as creation is its telos manifested.

If Christian theology were to develop a robust doctrine of creation and enable the church's confession of God as Creator and this world as creation, then we would also be confronting society with a new possibility. The major reason that we become nonteleological in our thinking and life is the failure of Christianity to bear witness to the universe as creation. When Christians fail in that witness, they leave the world only with possibilities that must fail. One possibility is to believe in no telos. This conviction may be explicitly articulated, but it is also often implicit, even deeply hidden, in society. When society reaches this conviction explicitly or implicitly, then humans must assume the burden either of making meaning in the universe or of abandoning the notion that there is meaning in the universe. Another possibility is to believe that the universe itself generates its own telos. Since the final reality of the universe is death, this conviction condemns us to fate. A final possibility is to provide an account of the telos of the universe that construes the universe's telos in relation to a different god from that of the Triune God of Christianity. None of these options can restore teleology since none of them is grounded in the one and only telos: Jesus Christ.

When Christians develop a trinitarian doctrine of creation in dialectic with redemption, then they have good news for society. The universe is not a burden or a curse that humans must bear as they try to construct meaning or try to escape the inextinguishable desire for meaning. Remember, I am writing as a theologian to exposit what the doctrine of creation should mean for society. Given our convictions about creation that I develop in the following chapters, we may know that the refusal to believe in Christ as the telos of the universe will lead to this despair, even as society develops strategies, practices, and products to ameliorate, deny, and manage the despair.[6]

Grace

On the basis of our doctrine of creation, we also have the good news that the universe cannot and need not generate its own telos. If the universe were self-generating, then this world in which we live would be the only world that

6. One analysis of these attempts by society may be found in MacIntyre, *After Virtue*, 73–78. I extend MacIntyre's analysis into the church in *Living Faithfully*, 32–37.

ever has been and ever will be. This would be the most real world, and all our possibilities, hopes, and dreams would either be limited by this world or would be dreams that are literally impossible.

But the Christian doctrine of creation declares to us that this world is not all that ever has been and will be. This present age is not "the most real world." The good news is that the one God—Father, Son, and Spirit—is the originator, sustainer, and completer of this world as creation through the redemption. In this confession, we testify to the telos of this world as God's creation: the most real world.

The telos of the world as God's creation is further elaborated and entered into when we develop a robust, mature doctrine of creation grounded in the doctrine of the trinity. As we understand the telos of the world grounded in the life of the Father, the Son, and the Spirit and redeemed by the work of the Triune God, we will be able also to give an account of why only the Triune God can create and sustain life that is not identical to God's life. Only the Triune God could create the cosmos as a gift and blessing that is free in its life, but only in dependence on God. Only the Triune God could create a world that is free to turn away from its given telos in the life that God gives and still be brought back to that life in God without either God or creation becoming something other than God and creation.

The very nature of teleology means that words are not enough to restore belief in a particular teleology or to restore discussion of teleology in general to society. The nature of teleology requires the display of a telos as a way of life. For Christians, this means the life of a community formed by and finding life in the Triune God and the dialectic of creation and redemption. One of the reasons that our society has abandoned teleology and even anathematized it is the failure of God's people to live teleologically—that is, to live in faithfulness to our confession that God is Creator and Redeemer. Instead we have lived as if this world circumscribed the possibilities of thought and life.[7] We have lived as if this world were all that ever has been and ever will be. In allowing this world to set the limits of our life and witness, we have contributed significantly to the absence of teleology in society.

Church in Creation and Society

One of the most significant contributions that theology can make in its recovery of the doctrine of creation is to establish the connection between the doctrine

---

7. Grappling with this situation has been the burden of three of my books: *Living Faithfully, Gospel Virtues,* and *Why Church Matters.*

of creation and the life of the church, not so that the church can make itself relevant to the concerns and pathologies of society, but so that the church may become a more faithful witness to the good news of the redemption of creation.[8] This witness would then offer society the possibility of recognizing its captivity to "the world"—the belief that the way things appear to be is the way they always have been and always will be.

At this point, we are ready to explore the ways that teleology may be misappropriated by the church and thus misrepresented in society. As we will later see, the telos of creation is realized in the new creation by the work of redemption. All of this is the work of the Father, the Son, and the Spirit. The telos of creation, then, is grounded in God. We participate in that telos in Christ because Christ is the telos. He is the new creation and the power of our life in the new creation. Thus, the telos is not something that we create; it is not something that we achieve; it is not something that we choose. The telos of creation is not the project that God assigns to us. Rather, it is God's project accomplished in Jesus Christ, to which we are called by the Spirit. As we are called by the Spirit, we become participants in what God has already accomplished.

Recovering and developing the doctrine of creation is essential to the church's witness. It is not a move calculated to enhance or increase the church's influence and numbers. Rather, the doctrine of creation is a requirement of the good news of Jesus Christ for the redemption of creation. At the same time, the doctrine of creation also enables us to begin to recover a Christian understanding of "blessing." This reality of blessing as the good news has been well developed by Ellen Charry in two volumes, *By the Renewing of Your Minds* and *God and the Art of Happiness*. The first book retrieves and advances the recognition that the gospel, and theology that faithfully serves the gospel, are intended for human flourishing. They are, in Charry's term, "aretological."[9] The second volume advances the argument of the first and argues that life with God is meant to unite goodness and happiness in what Charry calls "asherism."[10] Charry locates asherism within the matrix of the redemption of creation:

> Salvation is the healing of love that one may rest in God. Asherism works out
> that healing process in a life of reverent obedience to divine commands that

8. Though I differ significantly on many points, I still find a valuable conversation partner in Donovan, *Church in the Midst of Creation*.

9. Charry derives "aretological" from the Greek *aretē* for virtue or excellence. *Aretē* is given particular shape and content by the work of the Spirit in conformity to Christ that leads to human flourishing as creatures of God. See Charry, *By the Renewing of Your Minds*, esp. 19.

10. In *God and the Art of Happiness* (xi), Charry derives "asherism" from the Hebrew word for "happy" or "blessed."

shape character and bring moral-psychological flourishing and enhance societal well-being. Salvation is an excellent pattern of living that is personally rewarding because it advances God's intention for creation. It is a realizing eschatology.[11]

Yet there is a conflict between "the fallen world" and creation that relocates aretological and asherist expectations within the redemption of creation. This brings these blessings into greater conflict with the fallen world than Charry allows. To put it biblically, the psalms of lament, Job, and Ecclesiastes must also be a significant part of our happiness. To put it theologically, the doctrine of creation does indeed witness to and guide us into the excellence, goodness, and happiness of life as God intends it, but the doctrine of creation must also recognize the present reality of a fallen world that is ruled by death and in that way is dysteleological. Such recognition provides warnings about the difficulties and suffering that we encounter when we follow the way of the redemption of creation, so that our account of blessedness stands up to the realities of the fallen world and calls us into the hope of creation redeemed.

Exposing Lies and Illusions of Society

In a society that is alternately ateological or dysteleological, the world is suffered as a burden and a curse. Excitement and entertainment replace happiness and excellence. The Christian doctrine of creation can expose these falsehoods, illusions, and counterfeits as part of the lie that says this world is all that ever has been and ever will be. The ateleology and dysteleology of society make sense if this world is all that there is. But a faithful community of disciples of Jesus Christ will bear witness to another, most real world, in which the telos is the flourishing of the universe in the new creation. The mission of the disciple community is to participate in that "realizing eschatology" so that others may believe and enter into the good news of creation redeemed in the new creation.

Nature

One of the most far-reaching and damaging effects of the loss of teleology is what I will describe as the transformation of creation into nature.[12] This

11. Ibid.
12. We do not have a comprehensive and focused theological account of the transition from creation to nature. Taylor, *Secular Age*, covers much of this ground with brilliance that is very relevant to theological concerns. But I would still like to read an account that could be titled "At

transformation is not always accompanied by these precise terms. Nor is the occurrence of these terms necessarily an indication of this damaging transformation. But when the transformation is damaging, it occurs in two interwoven movements. In one movement, we turn away from the conviction that this world can be understood and explained only through some sort of account of this world in relation to God as Creator. In another movement, we turn to the conviction that this world is "self-explanatory"—that is, that it can be fully explained and understood without reference to anything other than itself. This is the damaging move from creation to nature.

This turn to "nature" is the conviction that this world is all that there ever has been and ever will be. By such a description I do not mean that this conviction regards the world as static. Rather, I wish to assert that this view of the world as "nature" limits the possibilities of the future and of reality to the forces and processes already at work in the world.[13] In this description, we may also recognize that people are most often "practical naturalists," confessing belief in God and creation and afterlife while living as if this world were all there ever has been and ever will be.

It may initially seem that the doctrine of creation is no improvement on this view since I argue that "creation" is teleological and that creation's telos is in Jesus Christ and is at work now, a "realizing eschatology" in Charry's terms. But such a conclusion forgets that the teleology of the world as creation depends on God—the Father, the Son, and the Spirit; it is not contained within the world but is a rupture in the world and redeems the world as creation.

At this point, I will appeal to an illuminating oxymoron and speak of an apocalyptic teleology. This term is an apparent oxymoron because "apocalyptic" stands for something new, something that cannot be extrapolated from the present, and "teleology" identifies something already present that is being worked out. But the oxymoron is only an apparent one; it is in fact an apt description of the work of God in Christ that is the redemption of creation in the new creation. The end (*telos* as in goal, aim, intent) of God's work is given to the world in Christ at the beginning and in the sustaining and completing of the universe. But this is truly a gift in that it is never contained or possessed by the universe.

---

the Origins of Modern Naturalism," which would tell a story parallel to Buckley, *At the Origins of Modern Atheism*. McGrath's *Nature* pursues a different aim with learning and insight.

13. In the work of some theologians, the use of "nature" instead of "creation" is relatively benign. But in many cases the use of "nature" reveals a captivity to the world's story and the imperium of the sciences. For an insightful account of this, see Nichols, *Sacred Cosmos*. I am indebted to Philip Rolnick for reminding me of this book.

Thus, the limited horizon and chains of cause and effect confessed by "nature" are exceeded and broken by the confession of "creation." Yes, we may achieve a persuasive description of nature and its chain of cause and effect. We may even achieve some degree of control in the chain of cause and effect. But we are still bound by those chains. The good news of creation is that "nature" has no hold on us. In Christ we are brought out of the bondage of nature and into the freedom of creation. We are freed from death, which rules nature, and freed for life, which rules creation.[14]

Creatureliness

To speak of creatureliness is to ascribe to those entities that we call "creatures" the primary relationship and identity in relation to the Creator. "Creatureliness" may be ascribed to many things. I will focus first on the creatureliness of humans, then on the creatureliness of other living things.[15]

To say that humans are creatures is to say that our identity, our meaning, our life depend on our relationship to the One who created us. This assertion runs counter to most of what we are taught. On the one hand, we are told that we are our own rulers. We have been set free from all external authority and power. We are dependent on no one but ourselves. This is not necessarily a crude individualism or solipsism. It is a statement about the human condition. We make ourselves. We determine our own destiny. This project may be pursued as a war of all against all or as a communal endeavor, but it is an entirely human project. The only limits are the limits of "nature." And even nature may be conquered, controlled, or escaped.[16]

On the other hand, we may be told (if we are not creatures) that we have no identity. There is no such thing as constructing our own selves and determining our own destinies. We are merely products of the forces to which we have been subject and other forces that determine our lives today. Our genes, our families of origin, our traumas, our failures and successes, our particular biochemical make-up, market forces, ideologies, brain chemistry, and more converge on the aggregation of molecules that constitutes our lives. These forces determine who each of us is. We have been constructed by these forces. The belief that I shape my life and determine my destiny is a fantasy that

14. See chap. 5, where I describe the one God—Father, Son, and Spirit—as life and as the source of all life that is not identical to God.

15. I am indebted to Norman Wirzba for a conversation that confirmed my intuition that "creatureliness" is an important description to recover.

16. See chap. 8.

gives me some comfort along the way, but in the end it is an illusion, a new opiate for the masses that makes me available to markets and ideologies and demagogues and demigods.

Very few if any of us live entirely by these convictions, but they have an enormous influence on our construal of what it means to be human and how we are to relate to one another as humans.[17] Given the absence of "creatureliness," society is vulnerable to all kinds of antihuman, antilife ideologies. Society, of course, having forgotten and even actively eradicated belief in human creatureliness, does not see the situation this way. When we have severed human identity from relationship to the Father, the Son, and the Spirit, who create and redeem us for life, then our very being is surrendered to nonbeing. Death becomes the final determining force in what it means to be human, and we develop many strategies and practices for coping with, suppressing, and denying this finality. In the end, these strategies and practices become simply another way that we deny our creatureliness and place ourselves outside God's gift of life.

If theology recovers a robust doctrine of creation and persuades the church of its significance so that the life and witness of the church is shaped by it, then one of the central features of that life and witness will be the display of our acceptance of and delight in our human creatureliness. Most of the time, church life is indistinguishable from society. We display the same anxieties and fears, the same susceptibilities and immaturity that are on display throughout society. They are displayed in the fearful and anxious way that we fight the "culture wars," participate in national politics, and tie the future of the gospel to legislative and electoral outcomes. They are displayed in the desperate ways that we depend on medical care, increasing prosperity, and national security.[18] These things are not bad in themselves, but the ways that we depend on them reveal our convictions that they are the source of our lives and our flourishing. In the way that we relate to them, we reveal our idolatry of money, nations, classes, health.

When we recover a robust belief in human creatureliness, we will learn that we do not belong to ourselves or to all the other forces that promise us "life." We belong to the Father, the Son, and the Spirit, who make us, sustain us, redeem us, go with us through death, and bring us to life in the telos of all creation: the new creation. To be creatures is to be cared for and sustained by life that is inexhaustible and unconquerable. To be creatures is to know that our identity is eternally guaranteed by the only One who is eternal. In

---

17. Again, see Taylor, *Sources of the Self* and *Ethics of Authenticity*.

18. For a perceptive and chilling account of how we seek to "create" our own lives, especially the lives of children, see Hall, *Conceiving Parenthood*.

this life, we are told many things about our identity, both good and bad, both life enhancing and life destroying. All these things must be aligned properly with the God who creates and redeems us. When we know that our identity is eternally secure in God, we can begin to discern what is true of us, the good and the bad. Since we are creatures whose lives and identity are guaranteed in dependence on God, we can trust God to judge us rightly. In our creaturely identity, we may be made one with Jesus Christ, who himself became human and bore our weaknesses and our sin so that we could become truly human in him.

Let me say this strongly: we are not truly and fully human until we believe that we are God's creatures and trust in Christ to remove our inhumanity, free us from all that makes us less than human, and bear away the consequences of our refusal to acknowledge our creatureliness and trust in God for life.

When we recover this reality of our creatureliness in Christ, we become witnesses to the inhumanity of society. When our society lacks a sense of creatureliness that is part of the very meaning of being human, we turn to other ways of construing our humanity, with tragic consequences. When we do not recognize that humans have their identity as human by virtue of our creatureliness before God, we become susceptible to other bases for our humanity. Throughout history societies have fallen into this error, often with horrifying results. We become divided by the things that distinguish us, things that delight God in the beauty of diversity. The gifts and blessings of our creatureliness become burdens and curses.

Or we may begin to construe "the human" according to our own particular likeness. We construct ways of identifying our particular identity markers as those that identify all that is human. These markers are commonplace: class, gender, race, nationality, religion, mobility, intelligence, usefulness, and so on. Instead of being wonderful variations that make creation beautiful and reveal God's delight in "dappled things," these variations become markers of inferiority, of status, and finally of human identity.[19]

We can see the denial of our creatureliness and the dehumanizing dynamic that often follows throughout history. It is present in many stories in Scripture, directed against both God's people and others by God's people. It may be seen in Aristotle's descriptions of slaves, women, and children. It may be seen in many stories of conquest and in a multitude of social structures. It is (unfortunately) almost commonplace in stories of the Shoah. One of the most illuminating accounts of this dynamic is given by Willie Jennings in his

19. Theological reflection on what it means to be human will be dominated in the foreseeable future by the magisterial work of Kelsey, *Eccentric Existence*.

analysis of the European "discovery" of the New World and the inability of Europe's theologians to draw on the doctrine of creation in such a way that they could "recognize" the humanity of the inhabitants of the New World.[20] Jennings's account exposes and analyzes the dynamic that takes over when we are missing a full, Christian doctrine of creation in society. Caught up in this dynamic, we cannot recognize others as creatures like ourselves before God. Instead, we place them in categories that deny their humanity and thus make them vulnerable and available to be used for our purposes. They are at our disposal, a chilling description that would seem inconceivable if it were not for the many actual horrors that have been committed precisely as part of this dynamic. We may hope and pray that Jennings's work and others that follow it interrupt this dynamic.[21]

For long periods of time and in many places, this dynamic of subjugating the "less-than-human" other occurs in oppressive and destructive ways that stay just quiet enough so that we do not see them or, seeing them, we do not pay attention to them. (Edmund Burke's aphorism "All that is required for evil to prevail is for good men to do nothing" needs a supplement: "Most good people avoid doing something by not paying attention to what is actually happening.") The eruptions of this evil that we identify with genocide, slavery, and the like reveal the dysteleology of this dynamic: it ends in the destruction and death of all that is human, creaturely, and created.

When we notice these eruptions, we tend to focus on the perpetrators, those who have seized control of "what it means to be human" and thus acquire the power to destroy and deal in death. But there is another side to this: the "victims." Sometimes, perhaps often, victims are simply on the weak side of the distribution of social power. But they are often doubly victimized: they are both crushed by the literal physical power wielded by the dominators and perpetrators, and they (the victims) also believe that this destruction is simply their telos. They believe that their destruction is simply what the working of society requires.[22]

This dimension of recognizing the creatureliness of humankind is present in Genesis with the man and the woman becoming one flesh. It is broken by

20. W. Jennings, *Christian Imagination*, chap. 5.

21. Another book that contributes insights and correctives to this dehumanizing effect of a deficient doctrine of creation is Tran, *Vietnam War and Theologies of Memory*. In the course of his argument, Tran develops an account of time that corrects a possible deficiency in my account of a doctrine of creation.

22. Although I do not believe that Rene Girard provides an exhaustive explanation of this dynamic and of society, I do find his work richly illuminating. See *I See Satan Fall Like Lightning*; *Scapegoat*; *Things Hidden*. See also works that extend Girard's insights: Bailie, *Violence Unveiled*, and Alison, *Raising Abel*.

our fall away from this telos. Healing begins with the promise to Abram that "all peoples on earth will be blessed through you" (Gen. 12:3). There are anticipations of the fulfillment of this telos throughout the Tanak (Melchizedek, Namaan, the prophecies of Isaiah and others). Its fulfillment begins in Christ, finds embodiment in the church (Gal. 3:28; Eph. 2; Col. 3:11; 1 Peter), and culminates in the new creation: "After this I looked, and there before me was a great multitude that no one could count, from every nation, tribe, people and language, standing before the throne and before the Lamb" (Rev. 7:9).

This is the healing and fulfilling of our humanity as our creatureliness is redeemed and the telos of creation is realized through Christ. In a society under the rule of principalities and powers that are fallen away from their original purpose, our differences as humans divide us and set us against one another. When we recognize that all these differences are marks of our creatureliness and gifts that sustain the flourishing of life, then the world is redeemed as creation. That is, the world is no longer the place where we compete with one another. Now, the "world" has become "creation," where life flourishes as our differences enrich us, and we are reconciled to one another in unity, not uniformity. Our differences become marks of God's grace and presence. Being "creatures" is the larger identity manifested in our differences, just as God is manifest in the triune identity of Father, Son, and Spirit.[23]

Createdness

Now that we have established the healing that may occur among humans as we believe in our creatureliness, we can extend that healing to other creatures and to all creation.[24] In recognizing this creatureliness and createdness of all things, Christians have a reason for caring for all creation and for recognizing our interdependence, not by leveling all relationships and all living things, but by properly relating all living things to God and then by relating to them in ways appropriate to their createdness.

Once again, we are challenged to think in teleological ways rather than in utilitarian or pragmatic ways. In society and in the church, we have often simply continued utilitarian and pragmatic ways of thinking even as we are confronted with crises in the universe that extinguish species and hasten death. We care for parts of creation other than humans because we humans see those parts as critical to our own survival and flourishing. If we oppose the clear-cutting of forests and the destruction of other habitats, it is often because we

23. See chap. 5.
24. See the recent, thorough exposition by Bauckham, *Living with Other Creatures*.

have become convinced that such actions are necessary for the sustaining and flourishing of human life. The same may be said of much of our response to "environmental" crises.

But if we truly understand our creatureliness, then we will care for that which is not human because we recognize in all things their createdness. We care for all things because they have their being and their existence by virtue of their telos in creation as it is redeemed for the new creation. They are not incidental to human life in this age; rather, they are integral to God's creation and redemption.[25] When we come to recognize our own createdness, we will begin to care for, nourish, and delight in all createdness because we will recognize that the love and sustenance and redemption that we receive from God's hands is directed to all creation. To the extent that we do not care and do not delight in all creation, to that same extent we have not yet learned that we are creatures who live by delighting in God—the Father, the Son, and the Spirit. To the extent that we have not learned and delighted in our creatureliness, we are in danger of not recognizing the creatureliness of others. We will treat them as useful for meeting our own needs, denying their true telos in the new creation.

Good Business

One of the places that manifests the pathologies of society that result from the theological neglect of creation is the realm of business.[26] (In a later chapter we will also consider the sciences and technology.) In this brief section, I will simply try to identify some ways that a robust doctrine of creation could reshape the way that we think about and practice business. It is in the practices of businesses that we see creatures, indeed all created things, captured and consumed for the use of others.

If we recover a robust doctrine of creation to guide our business practices, we will know that we operate in a world not of scarcity but of abundance. The discipline of economics and the practice of business that complements it are limited by the horizon of this world. They may help us understand how this world works, but they are studying a world that has fallen away from its telos in God and does not believe that in Christ creation is redeemed for the new creation. Creation and redemption depend on the inexhaustible and unconquerable life of the Father, the Son, and the Spirit. The world of scarcity is the

25. See chap. 7, under "Reconciling All Things: Colossians 1:15–20."

26. This section had been developing in my thinking, but I am indebted to encouragement from Peter Harris, director of A Rocha International, for pushing me to address this pathology. Of course, he bears no responsibility for the way that I engage the issues here.

fallen world; it is not the last word. The last word is the world of abundance, even superabundance, that will be fully revealed in the new creation. In this most real world, life is abundant and eternal.

In this vision of creation in our midst even now, all things are reconciled to God in Christ, and we, God's people and Christ's disciples, are called to bear witness to our lives in relation to God. We will resist the dysteleology of this fallen world and the practices that follow from it both in our refusal to follow in their way and in our organization of our lives to reflect the superabundance of the new creation. Yes, we know that the new creation is not yet fully present and that we seek to follow the way of the new creation in a world that is in rebellion against the God of creation and the new creation. We follow this way not because it is easy or prosperous in this fallen world but because we believe that God calls us to life along this path and only along this path.

Without the teleological vision of creation redeemed for the new creation, the world is simply a repository of "resources" and a depository of unclaimed and not-yet-created wealth. That is, if the only horizon that guides our language about this world is this world, then everything is available for our use. What we often do not see is that this understanding also means that we are available to be used. One of the ways that this is manifested most clearly and destructively is in the manufacturing of desire and the marketing of products purported to meet those desires.[27]

Without a doctrine of creation that calls us to worship and serve the Creator, we become captive to created things and serve them. We become, in a word, idolaters. That is strong and often offensive language in society. Certainly the surveys reveal that a large majority of people in North America (where the majority of my readers live) still believe in God. But such reports tell very little of the story. When Israel's prophets condemned the people of Israel for idolatry, the people too believed in God and engaged in religious rituals (see Isa. 1:10–20). Idolatry is worship and obedience to created things rather than to the One who creates all things and redeems them. Idolatry may also be worship of the One who creates and redeems, but for the misguided purpose of securing goods external to our relationship to God. That is, we may worship God not for Godself but for what we can get from God. The tragic irony is that if we understood creation and our createdness, we would know that in God—the Father, the Son, and the Spirit—is all that we need for life and all that we would desire if we knew God and ourselves truly.[28]

27. For a meditation on the way this works out in everyday life, see Cavanaugh, *Being Consumed*, and chap. 10 below.

28. See my brief reflections on idolatry in Wilson, *Living Faithfully*, 2nd ed., 22–23, and the larger context of our fragmented lives and society.

Good business, then, would arise over time from the discipline of learning to trust in God alone for life and all that we need for life. It would learn that scarcity is the consequence of our idolatry and our following the way of the fallen world; abundance is the gift of the One who creates and the blessing of following the way of the redemption of creation, which is the way of Jesus Christ. Good business is not a matter of making a few adjustments or changing a few practices or finding the right economic system in this world. Rather, good business is the result of a continuing conversion to the way of Jesus Christ, who is the telos of redeemed creation in the new creation.

Part 2

Imagine now that our adventurers have learned where they are. The next step is to learn the territory through which their journey takes them. They need a map for their journey that will complement the presence of their guide and help them find their way to the destination that is the place of life forever. They need to know what dangers they will face along the journey and what resources and promises their guide offers.

"Mustard Seed"

4

The Dialectic of the Kingdom

One of the gravest errors we can make in our witness to the good news of Jesus Christ is to separate creation and redemption from each other. The place and the meaning of creation are found in its redemption. The place and the meaning of redemption are its reclaiming and healing of creation. This is the good news of the kingdom of God in Jesus Christ. Apart from redemption, creation loses its purpose as declared in the gospel of Jesus Christ. Apart from creation, redemption has no purpose in the gospel. As we will see in detail later in this chapter, we recognize "creation" as creation only in relation to God's work of redemption. Likewise, we recognize "redemption" as redemption only in its relation to God's work of creation. When we sever the connection between creation and redemption, we lose both: we remove both creation and redemption from the gospel. In doing so, we may continue to perpetuate some version of the "good news of Jesus Christ" that we live and proclaim, but it will be a pale version that often drifts into a loud proclamation of "good news," which upon close examination turns out to be bad news.

If we come to the realization that we have neglected the doctrine of creation and rush forward to recover and reclaim the doctrine apart from its integral relationship with redemption, then we will have simply exposed gospel witness and Christian living to further vulnerabilities and pathologies. To put it another way: as we recover a Christian doctrine of creation we must root that recovery in Christ. In his reflection on Colossians 1, T. F. Torrance witnesses to this truth when he states that

> in the eternal economic purpose for the creation brought to redemptive fulfillment in the incarnation, Jesus Christ is the central and pivotal reality of the universe, for all things were created through him and for him. . . . With the incarnation, the death and resurrection of Christ in space and time a portentous change has taken place in the universe affecting the way in which we are to understand divine creation as proleptically conditioned by redemption.[1]

One of the most misguided notions in our current thinking is the belief that we can address the many pressing issues of our times—the degradation of Earth, what it means to be human, the use of technology, and more—without a robust doctrine of creation grounded in witness to Christ.[2]

When the church and its teachers explicitly or implicitly, intentionally or unintentionally, separate creation and redemption, our understanding of the gospel, our living it and witnessing to it become attenuated and even corrupt. This attenuation or corruption of the gospel often occurs so slowly that we do not notice what is happening. Eventually this attenuated or corrupt understanding of the gospel becomes so commonplace that we are almost incapable of recognizing our loss or imagining another account of the gospel and a life of faithfulness.

We are dangerously close to this tragedy and in many places have already slipped into an appearance of Christian faithfulness that does not participate in God's redemption of creation and has no awareness of that loss. Our situation is sufficiently dire that before I make my case for this diagnosis, I will first explore what it means to hold creation and redemption together in our understanding, living, and witnessing to the gospel of Jesus Christ.[3]

---

1. Torrance, *Christian Doctrine of God*, 204. In a footnote (204n1), Torrance references and quotes Mackintosh, *Doctrine of the Person of Jesus Christ*.

2. See, for example, Northcott, *Environment and Christian Ethics*, 222: "It becomes clear then that the recovery of an ecological ethics in the modern world requires the recovery of a doctrine of creation redeemed, and the worship of a creator who is also redeemer of creation." See also McGrath, *Nature*, 183: "Both creation and redemption are set within the one economy of salvation of God, with the latter recapitulating the former."

3. The integrity of creation and redemption in Christ was recognized, asserted, and defended throughout the early church and the Middle Ages. Only in modernity has this integrity been largely abandoned and forgotten. However, there are bright spots in modernity. Barth's presentation of covenant and creation bring creation and redemption together within the contours of the Reformed tradition. See Barth, *Church Dogmatics*, III/1. See also the work of T. F. Torrance, represented by his assertion that "the consubstantiality of the incarnate Son with God the Father . . . binds creation and redemption together in such a way that the creation is anchored in the love of God himself as its ultimate ground" (*Trinitarian Faith*, 135; see also Torrance, *Atonement*, 195–200).

The Dialectic of the Kingdom

"The dialectic of the kingdom" is a phrase that may be strange enough to help us think in new ways about the relationship between creation and redemption.[4] By *dialectic*, I simply mean the necessity of holding in relationship two works of God that cannot be properly and faithfully thought and lived apart from each other. I do not mean that creation and redemption are thesis-antithesis that result in synthesis. By *kingdom*, I am simply drawing on an image that Jesus used to bring into focus the many dimensions of the good news. This kingdom is not an ideal or a mere idea; it is the reality of God's redemption of creation.[5]

The dialectic of the kingdom, then, is a phrase meant to force us to keep in mind the necessity of thinking and living "creation and redemption" together. We must not separate the two from each other. We also must not confuse the two or absorb one into the other. Each has its own integrity but also only has its full significance in relation to the other.[6] How, then, are we to relate creation and redemption to each other, each with its own integrity, but having wholeness only in relation to the other? Here I will explore three ways of doing this.

Life

The first way to affirm the oneness of creation and redemption is to see them as the constituents of life. One very powerful description of the triune reality of God is, simply, Life. This is also an appropriate way of bearing witness to God's self-naming: YHWH, "I AM WHO I AM" (Exod. 3).[7] One way to reflect this truth about God in our doctrine of creation is to sustain the "dialectic of the kingdom" by recognizing that the God who is Life gives life to that which is not God through the work of creation and redemption.

This reality pervades John's Gospel. In the opening chapter, as creation and redemption come together in "the Word . . . made flesh" (v. 14 KJV) we

4. I adopt this phrase from Hartt, *Christian Critique of American Culture*, 75–76, where Hartt introduces the phrase, then says: "Without that dialectic the world of divine creation and of divine redemption splits into two unreal and mutually hostile parts." Hartt's work is dedicated to the good news that in Jesus Christ, God's work of creation and redemption is one.

5. For a brief presentation of the kingdom, see Wilson, *God So Loved the World*, 23–58.

6. Some may recognize in this an echo of the Chalcedonian definition of Christ's two natures in one person. That is an appropriate perception. However, that definition applies only to Christ himself. Nevertheless, it does give us some guidance in our present witness to the gospel. In the end, however, I propose that creation and redemption become one in the new creation. For an extended reflection on this idea, see Bulgakov, *Lamb of God*, 182–211. I disagree with some of the details of Bulgakov's account but still find it the most instructive reflection. I am indebted to Doug Harink for reminding me of this passage in Bulgakov.

7. Waltke, *Old Testament Theology*, 359–69; Goldingay, *Israel's Gospel*, passim; *Israel's Faith*, 26–43; for an account of the Triune God as life, see the following chapter and references there.

are told that "in him was life" (v. 4). Throughout John's Gospel, Jesus as the life of the world is declared in various ways:

> "Very truly, I tell you, anyone who hears my word and believes him who sent me has eternal life, and does not come under judgment, but has passed from death to life" (John 5:24 NRSV).
>
> "I am the bread of life" (John 6:35; see the entire discourse).
>
> "The words that I have spoken to you are spirit and life" (John 6:63 NRSV).
>
> "I am the light of the world. Whoever follows me will never walk in darkness, but will have the light of life" (John 8:12).
>
> "I am the resurrection and the life" (John 11:25).
>
> "I am the way, and the truth, and the life" (John 14:6 NRSV).

In these representative passages, we see creation and redemption coming together in the reality of life. There is no gospel more carefully grounded in creation than the Gospel of John. At the same time, there is no gospel more declarative of redemption. John, in the maturity of his thought, testifies to Jesus Christ as life.[8] This testimony recognizes that Jesus Christ—the "Word made flesh"—is the agent of creation: "In the beginning was the Word. . . . Through him all things were made; without him nothing was made that has been made" (John 1:1, 3). John goes on: "in him was life" (v. 4). As the rest of the story makes clear, without the redemptive work of God in Christ, the life that has been given to creation would be eternally captive to condemnation and would finally perish were it not for Christ. In Christ, the creation is saved from condemnation and enters the freedom of eternal life.

The interweaving of Christ's work as Creator and Redeemer brings life. We may say, then, that creation and redemption are two aspects of one reality: life. This affirmation is also declared in other parts of the New Testament and is assumed even where it is not made explicit. For Paul, the very life of creation is grounded in the life of redemption. Only in and through Christ does creation have its very existence, its continuation, and its purpose. (Among other passages, see Col. 1–2.) And the author of Hebrews begins with an echo of John 1:

> In the past God spoke to our ancestors through the prophets at many times and in various ways, but in these last days he has spoken to us by his Son, whom he appointed heir of all things, and through whom also he made the universe. The Son is the radiance of God's glory and the exact representation of his being, sustaining all things by his powerful word. After he had provided purification for sins, he sat down at the right hand of the Majesty in heaven. (Heb. 1:1–3)

8. See McDonough, *Christ as Creator*, chaps. 2 and 10.

Once again, in this passage we can see the interweaving of creation and redemption, which results in life. Here "the Son" inherits "all things" and is the one through whom the universe is made. (It may be significant that his inheritance of all things is announced before the declaration that through him the universe was made.) He upholds the universe and made purification for sins. Once again neither creation nor redemption is sufficient alone for life, but the two together bring the wholeness that is life.

In the way that this testimony to life through creation and redemption is grounded in Christ, it is also therefore grounded in the earlier witness of Israel to the coming of the Messiah as the Tanak testifies to life through creation and redemption. Israel during this time knew that life cannot be grounded merely in creation; life is promised and enjoyed only through God's redemption of creation.[9]

New Creation

In the midst of these passages on life through creation and redemption, another vital oneness appears. In the coming together of God's work of creation and redemption for life, our vision is directed forward to the new creation. Thus, creation and redemption may be known by faith to be one in their "end" in the new creation. By *end* here, I mean the telos, the purpose for which they exist. This is not their "end" as destruction or eradication, but their "end" as the fulfillment of their purpose.[10] We may say simply that God works creation and redemption for this: the new creation.

The new creation is neither the mere fulfillment of the purpose of God's creating work nor of God's redeeming work; rather it is God's work of creating and redeeming that together "end" in the new creation. In the gospel of Jesus Christ, this new creation is possible only through God's work of creating and redeeming.

The most powerful testimony to God's purpose in Christ to make all things new is found in Ephesians 1.

> Praise be to the God and Father of our Lord Jesus Christ, who has blessed us in the heavenly realms with every spiritual blessing in Christ. For he chose us in him before the creation of the world to be holy and blameless in his sight. In love he predestined us for adoption to sonship through Jesus Christ, in accordance with his pleasure and will—to the praise of his glorious grace, which

9. As we will see in detail in chap. 7, "Rereading Scripture," this conviction is declared "in the beginning."

10. See my comment on 2 Pet. 3:10–13 in chap. 6, footnote 17.

he has freely given us in the One he loves. In him we have redemption through his blood, the forgiveness of sins, in accordance with the riches of God's grace that he lavished on us. With all wisdom and understanding, he made known to us the mystery of his will according to his good pleasure, which he purposed in Christ, to be put into effect when the times reach their fulfillment—to bring unity to all things in heaven and on earth under Christ. (Eph. 1:3–10)

From this passage and many others, as well as from our theological reasoning about the dialectic of the kingdom in creation and redemption, we may assert the conviction that the new creation is God's eternal purpose.[11]

The Integrity of the Two Stories

We cannot tell the biblical story of creation apart from the story of redemption. Nor can we tell the biblical story of redemption apart from creation. We must first see the two in relation to each other before we bring one, then the other, into the foreground. Thinking dramatically, we will first give them equal billing before putting one, then the other, in the spotlight.

It may appear that we can tell the story of creation apart from redemption. It is quite commonplace to think of the biblical story in three acts: 1. Creation, 2. Fall, 3. Redemption, and sometimes 4. Consummation.[12] But if we pause to think carefully, we will recognize that the biblical story is one story in one act told through many different perspectives. Think, for example, of the story of creation in Genesis. This story assumes God's redemptive work in two ways: in its historical origins and in its theological character.

11. This, of course, raises two long-standing, knotty theological controversies: infra- versus supralapsarianism, and Barth's creative exposition of the relationship between covenant and creation. For the first, I will say without going into detailed analysis and extensive argument that the debate typically is set within a tension between creation and redemption and is seldom placed within the larger context of the new creation. This context, I think, could dissolve the question, though not everyone would be convinced. In short, to set the questions of God's decrees in relation to the new creation means that such would be God's purpose apart from sin entering the world. In a world without sin, one can easily imagine the incarnation (without crucifixion) as the means by which the creation would be apprehended for a new relationship with God. As to the second question, see my forthcoming essay "Is the Theater Redeemed? Creation and Redemption in Calvin, Edwards, and Barth." There I argue that although the language of "outer basis" and "inner meaning" are misleading and may cause a denigration or discarding of creation, nevertheless because creation is from the beginning included in God's covenant, Barth has a weak version of the dialectic of the kingdom for which I am presently arguing.

12. Barth may appear to follow this three-act sequence in his own way in the plan of volumes 3–5 of *Church Dogmatics*: creation, reconciliation, redemption. But an attentive reading recognizes that Barth is telling the same story three different ways and that his first two volumes of *Church Dogmatics* tell the whole story before focusing seriatim on the three indivisible works of the Triune God. R. Jenson does the same in the two volumes of his *Systematic Theology*.

Historically, this story as part of the Torah originates with the Israelites. Even if we push this story back to Moses, it has its place in the canon through the life of a people who have had their lives redeemed from slavery by I AM. They tell this story of creation retrospectively. None of them was there at creation to record what God did.[13] None of them has ever experienced this world to which Genesis 1–2 bears witness. The Israelites' experience has been an almost unbroken encounter with the broken world of Genesis 3. Theirs has been "an *almost* unbroken encounter" with the world of Genesis 3 because God has broken into the lives of their ancestors, Abraham, Isaac, and Jacob. The Israelites who receive and canonize the story of creation in Genesis 1–2 know only by faith that the world they live in is "creation"—an orderly, life-giving, gracious gift of the God who is worthy of praise—because they have been made participants in God's work of redeeming creation. We can recognize this world as "creation" only because of God's redemptive work. Or to put it differently, only a world open to and caught up in redemption can be recognized as "creation."[14]

We must avoid being misled and mystified by our use of the word "creation" for many views of the world. For the biblical story, which is our story, to confess this world as "creation" is to confess that the way things are now is not the way that they always have been nor the way that they always will be. The world as we know it is a world of pain and suffering. It gives life, then takes it away. The world, it seems, is an endlessly spinning wheel that generates life in one turn, only to grind it into pieces at the next turn, and recycle it into life that is then once again ground into pieces.

For Christians, the biblical doctrine of creation—that this world has not always been as it presently is and will not always be so—is rooted in the realization that God is redeeming this world. This conviction—that God is redeeming creation—changes everything about how we live in this world. If this world as it is today is the way that the world always has been and always will be, then we should live in it accordingly: accepting its conflicts and struggles, death, disease, and destruction and in the midst of this try simply to make the best of it. But since in Christ we know that this world is the creation that God is redeeming, then we live in it with trust, expectation, and joy that anticipates and even participates in the fullness of the redemption that is already at work and will one day be complete.

Thus, Christians can begin faithfully to confess and to live their convictions about "creation" when they learn that it is creation only through God's

---

13. Wiseman offers an intriguing variation on this in *Clues to Creation in Genesis*.
14. See chap. 7 for an extended treatment of this aspect of Gen. 1–3.

redemptive work. The contrary also holds true. If we fail to live our convictions about redemption and to connect our confession inextricably to creation, then we fail in faithful witness. In such cases, where creation is not kept in relation to redemption, creation then becomes an unreal world. Creation becomes a world without meaning because we cannot locate it in the biblical story. We must remember that in the biblical story, creation is not just that which God made but that which God is redeeming. From the beginning of its appearance in the biblical story, creation is located within God's redemptive acts. If we set this location—redemption—aside and then try to locate creation in the biblical story in some other way, "creation" soon becomes something other than creation. We may still use the term, but it no longer has meaning within the biblical story.

Of course, we often fall into the temptation to render an account of "creation" apart from redemption. Certainly we can study the life of plants and animals, the economic transactions of people, the political life of nations, and so much more without an active, explicit doctrine of creation located in relation to redemption. But we cannot discern the purpose and full significance of flora and fauna, economics, politics, and more apart from placing them within an account of this world as creation—that which God is redeeming in Christ.

Consequences of Separating the Stories

When we no longer locate "creation" within the biblical story inextricably connected with redemption, several different things may happen to "creation." One of the most common consequences is that "creation" becomes a realm independent of redemption. In this case, creation is regarded as following its own laws that may be discovered apart from redemption. I have argued above that this sort of move is a theological error. But is not this precisely what modern sciences have done quite successfully?

In the face of this widespread and seemingly undeniable claim to scientific success, three convictions come to bear. First, we must note that the sciences, as we know them in the West and those places where the West has significant influence, arose precisely in the context of conviction that the God of Jesus Christ is dependable in the rule of creation and that God is not identical with creation.[15] But this does not go far today because the sciences quickly moved away from this foundational conviction into work that practically and then theoretically operates without "the God hypothesis."

15. This main story line must be supplemented by the European reengagement with Islamic culture and science.

A more telling conviction is the realization that contemporary sciences operate within a very limited horizon.[16] They work on the basis that the way the world is today is the way it always has been and always will be. I do not mean this as a restatement of the criticism that the sciences presuppose a uniformitarian view of natural processes. That critique has often been advanced in crude and sophisticated versions by various defenders of "creation" over against "evolution" and scientific practices. But that critique itself actually perpetuates the basic limitation of the sciences. That is, the uniformitarian critique of the sciences remains at the level of material processes. The Christian doctrine of creation inextricably connected to redemption asserts a more fundamental challenge. It is not that the material processes of this world have changed so that, for example, the geological age of the earth cannot be accurately determined by sciences that presuppose a uniformity of processes. Rather, the very character of *creation* is different from that assumed both by contemporary sciences that set God aside and by the sciences that want to put God back into the process. In other words, the Christian doctrine of creation asserts that there is in fact a completely different process going on in creation—its redemption.[17]

This work of redemption points us to the most fundamental reality of creation: it is reconciled to God in Christ.[18] We can know many things about visible and invisible phenomena, but until we know this word of reconciliation about them, we do not know the world fully as creation. If reconciliation is absent from our understanding of the things of this world, then our knowledge, confession, and life fall short of faithfulness to the biblical story of God's redemption of creation.[19] It is here ultimately that any separation of creation from redemption ends up losing the fullness of Christian conviction about the cosmos as creation.

16. For accounts of this limitation, see Gorringe, *God's Theatre*, esp. chap. 2; Hardy, *God's Ways with the World*, 156–57.

17. Gorringe, *God's Theatre*, 32, remarks on God's grace and love, which are foundational to creation.

18. Here I am melding together the work of God that Barth treats under two rubrics, reconciliation and redemption. Barth famously never arrived at the doctrine of "redemption," but if we recognize that his dogmatics narrates the same work of God under different rubrics, then we may also discern a sketch of a doctrine of redemption implicit in the written volumes of *Church Dogmatics*.

19. This suggests some ways of thinking about other forms of knowledge in the world that we will explore in chap. 8. Note also that I do not say, "If reconciliation is absent from our understanding, then we fall short of *perfection*." Even when we know that all things are reconciled to God in Christ, our knowledge still falls short of perfection. Only God has perfect knowledge. Those who would argue that we always also fall short of *faithfulness* should remember the many calls and affirmations of faithfulness in the NT.

But such loss is not confined to the sciences. It is also present in theology itself, in the many theologies that over the centuries have thought that there is an "order of creation" to which we have access apart from the "order of redemption." This is a far-reaching claim that runs against much of the tradition of theology. To make the case fully would require another volume that carefully delineates the ways that this separation of creation and redemption in theology has led to various mistakes.[20]

The biggest mistake is made when "the order of creation" is separated from "the order of redemption," as has often but not always occurred in the Lutheran and Reformed traditions. When the order of creation is separated from the order of redemption and treated as if its purpose and meaning could be discerned apart from redemption, we end up with a bifurcated account of the Christian life, on the one hand, and life within an imagined order of creation that does not bear witness to Jesus Christ, on the other hand. We interpret the way things are now as part of the order of creation and simply try to make the best of the circumstances instead of realizing that the present situation is the way of the world, which has been publicly humiliated and defeated by Christ.

My own Baptist and pietist tradition has often failed in another way, having only "the order of redemption."[21] When this mistake matures, our account of salvation becomes an account of our being rescued from the world into an ethereal and other-worldly "heaven." In this case, our account of salvation and the Christian life become gnostic, and our witness is a pale reflection of the good news of Jesus Christ. We seek to save souls (the language of my tradition was "soul-winning") and imagine ourselves engaged in a rescue operation. Among several issues embedded in this language that we will consider throughout this book, we must here recognize that the good news of Jesus

20. The works of T. F. Torrance and Alister McGrath reconceive a "natural theology" that is theologically committed from the beginning. See Torrance's many works and McGrath's *Scientific Theology* (3 vols.). This reconception of "natural theology" is summed up by McGrath: "At the heart of this process of reconception is an insistence that natural theology is not an autonomous intellectual enterprise conducted from outside the Christian tradition, but a legitimate consequence of the Christian vision of reality. Natural theology presupposes the core doctrines of the Christian faith, which impels the theologian to view nature through the lens of a trinitarian vision of God. Natural theology is the proper outcome of faith, not its foundation; its consequence, not its presupposition" (*Order of Things*, 86). My one addition would be that such a natural theology also presupposes that we know "nature" as "creation" only through God's redemptive work. McGrath seems to agree with this in his locating this reconceived natural theology within the community of faith and a reference to J. Haught's inclusion of "the economy of salvation" within such a natural theology. In this respect, a mature example of such a "natural theology" may be set forth in Hauerwas, *With the Grain of the Universe*.

21. See my essay "Do Pietists Need a Doctrine of Creation?"

Christ is for the whole person, not just for some immaterial part of humans ("souls" separate from bodies), and that God's "rescue operation" redeems the world as creation. God saves us from the world by redeeming the world and giving life to the new creation.

The mistakes that we make when we separate creation and redemption are nearly endless in their ramifications. They have contributed to the rise of many heresies and reactions against those heresies.[22] What we need is a recovery of "the dialectic of the kingdom"—the redemption of creation for the new creation—so that we may enter into the fullness of the gospel and bear witness to it.

Redemption

The biblical story of redemption cannot be told, understood, or lived apart from creation. Together the Christian doctrines of creation and redemption give us rules for how to hear this story, see this work, and participate in it.

But first, imagine a different "Christian" account. This world is not creation. That is, it is not the free act of the One God, who is Father, Son, and Spirit and known to be so through the work of Christ. Rather, this world is from somewhere else, someone else. Or it is from no one and nowhere. But here it is. What is to be done with it? Well, it so happens (we imagine) that there is a triune god who comes across this world and decides to do something about it. Somehow this god, who has no prior relationship with this world, decides to claim it. This god does so by taking responsibility for its upkeep and sustenance. And eventually, the god decides to do something more. So the "second person" of the god comes into this world. This coming is not based on any original or purposeful relationship with this world. This is not a creator-creation relationship that we are imagining. It is not "redemption" because the relationship between this world and this god is purely accidental.

We could continue with this fanciful account and even imagine others. But such an exercise is futile. If this world is redeemed—as we believe that it is in Jesus Christ—then it is redeemed as creation by the God who is Creator—Father, Son, and Holy Spirit.

If we accept that this is God's creation, then we face another temptation: to think that redemption can take place apart from creation. This temptation is subtler than the temptation to think that we can know and live in creation

---

22. Although they are not precisely concerned with this question, relevant discussions appear in Burrell, *Freedom and Creation in Three Traditions*; Burrell and McGinn, *God and Creation*. In this latter work, see esp. chap. 3 by Burrell.

apart from redemption. Nevertheless, it is widespread. It most often takes form in the belief that "redemption" is God's work of saving us *from* our life in creation.[23] This commonplace denial of the interweaving of creation and redemption is deeply enshrined in beliefs and practices that regard this world merely as a container for God's work of salvation, not as an actual participant in God's work of salvation. It is as if this world were the stage set for God's work of redemption.[24] Once that work is done, the set is taken down and discarded because it is no longer needed.

This set of beliefs and practices finds expression in talk about "heaven" as an eternal dwelling for disembodied spirits; in practices that treat the cosmos as at best a tool for redemption and at worst an obstacle to redemption; in talk about "saving souls" (which are by nature immortal) from their captivity to bodies (which are by nature mortal); and in practices that locate "spiritual maturity" apart from bodily life.

Heaven on Earth: God's New Creation

To counter these mistakes, we must be vigilant in retrieving and guarding the biblical teaching about the interweaving of redemption and creation. The biblical vision of "heaven" is the vision of life in God's presence.[25] The vision of this heaven as the fulfillment of God's redemption of creation is given to John and to us: God will dwell with us in the new creation (Rev. 21). That is the fulfillment of the prayer that Jesus taught his disciples: "Your kingdom come, your will be done, on earth as it is in heaven" (Matt. 6:10). This fulfillment is "heaven on earth," where we will live in our resurrected bodies forever. We learn very clearly in the New Testament that the cosmos is not merely a tool of redemption or an impediment to redemption but is the very "objective" of redemption. We have objectives that we aim to accomplish by our actions

23. As I have noted earlier, the historic word for this is "gnosticism," which among other things teaches that "matter" is evil in its very nature and thus incapable of redemption; only "spirit" is good and thus in need not of "redemption" but only of release from its imprisonment in "matter."

24. Burrell speaks of "Christians so preoccupied with redemption that creation is simply presumed as its stage-setting" (*Freedom and Creation*, 41). I worry that Calvin's description of creation as "the theatre of God's glory" can and has too easily led to thinking that creation is the theater in which the drama of redemption is played out: the theater itself is not part of the drama, and when the play ends, the theater may be abandoned. See Calvin, *Institutes*, 1.5.1–2, 8; 1.14.20; 2.6.1; also Schreiner, *Theater of His Glory*. Several passages in Calvin mitigate against this conclusion (such as the celebration of God as Creator and Redeemer, *Institutes*, 1.6.1.), but the language of theater lends itself so strongly to the "stage-set" understanding of creation that more needs to be said to prevent that conclusion.

25. See Morse, *Difference Heaven Makes*; Willard, *Divine Conspiracy*, 66–84; Kreeft, *Heaven*.

but never accomplish fully. With God, however, there is no gap between God's intentions, actions, and accomplishments. God's aim in Jesus Christ is accomplished: "Through [Christ] God was pleased to reconcile to himself all things, whether on earth or in heaven, by making peace through the blood of his cross" (Col. 1:20 NRSV). Earlier in this passage, Paul has denoted "all things" as "things visible and invisible, whether thrones or dominions or rulers or powers" (Col. 1:16 NRSV). The "things" of the cosmos may set themselves as obstacles to redemption, but they are no match for their Creator. And the "peace" that God makes by the blood of the cross is picked up by the image of God weaving creation and redemption together into a new creation.

In John's vision, we also hear the declaration that God is "making all things new" (Rev. 21:5 NRSV) not "making all new things." This declaration requires us to think of God's redemption of creation, not God's annihilation of creation. The images that follow in John's Revelation make clear that although this new creation is not identical to the present cosmos, it is continuous with it. There is no sorrow, no death, no evil, no sea, no celestial sources of light. There is day but no night, a city, a river and a garden, the wealth of the peoples, and the glory of kings. Most tellingly, there is the tree of life. Some of this is straightforward language; much of it is imaginative. All of it is true and at a minimum conveys the unimaginable glory of the new creation in terms of life continuous with the present cosmos as the work of God's creation and redemption.[26]

Resurrection

As far as our bodies are concerned, we need to retrieve and guard the confession of physical resurrection. In evangelical communities, we often affirm vigorously and centrally the evidence for the bodily resurrection of Christ and its place as proof of Christ's divinity, but we seldom develop a strenuous and centrally important account of the theological significance of Christ's bodily resurrection as the promise of our own.[27] In some Christian communities, especially liberal Western Christianity, the "resurrection of Christ" is often affirmed as something that happened to the disciples.[28] That is, nothing changed for Jesus of Nazareth: his body was in the tomb until "natural processes" took their course. But the spirit of his message and his way of life lives on in the disciples. From frightened, discouraged followers of one who had been cruci-

---

26. These images in the book of Revelation are drawn mostly from Isaiah and some from Ezekiel. For a powerful exposition of the Isaiah connection, see Mouw, *When the Kings Come Marching In.*

27. A recent and welcome exception is N. T. Wright, *Surprised by Hope* and *Resurrection of the Son of God.*

28. This is true of popular authors such as Marcus Borg and John Shelby Spong.

fied and buried, they were transformed into people in whose lives the spirit of Jesus's teachings live on. Moving onto and beyond the fringes of Christian conviction, some teachers today view the "resurrection of Jesus" as a symbol of the constant renewal of life and the resilience of the human spirit, which in the face of death's inevitability, still affirms the continuation of life.

None of these views reflects the biblical testimony to Christ's resurrection or the absolutely essential place of the resurrection in the whole biblical story. To deny the significance of the bodily resurrection requires us to distort the testimony of Scripture and to affirm the present order of things. There simply is no story of the redemption of creation apart from the bodily resurrection of Jesus of Nazareth as the Christ. Yes, one can tell a different story with "Israel," "Jesus," and "God," as central characters in the story: a story that has no need of Christ's bodily resurrection. But that story is truly a different story. In various ways it leaves in place and unchallenged the dreary story of a world in which death is the ruling force. When it seeks to affirm life, it does so through sleight of hand and provides only an imitation of life, not its reality. The life these accounts offer is a pale, thin substitute for the life promised through the redemption of creation by "the blood of his cross."

Life in the Spirit

The life that is given to humankind and to all creation through Jesus Christ is the life that begins now in the Holy Spirit: the righteousness, peace, and joy that comprise the kingdom of God (Rom. 14:17), the fruit of the Spirit (Gal. 5:21–22), which in another setting Paul describes as "the firstfruits of the Spirit" (Rom. 8:23). If we are tempted to separate "spiritual life" from "bodily life" and conclude that only some immaterial, spiritual life really participates in redemption, we have only to ask ourselves one question: "What can we do 'spiritually,' as our participation in redemption, apart from our bodies?" The truth is, even though our bodies are dying physically, they are also even now being made to participate in redemption. Our bodily participation in the work of the Spirit is the first sign, the guarantee that we are indeed now participating in God's work of redeeming creation so that we may trust that our bodies will one day be raised to life in the new creation (Rom. 8).[29]

Incarnation

The doctrine of the incarnation—the Word became flesh—is one of the most powerful reminders of the work of God in Christ to weave together creation

29. Fee, *God's Empowering Presence*, 515–91.

and redemption. In the incarnation (not the doctrine but the mystery-laden actuality of the one who is fully human and fully divine yet one person), God weaves together creation and redemption in the person of Jesus of Nazareth. We often, even usually, confess the incarnation with firmness of faith but then go on to reduce its significance to redemption and fail to recognize the way that God engulfs creation with this act.

We reduce the incarnation by regarding it only as a necessary step toward God's act of redemption. In this reduction, the Word became flesh to bear our sins and live long enough as a human to teach and perform miracles that display and confirm his divinity before being crucified. In variations on this reductionist account of the incarnation, the Word becomes flesh as an instrumental act necessary to the work of redemption.

But that understanding of the incarnation reduces the Word becoming flesh to a skeleton with some flesh hanging on it. In contrast to this deracinated image, we must retrieve, celebrate, and live the fullness of the incarnation as the climactic act of God's love for God's creation. The Word became flesh not as an instrument toward our salvation but as an embrace of the whole of creation in this one person—an embrace that redeems all creation. As it is, this "one person" is the one by whom, through whom, and for whom all things were made. It is this very one who enters fully, deeply, passionately into the life of the creation. This is the action of love, love that began before the creation of the cosmos, gives life to the cosmos, holds the cosmos together, embraces and enfolds the cosmos into the life of God through Jesus Christ, and promises life eternal for the cosmos by weaving together creation and redemption in a new heavens and a new earth.

Creation

We cannot recognize or describe this world as "creation" apart from God's work of redemption. Yes, we often use the term "creation" without reference to redemption. But if we are truly thinking of this world as God's creation and living in it, then we implicitly understand this world as God's creation redeemed in Jesus Christ. Again, this simply *is* the grammar of the gospel. If we are using "creation" in some other way, then we are employing a faulty grammar or telling a different story from the story of Jesus Christ.

Tragically, we have often, perhaps more often than not, misspoken the good news of Jesus Christ when we have spoken of creation. Many times, the church and its teachers and preachers have spoken of creation as if it were a realm separate from God's redemptive work. We have spoken as if "creation" were simply a stage set for the drama of redemption. In cases like this, once the drama has come to its end, the stage set may be folded up and taken away. This world as stage set, misnamed creation, is incidental rather than integral to the work of redemption.

Worse yet, we—the church, its teachers and preachers—have portrayed this world as a (misnamed) "creation" that is an impediment to God's work of redemption. Here we are confusing terms. The biblical proclamation of the gospel knows of a "world" in rebellion against God and God's purposes. To be sure, the New Testament uses *world* in different ways. It may refer to all created things; it may refer to the human construal of reality, a kind of cosmology; and it may, as we are using it here, refer to everything that is in rebellion against God. In this last case, *world* is all that refuses to acknowledge God's love and the lordship of Jesus Christ. Here *world* is not creation: it is death, not life; it is anticreation, not new creation. But this biblical teaching is sometimes confused in the church and even opposed, so that "creation" becomes the "world" that is in rebellion against God.[30]

This confusion is often compounded by our use of *creation* to describe not the work of God but simply "everything that isn't God." So creation becomes a category of things rather than a characteristic of things that are the work of God. We misuse *creation* as a noun denoting a collection of things rather than the continuing work of God as God keeps this world in existence and works for its redemption.[31] In light of this, we do well to use occasionally, even frequently, the active form "creating." There is no creation apart from the continuing creating work of God. So creation properly understood is not an obstacle to God's purpose and God's redeeming work; instead, it is the very work of God.

There is most certainly a "world" that is in rebellion against God and refuses to acknowledge the rule of God in Christ. But even that world is made to be creation as God sustains and provides for it. God's providence is, in this respect, God's work of claiming even this rebellious world as creation. It provides no impediment to God's work of redemption. By God's sovereign love, the "world" is made to participate in God's purpose, which is life.

This testimony to God's providence leads to one further way in which "creation" may be distorted in our proclamation. In the course of our history, the church has many times fallen into the trap of portraying creation as this world from which God rescues us. This is one form of the persistent heresy

30. See chaps. 8 and 9.
31. After writing this, I discovered the elegant statement of Hardy, *God's Ways with the World*, 169: "Creation keeps the universe (or anything in it) from ending, and then ends it (or anything in it)."

that views material things as evil simply because they are material. Sadly, Christians have thoughtlessly and carelessly fallen into this trap many times.[32] We see this world as beyond God's redemptive work. So rather than redeem this world, God's saves us out of it for life in a new world to come. This error is reinforced by some popular preaching and hymnody. When we think of the church as a lifeboat in which we who are being saved huddle together while we await rescue—the return of Christ—we have mistaken the relationship between the world and creation.

This world is not unreal or illusory. This is not a passing phase or a temporary set. This world—wounded, broken, fallen, sinful, suffering, rebellious—this world is, by God's gracious rule, *creation*, the stuff of redemption. Apart from this, there is no redemption; there is nothing. If this world is not the stuff of redemption, then it will simply go on meaninglessly forever, or it will come to . . . nothing. The very fact that I can reason in this way and that you can agree or disagree reveals to us, quietly and gently, the meaningfulness of this stuff—its hope, our hope—in God's creating and redeeming work.

Difference

The joyful difference that this makes will be explored in part 3. But it will be helpful here to indicate some of that difference so that we may begin to grasp the significance of the "dialectic of the kingdom." Among many possibilities, I will briefly note three differences that this dialectic makes in our verbal witness, our way of being, and our ethics.

Verbal Witness

In our verbal witness to the good news of Jesus Christ, the dialectic of the kingdom grounds us theologically. We may often be lured into the mistake of describing the good news as an escape from the trials and sorrows of this world. This presentation may give us some competitive advantage in the marketplace of ideas and increase interest in our message. This message may be very successful in attracting people when it is done well by charismatic leaders. But it is not the gospel, and it does not create disciples of Jesus Christ. God in Christ is reconciling this world—all things—to its proper relationship to God. To put it in everyday terms: it is a mistake to tell people as they come into worship that they are to leave their burdens at the door. That is a tragic and dismal declaration of bad news. Instead, guided by the dialectic of the kingdom, we

---

32. See the wide-ranging, instructive jeremiad by Lee, *Against the Protestant Gnostics*.

invite people to bring their burdens, their sorrows, their sin into worship of the Father, the Son, and the Holy Spirit because the Triune God is the God of creation and redemption. It is the very stuff of our lives that God creates and redeems, weaving everything together into the new creation.

The dialectic of creation and redemption also protects us from another mistake in our witness, the error of proclaiming the "good news" that God's intention is to make us healthy and wealthy in this life. This dismal news falls into the error of unbelief by capitulating to the lie that this world in its fallenness and brokenness is simply the way things are. The "good news" of this "health and wealth" gospel is that Jesus Christ can give us the skills and blessings to make it here, to be prosperous financially and physically. This is a pretense of "good news" that distorts the redemption of all creation into a plan of success for the individual here and now.

The dialectic of the kingdom teaches us that God's creating and redeeming work is for the whole cosmos and will one day end in the new creation. That this world needs redemption tells us that there is something deadly wrong with it. God is making right that wrong. (Righteousness and justice testify to this: God is making the world right and lining all things up just the way that they should be. This includes, among many things, both identifying and condemning evil and extending grace and mercy to all who believe in God.) But the way that God is "righting" creation is not according to the world's desires but according to God's intention for life. The bad news of "prosperity" is that the world sets the expectations for how God will work in the world. Tragically, then, the world simply remains the world, and we remain captive to it, though with new resources and "blessing" to prosper in the world. When the church's "witness" is distorted by this error, this world is not "creation" but continues to be "world," and there is no redemption for it. Here is how C. S. Lewis exposes this tragedy in a classic passage:

> Indeed, if we consider the unblushing promises of reward and the staggering nature of the rewards promised in the Gospels, it would seem that Our Lord finds our desires not too strong, but too weak. We are half-hearted creatures, fooling about with drink and sex and ambition when infinite joy is offered us, like an ignorant child who wants to go on making mud pies in a slum because he cannot imagine what is meant by the offer of a holiday at the sea. We are far too easily pleased.[33]

Yes, God will bring into being the unimaginable blessing of the new creation through the redemption of creation. The message of "prosperity" is a sad, pale, insipid imitation of the new creation.

33. Lewis, *Weight of Glory*, 26.

Way of Being

In addition to our verbal witness, the dialectic of the kingdom makes a difference for our way of being in the world. By "being in the world," I mean something that is really about our witness as well. But it is more about our overall disposition in the world, our way of life, what we may sometimes consider under the label "ethics." To the extent that I am addressing our understanding of ethics, I am also trying to subvert and even overturn that understanding. Christian ethics should not be primarily about asserting a (or the) Christian position on an issue; nor should Christian ethics be primarily a study of what Christians do in the quandaries that "ethics" is so often thought to concern. Rather, Christian ethics is the work of discerning and participating in God's creating and redeeming work that sees them being woven together into the new creation. Much of our "Christian ethics" leaves the systems of this world intact, accepts the limits that they place on our character and life, and seeks then to make the best of this situation in the name of "Christian realism."[34] To counter this, I am proposing an approach to Christian ethics grounded in biblical or gospel realism: the dialectic of the kingdom sets the "limits" for our character and life. It is not easy to live in faithfulness to the kingdom; its "effectiveness" by the world's measure may be paltry, nonexistent, and even counterproductive. Forgiving our enemies is a very dangerous practice, as is blessing our persecutors. We can live this life only if we are captured by the vision of the new creation guarded by the dialectic of the kingdom.

When we turn to the dialectic of the kingdom for guidance in our way of being in the world, we discover the good news that affirms the goodness of this world as the creating work of God while at the same time asserting the necessity of the redeeming work of God. What we will always seek to discern in the world is where and how God's goodness and redemption is at work and being made known so that we can bear witness to it.

We develop this discernment by knowing the Father's love for the world and his sending of the Son. We further learn this discernment by dwelling in the story of Jesus Christ as the incarnation of the love of God. To dwell in this story as the story of the Messiah of Israel (Luke 24) and the Lord of all creation (Col. 1; Phil. 2) is to begin to develop eyes and ears and heart, whole disciples in the disciple community who can participate in God's redemption of creation and thus bear witness to its goodness as the stuff of the new creation. Finally, we must receive and live in the Holy Spirit, who today gathers

---

34. A prime example of this is Stackhouse, *Making the Best of It*. John is a warm and supportive friend. Our friendship thrives alongside our differences on this and other matters.

the disciple community, forms us in Christ, and scatters gifts among us so that only together may we learn how we are to be in this world.

Ethics as Witness

As we practice this discernment and learn how to be in the world in light of the dialectic of the kingdom, our life will be a witness to the new creation that is the end of this world. This witness will be our ethics, not as advice for people wanting to be good, not as the means of improving the world, nor as the ability to discern good and evil.[35] Rather, in light of the dialectic of the kingdom, our way of being in the world will reflect the insights of Dietrich Bonhoeffer:

> When the ethical problem presents itself essentially as the question of my own being good and doing good, the decision has already been made that the self and the world are the ultimate realities. All ethical reflection then has the goal that I be good, and that the world—by my action—becomes good. If it turns out, however, that these realities, myself and the world, are themselves embedded in a whole other ultimate reality, namely, the reality of God the Creator, Reconciler, and Redeemer, then the ethical problem takes on a whole new aspect. Of ultimate importance, then, is not that I become good, or that the condition of the world be improved by my efforts, but that the reality of God show itself everywhere to be the ultimate reality. (Bonhoeffer, *Ethics*, 48)

The public witness of our life as the disciple community, then, will not follow the easy way of denying life in this world or of fully affirming life in it as the world but will instead affirm the goodness of this world in light of *God's creating and redeeming work*.

Maintaining this reality of creation and redemption that looks forward to and lives toward the new creation is the dialectical tension that only God's grace can sustain. This is one of the central and pervasive insights of Bonhoeffer's *Ethics*: to think that Christian ethics can be based on any combination of rules, principles, decisions, and outcomes denies the ongoing reality of God's presence and work in the world through Christ. We come close to Bonhoeffer's argument when we say that we are "in but not of the world." But that formulation falls short of the deep reality that Bonhoeffer identifies and that I have tried to capture as the "dialectic of the kingdom."

Why are we "in but not of the world"? What meaning does that actually have beyond sloganeering—a phrase that serves as a "secret handshake" that

---

35. Remember, the first temptation and source of sin was our desire for "knowing good and evil" (Gen. 3:5). For a powerful exposition of this temptation in the form of ethics, see Bonhoeffer, *Ethics*, 299–302.

tells us we are members of the same group? In the dialectic of the kingdom, we find the inner dynamic of this phrase and are pushed beyond a superficial, nearly empty slogan. This "world" that we are in is the substance of God's creating and redeeming work. As the community of Christ's disciples, we confess that this world is reconciled to God in Christ and give our life to learning that reality more deeply and bearing witness to it more faithfully.

In our journey together, we are always vulnerable to two opposite errors. One error arises from our belief that this world is God's creation. If we begin to take this for granted, we can easily slip from "this world is good because of God's creating work" to "this world is good." We must realize and sustain the conviction that this world has its goodness only by God's gracious, creating work. The second error arises when we think that the goodness that we see in this world belongs to the world in itself. This serious mistake will inevitably lead us to all kinds of heresies that also make us vulnerable to various ideologies. One horrific example is the heretical ideology promulgated by the German Christian movement in its adoption of Nazi ideology. But in adducing a horrific example such as this, I am concerned that we be clear-eyed about other heresies and ideologies that keep a lower profile but do immense evil.

The language that we use here about goodness must be carefully guarded. It is not that only the disciples of Jesus can see the goodness of the world. That goodness is often evident to many and at times is seen more clearly by those who are outside the disciple community for reasons that I will identify below. What the dialectic of the kingdom teaches the disciple community is that all the goodness of this world is the result of God's creating and redeeming work. We are the ones called by God to learn this and therefore be able by God's grace to judge and bear witness to what in this world truly is the goodness of God (Phil. 4:8–9).

To accomplish this mission, the church must learn the justice and righteousness of God in Christ. To ask the question of justice is to ask, "Does this structure, this policy, this practice, this institution truly line up with God's intention for life?" To ask the question of righteousness is to ask, "Does this action, this person, this relationship restore God's intention for us?" This language is illustrative, not prescriptive. The terms that I use in asking the "justice" question might be used to ask the "righteousness" question. In our present circumstances, justice and righteousness require further reflection and discussion.[36] From this learning we may be able to bear public witness to what

---

36. One of the great needs for the church today is more works on God's justice. We have many works about justice in philosophy and political theory but few in biblical studies, theology, and the history of Christianity. I suspect that our relative neglect of justice is connected with the same dynamics that drive our relative neglect of the doctrine of creation.

is and is not the goodness of God. If we are content simply to follow common sense, intuition, or opinion polls to discern the goodness of this world as God's creation, then we have surrendered our life in God marked by the dialectic of the kingdom and have capitulated to this world.

One way of identifying this capitulation is to say that we have given up the gospel for religion or spirituality. Both *religion* (as I am using it here) and *spirituality* identify ways of managing "the way things are" instead of living in light of the dialectic of the kingdom toward the new creation. Religion binds us to the way things are. It gives us rituals and convictions that help us adjust to the way things are and manage our coping with them. This spirituality likewise binds us to the way things are but promises to create a space where we can cope with what the world has done to us or, alternatively, to escape the world for a while. It promises us another space, not the redemption of this space. The understanding of *religion* that I have just articulated recalls the overall trajectory of Bonhoeffer's theology and his call for "religionless Christianity."[37] His work is directed at a "Christianity" that distorts the gospel by accepting the way things are, seeking to discern God's work in the world apart from a Christian doctrine of creation rooted in the dialectic of the kingdom and the one God—Father, Son, and Spirit.

Bringing together Bonhoeffer's early emphasis on "the church against the world" and his later thoughts on the "worldliness of the church" and "religionless Christianity," we may say that guided by the dialectic of the kingdom the church is *against* the world and *for* creation. This is the public witness of the church as the people whom God calls to participate in and bear witness to the redemption of creation in Christ.[38]

---

37. Bonhoeffer, *Letters and Papers from Prison*, 362–64; see also the discussion of this phrase in the editors' introduction, 20–30.

38. For an accessible exploration of "salvation" set in the context of the whole creation and the church's responsibility, see Snyder, *Salvation Means Creation Healed*.

5

One Creator: Father, Son, and Spirit

W e Christians confess one God—Father, Son, and Holy Spirit.[1] These three-and-one work together in creation and redemption.[2] This confession is critical to the development of a robust, mature doctrine of creation and practices that enable us to participate in God's creating work. When we separate the work of redemption and creation and assign each work solely to one of the three, we open the door to many erroneous ways of thinking and living that rush into the church with sinister glee. To develop a robust doctrine of creation guided by the dialectic of the kingdom, we must also be guided by a robust doctrine of the trinity. But before we turn to an exploration of the creating work of the Triune God, I must first introduce those aspects of the doctrine of the trinity that will guide us in developing an understanding of creation as the work of the Father, the Son, and the Holy Spirit.

After centuries of relative neglect, the doctrine of the trinity exploded as a focus of theological reflection beginning in the mid-twentieth century. One of the most influential agents of this renewal was Karl Barth (1886–1968), who retrieved the doctrine of the trinity and demonstrated its fruitfulness for theological work in his *Church Dogmatics*. Since then, theological discussion and debate about the doctrine have become so vigorous and varied that one almost has to specialize in that area of doctrine to keep up with everything written.

1. I use the unusual and somewhat awkward phrase "one God—Father, Son, and Spirit" to keep us mindful of the limitations of human language when directed to God. I do not use the more familiar "trinity" or "Triune God" because I think that those terms have become so familiar that they are nearly empty of meaning. We confess "one God—Father, Son, and Spirit."
2. For a concise statement of this work, see Rust, *Science and Faith*, 184–85.

I will not try to summarize the discussions or adjudicate the debates here. That is a topic for another book.[3] Instead, here I will draw from the wider theological literature for three aspects of the doctrine that are directly relevant to the doctrine of creation: grammar of the trinity, life, and creation by Father, Son, and Holy Spirit.

Grammar of the Trinity

When we confess one God—Father, Son, and Holy Spirit—we commit ourselves to several rules for how we think about God, worship God, bear witness to God, participate in God's creating and redeeming work, and develop other teachings of Christianity. These rules are only one aspect of the doctrine of the trinity; they do not exhaust the meaning of the doctrine and its significance for followers of Christ.[4]

Faithful followers of Christ are always growing into the reality identified and guarded by the doctrine of the trinity. We will never fully and completely understand the one God who is Father, Son, and Spirit. If we did comprehend God fully, then we would have either reduced God to human size or leaped over the divine-human difference. We can have trustworthy knowledge of God to guide us, but if we aspire to become God, we have lost the good news that God redeems our humanity.

One other observation is necessary before we explore the grammar of our confession of one God—Father, Son, and Holy Spirit. You may have noticed that I have not said that we confess "the doctrine of the trinity." Nowhere in the ecumenical creeds does the church confess belief in the "trinity." Rather, our confession of belief in God is trinitarian in its shape. The doctrine of the trinity is a rule or guide arising from our confession of one God—Father, Son, and Holy Spirit—and subsequently serves to extend, guide, and guard our confession.

When we confess our belief in one God—the Father, the Son, and the Holy Spirit—we deny that these three are identical. The Father is not the Son or the Spirit; the Son is not the Father or the Spirit; the Spirit is not the Father or the Son. So we affirm that these three are differentiated from one another. But in our confession, we also deny that these name three different gods. At the same time,

---

3. For my contributions to this discussion, see my reviews of R. Olson and C. Hall, *The Trinity*, and P. Molnar, *Divine Freedom and the Doctrine of the Immanent Trinity*; and my introductory account in *Primer for Christian Doctrine*, 22–27. The foundational documents are helpfully collected in Rusch, *Trinitarian Controversy*. For a review and analysis of the literature, see Grenz, *Rediscovering the Triune God*.

4. See another application of this "trinitarian grammar" in Wilson, *Why Church Matters*, chap. 4.

however, we affirm that they are each divine in the same way. Each shares the same attributes and descriptors that characterize the other two, but not the names.

Thus, the doctrine of the trinity is not a mathematical formula, nor is it a pattern for apportioning divinity among the three persons, as if each were one-third of God and the three together add up to one God. Rather, the doctrine of the trinity, as I follow it here, is a rule for how to apply the language of "three" and "one" to God in ways that faithfully bear witness both to God's own life revealed to us and to God's work of creation and redemption. All these statements could be heavily qualified in light of the theological development of the doctrine of the trinity and the particular debates about more precise language for the interrelations of Father, Son, and Spirit and the way we understand the oneness of God. Some of these differences go back to the schism between the Eastern, Greek-speaking church and the Western, Latin-speaking church. More differences have developed in recent decades.

These differences and the special theological attention that they represent can help us to enter more fully into the mystery of the Triune God. They also give us boundaries that rightly guard the proper confession of God's oneness and threeness. But when the fine distinctions made by theologians become tests of fellowship or divisive of friendship in Christ, we have brought dishonor rather than honor to the Father, the Son, and the Holy Spirit. Before the face of the Triune God, surely it is good and right to confess our wonder, even in words drawn from the fine distinctions of theology, while also acknowledging with good humor and humility that we confess in fear and trembling, dependent on God's grace and forgiveness for all that we say wrongly about our marvelous God.[5] Our attitude should be that of the apostle Paul, who, after eleven chapters of Spirit-inspired writing, confesses:

> Oh, the depth of the riches of the wisdom and knowledge of God!
>> How unsearchable his judgments,
>> and his paths beyond tracing out!
> "Who has known the mind of the Lord?
>> Or who has been his counselor?"
> "Who has ever given to God,
>> that God should repay them?"
> For from him and through him and to him are all things.
>> To him be the glory forever! Amen.
>
> Romans 11:33–36

5. Let us learn from Saint Augustine, who at the end of his magisterial work on the doctrine of the trinity prayed, "O Lord the one God, God the Trinity, whatever I have said in these books that is of Thine, may they acknowledge who are Thine; if anything of my own, may it be pardoned both by Thee and by those who are Thine. Amen." Augustine, *On the Trinity* (*De Trinitate*), 15, 51.

Life

God is life. God is not merely "the living one," as if we had some access to life apart from God, of which God is the greatest exemplar. It is not as if there were various ways of life, in spite of our persistence in thinking that we can choose a lifestyle: "This is the way I choose to live." No. Apart from God, any choice we make is merely the way we choose to die. The life-and-death choice that Moses set before the Israelites (Deut. 30) is the same for all people. God is life; all else is death.

God simply is Life. This is one very fitting and powerful way to bear witness to God's name, YHWH. Bruce Waltke has argued cogently that a proper translation of YHWH is "I AM."[6] As followers of Jesus Christ, we are taught to confess belief in one God—Father, Son, and Holy Spirit.[7] This confession brings us right back to "I AM" and the marvelous unfolding of the meaning of God's name as we see that the life of I AM is the living actuality of the Father, the Son, and the Spirit.

When we understand something of God's life as Father, Son, and Holy Spirit, we may begin to realize that this trinitarian life is the only way that there can be life. Otherwise, there would be nothing. This is not an easy or quick thing to learn or teach. I have taught the doctrine of the trinity to thousands of students over many years. Yet it was only as I began to think more carefully about the doctrine of creation in preparation for writing this book that I began to find myself drawn more fully into this mystery.

To approach my argument that the one God—Father, Son, and Spirit—simply is Life, I will set it in the context of two other arguments in the history of theology and Christian philosophy. In the history of theology, Saint Anselm (1033–1109) articulated a worshipful, prayerful account of God as "that than which nothing greater can be conceived."[8] This account has often been taken as an argument for the existence of God. More recently, a twentieth-century philosopher of religion, Alvin Plantinga, has articulated a contemporary version of Anselm's argument.[9] There are significant differences between Anselm and Plantinga in both style and substance, but both challenge us to imagine the (im)possibility of God not existing and conclude that such a state of affairs—God not existing—is not possible.

Neither version of this argument made much impact on me before I began writing this book. They seemed merely to argue for the existence of God,

6. Waltke, *Old Testament Theology*, passim, esp. 359–69.
7. Torrance, *Trinitarian Faith*, 302–40.
8. Anselm, *Proslogium*, various editions.
9. Plantinga, *God and Other Minds*.

and that did not seem very interesting or important. What God is like, *if* God exists—now that seems important. And that is what I have found in bringing the trinitarian doctrine of God into my reflection on the work of creation. If God were not "One God—Father, Son, and Holy Spirit"—there would be no creation. There would be nothing and no one to know that there is nothing. The answer to the haunting question, which some label the biggest of the big questions, "Why is there something rather than nothing?" is "God, the Father, the Son, and the Holy Spirit."

How am I to explain this? Here I feel much like Anselm must have felt when he begins his *Proslogium* with prayerful adoration and confession. This mystery is not immediately open to us; it takes persistence, quietness, and receptiveness. If you will continue to turn it over and over in your thinking and living, it will at the very least teach you the joy of wonder, delight in the mystery, and the marvels of friendship with the Father, the Son, and the Holy Spirit.

To confess belief in one God—Father, Son, and Spirit—is to believe that God lives by relationship.[10] It is not enough to say that God lives in relationship because the very relationships of Father, Son, and Holy Spirit are the life of God. Think about it this way: the Father is "Father," only in relation to the Son. Without the Son, the Father would not be. Likewise for the Son: there is no Son without the Father. And apart from the Spirit, the Father and the Son would be enclosed in a mere back-and-forth exchange of identity that would leave them engaged only with each other. But the life generated by the Father in relationship with the Son also generates relationship with the Spirit. Expressed yet another way, the Spirit is the life shared by the Father and the Son. We might represent this by saying that if there were only Father and Son, life would be an exchange. But with the Father, the Son, and the Spirit, life is an interchange. Life is not merely reciprocal.

Consider the alternatives. If there were one god, solitary, not triune, what would "life" look like? We would be restricted to one of two possibilities. If this one, solitary god were to be "alive" in any way, then life would not look as it does today. Life as we know it is relational; life as we know it is an interchange of energy and of lives being given for other lives. In the case of one, solitary god, we could not speak of "life" in any real, recognizable way. Alternatively, this god would have to "create" in order for there to be a relationship that we could perhaps in some way call "life." But where would this solitary god find the resources, the energy, to "create"? In this case, the

---

10. We must be careful, however, to note that these relationships do not exhaust the identity of the Father, the Son, and the Spirit. Indeed, I am convinced that there could be no relationships if "relationships" was all there is to God.

god would be as dependent on the world as the world would be on the god. And neither would actually be "dependable." That is, the god would not have "life" until the god "created" the world. So where would the life that is given to the world come from? Likewise, if the god only had life once the world was created, then where would the world find the energy of life to sustain the god in relationship?

Only God who is Father, Son, and Holy Spirit has life in Godself so that the world is created not to give life to God or relationship to God but purely out of God's grace flowing from God's own self-sustaining, relational life. The God who is triune creates not from need for relationship but in complete freedom from any external force or necessity. The Father, the Son, and the Holy Spirit create out of God's own life. In the life of the Triune God, the Father freely gives himself to the Son, so that he is both fully and eternally the Father and the Son is fully, eternally the Son. Likewise, the Son gives himself freely as the Son to the Father, so that each is fully and eternally Son and Father. Their giving to each other is the life of the Holy Spirit, who in receiving from and giving to the Father and the Son, is fully and eternally the Spirit. Moreover, the Spirit is the very gift that the Spirit gives to the Father and the Son, desiring that the Father and the Son love each other.[11]

From this mutuality of giving and receiving, which simply *is* life, and which may also be named as love, the Father, the Son, and the Holy Spirit give life to something other than God: creation. We believe in One Creator—Father, Son, and Spirit.

Creation by Father, Son, and Holy Spirit

In the biblical witness to creation and redemption by the Father, the Son, and the Spirit, the language used is the language of praise, thanksgiving, testimony, invitation, lament, and wonder.[12] This witness is trinitarian in its grammar, but it is not the careful language of the creeds and confessions, nor is it the analytical language of most theology. Much of the time, our own language for God and God's work follows this same trinitarian grammar. But at times our grammar gets corrupted, our language becomes confused, and our witness falls short of the reality of God's work. At those times, we need to return to the biblical witness and reflect more carefully on it. As we do so,

11. I am indebted to Scott Kohler for this description of the Spirit. Kohler draws insights from Jenson, *Triune God*, 146–61.

12. For recent expositions, see Torrance, *Christian Doctrine of God*, 203–34; Jenson, *Triune God*; and Gunton, *Triune Creator*.

we will temporarily disrupt the passionate flow of words in order to relearn the basic grammar. Once we have done so, we must then regain the liveliness of the language of praise and the other modes of participatory language that we briefly set aside. That is, given our loss of a robust trinitarian grammar of creation, we must temporarily distance ourselves from what we are doing in order to correct it. In so doing, we may recover the faithful language that we need in order to know and live in light of God's redemption of creation.

In a way, we are doing what professional golfers do when they lose control of their swing. They work with their coaches to discern what has gone wrong. Are they dropping their shoulders? Taking too long a backswing? Compensating for an unidentified injury by shifting motion imperceptibly? For us, we will step away from our everyday language and practice of the faith and return to our confessions and to Scripture in order to regain a faithful, lively, trinitarian account of creation.

Grammar of Redemption

To develop conformity to the trinitarian grammar of creation, we will begin with a more familiar grammar: the trinitarian grammar of redemption. As we do so, we will also see how we cannot really speak of redemption in trinitarian terms without also speaking of creation.

In Scripture, God's people confess the work of the Father, the Son, and the Spirit in redemption. As we do so, we realize that this redemptive work is the redemption of creation. The God who comes to us in Jesus Christ is also the God who creates the world. As we come to recognize both the *roles* of the Father, the Son, and the Spirit in redemption and the *identity* of this Triune God as Creator, we realize that the Creator is the Triune God. That is, in the clear revelation of the Father, the Son, and the Spirit in Christ's work of redemption, the Father, the Son, and the Spirit are also revealed to be Creator.

To say that there is one God who both creates and redeems is an inextricable part of the confession that Christ is Lord. This confession has a two-part meaning. First, it identifies Christ with God.[13] Since the work that the Tanak ascribes to God is ascribed to Jesus Christ in the same language, this Jesus of Nazareth is being recognized and declared to be God.[14] Second, it is as Creator of the universe that Jesus Christ claims lordship over all creation—the "all things" of Colossians 1:15–20.

13. This question of Jesus's identity with God has been brilliantly argued recently in two very different ways. See, among others, Bauckham, *Jesus and the God of Israel*; and Hurtado, *How on Earth Did Jesus Become a God?* and *Lord Jesus Christ*.
14. See Bauckham, *Jesus and the God of Israel*.

Similarly, to say that the Father sends Jesus Christ and that Jesus Christ does the will of the Father in the work of redemption is also to say that the Father is the one who initiates the work of creation. This confession of the Father as Creator is enshrined in our creeds: "I believe in God, the Father Almighty, maker of heaven and earth" (Apostles' Creed). To confess God as "Father" before confessing him as "maker of heaven and earth" represents the church's recognition that in Jesus Christ, the one God who is Father, Son, and Holy Spirit is both Redeemer and Creator. That is, confessing God as Father before we confess God as "maker of heaven and earth" presupposes the Son, which in turn directs us to the work of redemption.[15] Finally, to acknowledge that the work of redemption is completed by the Spirit, who gives us life in Christ by the gift of faith, sustains that life in the church ("the Body of Christ"), and brings it to completion in our glorification, leads us also to confess that the Spirit is the one who gives life to creation, sustains it, and brings it to its glorification through the work of Christ.

We may imagine this trinitarian economy of redemption as a story arc in which creation comes from the Father, through the work of the Son, by the life of the Spirit and is returned to the Father by the life of the Spirit through the work of the Son. Once again, we must follow the dialectic of the kingdom and articulate creation and redemption together. We are now also beginning to learn that the dialectic of the kingdom must be governed by trinitarian grammar that bears witness to trinitarian economy.[16]

Many biblical passages contribute to the telling of the story in this way. None of them tells the whole story in this way, so none of the passages may serve as a proof text for this telling of the story. Indeed, we must be careful to recognize that this bare-bones story arc as I have written it here is not the story itself but a guide to telling the story. As we tell the story of the dialectic of the kingdom, this trinitarian economy serves as a guide for discerning where we are in God's work of redeeming creation at this time and in this place. The story becomes inescapably particular as soon as we locate this story in Jesus of Nazareth and recognize that he is the fulfillment and promise of the redemption of creation. Yes, all the cosmos is the creation of the Triune God, who also redeems the entire cosmos. But that cosmic work is accomplished

---

15. See Torrance, *Trinitarian Faith*, 76–84.

16. Torrance, *Christian Doctrine of God*, 204: "Moreover, since it is in the life and work of Jesus Christ that God has been manifested to us in his reality as Father, Son, and Holy Spirit, our knowledge of the Sovereign Creator may not be abstracted from the incarnate power of the saving love of the triune God mediated to us and activated among us in salvation history or from the creative power of the Holy Spirit poured out upon all flesh who sheds abroad that love of God in our hearts." (Note: Torrance uses "salvation history" in a way different from the use that I critique in chap. 1.)

through *this one man: Jesus of Nazareth*, who is also God *in this flesh*. So the "economy of creation" as the work of the one God—Father, Son, and Holy Spirit—is inextricable from "the economy of redemption."[17]

Having acknowledged the interweaving of creation and redemption in our understanding of the trinitarian economy of creation, we may now explore this in more detail by recalling the trinitarian grammar that I outlined earlier. We confess that the Father, the Son, and the Holy Spirit are not identical to one another; there is real difference in the one God. At the same time, we confess that there is real oneness of the three; they are identically God. One of the ways that we maintain these "rules" is by recognizing that the Father, the Son, and the Holy Spirit are each active agents in all the works of God. To take the clearest example of this: in the work of salvation, we acknowledge that the Father sends the Son; that the Son is incarnate, dies for us, and is raised from the dead; and that the Spirit brings us to faith in Christ and conforms us to Christ.[18] We may learn something else about the rule of trinitarian grammar by recognizing that we must not apportion different dispositions or motivations among the three. One of the ways that this "grammatical error" is sometimes committed is by describing the Father as angry, the Son as merciful, and the Spirit as gentle. But these ascriptions of disposition and motivation fall under the trinitarian rule of oneness; the Father, the Son, and the Spirit are one in all their attributes: anger, mercy, patience, and so on. There are other things that we could add to this account, but these few descriptions serve as an example of the "economy," or crudely "the division of labor," among the three in the one work of the salvation of humans.

Grammar of Creation

What is true of the trinitarian economy of God's salvation is also true of God's work of creation: in both works, the Father, the Son, and the Spirit have

17. I am here offering brief guidance for the perceived tension between particularity and universality. Sometimes this has been construed as a tension between creation, which is regarded as universal, and redemption, which is regarded as particular. Those who feel this tension strongly often resort to two flawed notions: on the one hand, they may universalize Christ, so that he is simply representative of a universal spirit or some power in the universe, which finds instantiation in his life and teaching; or, on the other hand, they may deny the reality of creation in redemption, maintaining that redemption is the salvation of particular individuals, not the redemption of all creation. In this chapter, I seek, among other things, to demonstrate and follow the conviction that creation and redemption are particular, in that they are both the work of this God—Father, Son, and Spirit—and have their center in Christ. For further elucidation, see chaps. 6 and 7.

18. Here I am using *salvation* not as a synonym for redemption but as a term for describing how God specifically works to redeem humans. These terms are used in different ways theologically. Here I am treating *salvation* as a subset of redemption.

differentiated roles. These roles in creation are not as clearly demarcated in theology as are the roles of the three in salvation. This is the case for at least two reasons. One reason is the relative neglect of the doctrine of creation. Although the teachers of the early church gave considerable attention to the doctrine of creation, as we have noted, theology since around the mid-seventeenth century has been retreating from the doctrine of creation with few exceptions. Another reason is that Scripture itself seems a bit less clear on the roles of the three in creation than in salvation. However, once we begin to pay attention to the doctrine of creation and seek its trinitarian grammar in Scripture, the trinitarian economy of creation will begin to come into focus.

As we work from the greater clarity of the trinitarian grammar of salvation, we will gain greater clarity of the trinitarian grammar of creation. In the trinitarian grammar and economy of salvation, we recognize that salvation is the will and work of one God. In that will and work, the Father is the agent who sends the Son into the world (John 20:21). The Son is the direct agent of salvation through his incarnation, crucifixion, and resurrection. The Spirit is the agent of the continuation and completion of salvation through the work of conviction, faith, and sanctification. Again, my purpose here is not to articulate a full trinitarian doctrine of salvation but to move from the clarity and maturity of our understanding of this economy to an account of the economy of creation.

Following the trinitarian economy of salvation, we may begin an account of the trinitarian economy of creation. In creation as the will and work of one God, we may distinguish the agency of the Father in initiating this work. Much in Scripture indicates the initiating agency of the Father's will. As we assemble these passages, we have not yet reached a trinitarian grammar of creation. Rather, we are discerning a consistent, unbroken pattern in the trinitarian economy of the Father, the Son, and the Holy Spirit. In Scripture, we hear from the incarnate Son, Jesus Christ, that he does only the will of the Father.[19] As we move further into the doctrine of salvation, we also learn from Jesus that he "will ask the Father, and [the Father] will give you another advocate to help you and be with you forever—the Spirit of truth" (John 14:16–17).

19. Many times when the NT refers to "God," the reference is to the Father. This takes us into another aspect of the development of the doctrine of the trinity as we realize that the doctrine is not itself identified in Scripture but is nevertheless necessary for reading Scripture coherently, coming to faith in Jesus Christ, and bearing witness to God's creating and redeeming work. Once we have been taught the oneness and threeness of God in fuller measure by the work of the Spirit in the church, the representation of that teaching by the doctrine of the trinity becomes a guide for faithfully reading Scripture and telling the good news of Jesus Christ.

These passages reveal that the Father generates the work that the one God does in salvation—the Father sends the Son and the Spirit.[20] This sending or generating role of the Father in salvation also marks the Father's role in creation. Just as the work of redemption originates in the will of the Father, so also does the work of creation.

But as with the work of salvation, the Father is not alone in the work of creation. If we were to ascribe the work of creation to the Father alone, we would not be reflecting the life of the Triune God, nor would we be able to give an account of life as one of relationship. So with the doctrine of creation, as with the doctrine of salvation, we also learn that the Son and the Spirit work with the Father.

The role of the Son in creation is analogous to his role in redemption. The Son is the one who directly engages with the world in creation and salvation.[21] It is the Son, not the Father, who is incarnate for our redemption. It is the Son, not the Father, who shapes creation.

Here we may learn something from trinitarian theology about how to read earlier Scripture. During the modern period and even in some thinkers preceding modernity, Scripture was read with a strict and rigid chronological rule imposed on the reading: one must not read back into earlier passages what is revealed later. But in recent years both biblical scholars and theologians have begun to recover a reading of Scripture that recognizes that if all Scripture is the work of the one God whom we know through Christ as the Father, the Son, and the Holy Spirit, and if all the work of God to which Scripture bears witness is the work of the Triune God, even though this was not always known, then we who know God as Father, Son, and Spirit may reread Scripture for the ways in which the author of Scripture, the Holy Spirit, reveals to us how the Triune God has been at work from the beginning.

With this in mind, we may reread the story of creation "in the beginning" as the work of the Father, the Son, and the Holy Spirit. Remember, it is reverent faithfulness to expect that the Father, the Son, and the Spirit are present in this testimony. Though it would not be clear to God's people until the coming of Christ, we should expect and celebrate the presence of the Father, the Son, and the Holy Spirit in this testimony. And that is what we find concealed but now revealed in the text of Genesis 1. God who speaks the cosmos into creation is

20. The Eastern Orthodox (Greek) doctrine of the trinity argues that the Spirit proceeds from the Father alone; Western (Latin) theology argues that the Spirit proceeds from the Father and the Son. These arguments relate to the intra-trinitarian relations of God. Here I am concerned with God's work in the world, what is often called the "economic trinity" in contrast to the "immanent trinity." This disagreement is quite tangled and need not occupy us here. My purpose is to establish a basic trinitarian economy for creation; advanced grammar can wait for another occasion. Both East and West agree that the Father initiates the work of God.

21. See McDonough, *Christ as Creator*, and below, chaps. 6 and 7.

the Father. The Word that he speaks and that is effective in bringing the world into being is the Son. And the Spirit who broods over the waters (Gen. 1:2) is the Spirit who gives life to all that the Father speaks into existence through the Son.[22]

From this passage we can move to a brief reflection on the role of the Spirit in the economy of creation. Just as the Spirit is the immanent God brooding over the waters (Gen. 1:2), so the Spirit is to be the divine agent of continuing engagement with the world.[23] The "Spirit" is the one who gives life to creation by the presence of the Spirit and who withdraws life from the world when the Spirit withdraws (Ps. 104:27–30). Just as the Spirit is the life generated by the relationship between the Father and the Son, so the Spirit is the life that is generated by God's relationship to the world. The world is "created"—that is, given life in the Spirit—by its relationship to the Father through the work of the Son. When that relationship is violated, the life of the world languishes. By God's grace and the atoning work of Christ, the world is never given up by God. But the faithfulness of the world to God's work and will in Christ does measure the flourishing of the life of the world—its being as God's creation.[24]

Trinitarian Grammar of Creation and Justice

This reality is declared over and over again in the Prophets: the languishing and flourishing of the world and the ability of the land to produce the stuff of life is directly connected to the conformity of the world to God's justice. In other words, God's justice revealed in the Tanak is the way in which the world becomes God's creation and sustains life. To the extent that we violate God's justice the land does not flourish and sustain life. That is, "the land" is not a closed, natural system that operates apart from the relationship between God, the land, and the people.

We must read these prophets carefully; those who have no power and thus are the ones who lose their lives in the midst of injustice are known and kept

22. We will consider this passage in further detail in chap. 7.

23. Catherine Keller has constructed an entire theology out of the image of the Spirit brooding over the waters in her *Face of the Deep*. Keller's theology is heterodox at best. In another setting, I would pursue the deleterious consequences of Keller's theology. It is not merely that she violates "orthodoxy" and imagines a whole new beginning, but her theology leaves us without the hope of the new creation in Christ. More helpful are the wise comments of Saint Basil, summarized with references in Wilken, *Spirit of Early Christian Thought*, 143. Basil sees the trinitarian economy of Gen. 1 and in Wilken's summary "reminds his congregation . . . [that] the Holy Spirit is like a bird that covers her eggs with her body and by her body's warmth imparts the vital force that will give them life. In Genesis the Holy Spirit plays 'an active role in creation' because the Spirit gives the water the power to produce living things."

24. In Rom. 8, Paul weaves together this work of the Spirit in creation and redemption through insights generated by the resurrection of Christ. The Spirit is the immanent power of life.

by the God of justice. Those who appear to save their lives and flourish in the midst of injustice—the powerful and the wealthy—are the ones who ultimately lose their lives. Once again, we must be careful not to read "creation" and God's work of creation from a naive approach to the world as if it were God's creation to which we have direct access apart from the long story of God's redemption from the garden to the new creation.[25]

We must also recognize that this judgment upon the world is both an act of the dialectic of the kingdom—creation and redemption—and an act ruled by trinitarian grammar. As an act of the dialectic of the kingdom, God's judgment-in-justice is for the redemption of creation. It is not ultimately an act of condemnation but an act of grace, revealing to us the life-destroying consequences of our denial of this world as God's creation and inviting us, urging us, compelling us to turn to the life-giving justice of God in redemption. God's justice sets this world right as God's creation by redeeming it from the consequences of sin. In this way, the end of this world is the new creation: "God did not send his Son into the world to condemn the world, but to save the world through him" (John 3:17).

As ruled by trinitarian grammar, God's judgments are acts of the Father, the Son, and the Holy Spirit. As an act of the Father, judgment on our violations of life are judgments of our distance from the vision of the Father for creation. As an act of the Son, judgment is the measure of our rebellion against the way this world is made for life and our refusal to receive Christ's life as the renewing of what we have lost in sin. As an act of the Holy Spirit, judgment is a measure of our turn to illusory sources for our lives. These judgments reveal that we look but do not see, hear but do not understand, exist but do not live.

In other words, we believe the lie that we live in "the world" rather than creation. To live in the world is to live in the illusion that we have control of life, that we can gain understanding by ourselves, that we can choose our own destinies. When this illusion collapses, we stoically resign ourselves to fate, turn to a plurality of gods or powers that rule over us (new age), or turn back to the one God—Father, Son, and Spirit—who redeems creation. If we turn to the God who redeems creation, then we discover that we have now been given our destiny. We begin to understand this destiny as we humbly submit to our Creator and Redeemer and receive from God the gifts that fulfill our lives and cause us to flourish not in our own strength but in the strength we are given as we live in relationship with God. That is, when we believe in God the Father, the Son, and the Holy Spirit, God brings our lives into alignment with the life that God gives through creation and redemption.

25. Davis, *Scripture, Culture, and Agriculture*; Marlow, *Biblical Prophets and Contemporary Environmental Ethics*.

This is simply the act of following Christ. He shows us how to make our way through this world as God's creation. He shows us what it means to live in this world as God's creation. This life in Christ is made possible by the Spirit. With the Son and the Spirit, we are guided off the path that leads to death and onto the path that leads to life—that is, the path that leads to, and already is, life with God.

Trinitarian Grammar of Creation and Providence

In addition to revealing something about God's justice, the trinitarian economy of creation also reveals to us the way that the life of creation is sustained. In the intra-trinitarian relationships of the Father, the Son, and the Spirit, each of the three lives fully gives, as individuals, to the others. That is, as the Father gives himself fully to the Son, his identity as Father is not lessened but continually, eternally fulfilled. And we may say the same of the Son and the Spirit in their self-giving. This self-giving, which is also self-fulfilling, is the very shape of Life. When this Life, who is named "I AM," creates, that which I AM creates also lives this way.

Thus, creation lives as it gives itself fully to the one Creator—Father, Son, and Spirit. Creation does this through praise. This praise is simply the outpouring of created life toward I AM in adoration and obedience. These acts are the very source of the life of the world as creation. Therefore, when the world adores other (created) things and turns away from life as I AM creates it, to seek life in created things, then the world dies, quite simply because the world has turned away from Life.

At this point we may bring together our trinitarian account of justice and of life in order to note that both justice and life are God related. It is not that God has created an order for life that we violate by injustice and thus suffer the consequences of being out of order. Since justice and life are intrinsic to God, when we violate them, we are not violating an order that is extrinsic to God. Instead, we are violating God's own character, which forms the justice and life of creation.

In this way, a trinitarian grammar of justice and life guards against two opposing errors. One error is to conclude that God created an order that is self-sustaining and self-governing so that God need not have any direct involvement in sustaining and governing the order of creation.[26] The opposite error is to identify God with the order of creation and reduce God to "nature" or the natural order of things.[27] The first error distances God from ongoing creation.

---

26. This is, roughly, the teaching of deism, found in thinkers such as Matthew Tindal.

27. This is Baruch Spinoza's "Deus sive natura" ("God or Nature"; that is, they name the same things; the terms are interchangeable). In recent years, the work of James Gustafson seems

The second error identifies God with "creation" now conceived as "nature." Only a trinitarian economy of creation can account for God's continuing care, which sustains the world without collapsing God into the world and identifying God with nature.

Summary of Trinitarian Grammar and Economy of Creation

The one God—Father, Son, and Holy Spirit—is the one God who creates. Although creating is the act of the one God, the Father, the Son, and the Holy Spirit are not identical in their participation in the work of creation (and redemption). The Father initiates the work of creation, the Son implements that work, and the Spirit completes it. Each work anticipates and depends on the other work. This trinitarian grammar and economy cannot be disconnected from the work of redemption, which the Father initiates, the Son implements, and the Spirit completes.[28] When we bring God's work of creation and redemption under the trinitarian rule and economy of God, we also see how God's continuing rule of justice and sustaining of life are intrinsic to the life of the Father, the Son, and the Spirit.[29]

Scripture witnesses to the continual unfolding of our knowledge of this God in the work of creation and redemption. The God who is Life sustains a world that has turned to death and is now ruled by death. Why would, how can, the God who is Life be justified in sustaining such a world? God sustains this death-ruled world without violating life because death is no match for the life that is God's gift and that is so grounded in God's own living that it cannot be destroyed. God has revealed this to us despite our submission to death and made life available to us by coming to us in the incarnation, crucifixion, and resurrection of the Son. These events (and the doctrines that teach and bear

---

to reclaim some of Spinoza's teaching. See Gustafson, *Ethics from a Theocentric Perspective* and *Sense of the Divine*. Most commentators liken Gustafson's thought to stoicism. For an illuminating and high-level exchange about the likeness of his work to that of Spinoza, see Hartt, "Concerning God and Man"; Gustafson, "Response to Hartt"; and Neville, "On the Architecture."

28. Without getting into fine distinctions between "perichoresis," "circumincession," and other terms that may be used to describe the relationships of the threeness and oneness, we may say here that the works of God interweave, interpenetrate, and enfold one another, so that they cannot be separated.

29. As I note below, one lively debate today is the contribution of Irenaeus to a contemporary retrieval of the doctrine of creation. Colin Gunton has been vigorous in his commendation of Irenaeus, especially as an alternative to Augustine and the Augustinian tradition. See Gunton, *Triune Creator*. I too find Irenaeus helpful in many ways, and my own work offers an alternative to Augustine at several points. But I am also leery of Irenaeus's central image of the Son and the Spirit as the right and the left hand of the Father. I worry that this imagery denies real agency to the Son and the Spirit and tends to make them tools of the Father. Both the Son and the Spirit have direct, continuing engagement with creation.

witness to them) are as much about God's work of creation as they are about God's work of redemption. Only through this work is this world "creation."[30]

Grammatical Errors in the Doctrine of Creation

If good trinitarian grammar sustains and guides a Christian doctrine of the creation, then errors in "grammar" can lead to tragic results in our understanding of life as God's gift and rule of the cosmos. Sometimes a trinitarian grammar of creation is violated or dismissed deliberately by people who view such a grammar as obsolete or parochial. Many other times, people simply drift carelessly and thoughtlessly into bad grammar until they have lost the meaning of words, even though they continue as if the words actually communicate real and truthful things.

As I outline the various possibilities of a bad trinitarian grammar of creation, I do not name actual culprits. Rather, I am concerned with describing bad grammar and its consequences in sufficient detail that readers can discern for themselves actual instances and practices of bad grammar in their own lives, in others' lives, and in their communities. The tragedy of bad grammatical practices in the doctrine of creation is not that such practices violate the rules of grammar or offend the guardians of grammar, but that bad grammar leads to bad thinking and bad living. To show that such is the case is the aim of the following analysis.

Before we consider possible grammatical errors, it is good for us to reflect on what we will be doing in this exercise. As we move through the various possible errors, we will not always be considering occasions when the grammar has been deliberately denied nor will we always be examining thinkers who explicitly reject a trinitarian account of creation. Rather, we will begin by identifying potential errors. After we reflect briefly on the nature of the error, we will then consider what that error might look like in its consequences for thinking and living in the good news of Jesus Christ. Along the way we will also sometimes discover why distortions of the trinitarian grammar of creation may make alternative doctrines and lives more attractive.

Father, Son, _____. What happens to the Christian doctrine of creation if we have a grammar in which the Father initiates the work of creation

---

30. There is continuing debate today about resources in the Christian tradition for the doctrine of creation, with strong recommendations being submitted for Irenaeus, Augustine, Thomas Aquinas, Calvin, Edwards, Barth, and Balthasar. The main focus is the differences between Irenaeus and Augustine, with Thomas very close behind. Entering into this debate is beyond the scope of this book. But the debate is one way that we may develop a more robust theological account of creation. I think that we need to learn from them all and be critical of various aspects in each of them.

and the Son implements that work, but there is no Spirit to complete it? In such a case, God plans creation and brings it into being but then has no continuing relationship with it. Even the incarnation is lost, since the conception of Jesus in Mary is the work of the Holy Spirit. Once again we confront the impossibility of separating creation and redemption.

In this loss of any account of God's ongoing relationship with the world, we lose "creation" as a description of this world, and "nature" takes its place. This is not quite deism, which would still give us some sense of God "invading" this world. But we would locate God's continuing work in the world as a rescue mission directed only toward humans, not as a redemptive mission directed toward all creation that is sustained and completed by the work of the Spirit. In accounts of this type, we would see the world as wholly marked by the fall, by sin, and by death. We would have a rather dismal view of the world and see the Christian life as simply holding on in the midst of evil.

One can imagine that the circumstances of some people's lives could push them in this direction. One can also imagine that some people's temperaments could incline them in this direction. Others may be led here by their study of the world and conclude that while God may have initiated and implemented the creation of this world, God did so in such a way that it was "maintenance free" in regard to creation though in need of intervention for redemption. This teaching, then, would have a disengaged Creator but an intervening Redeemer.

In this violation of trinitarian grammar, we would have no basis for a continuing relationship with God in creation. If those holding a position like this perceive beauty in the world (and that is far from certain or consistent), they perceive it as a "leftover" from creation or as a product of "natural" order. It does not occasion in them an awe of God's own beauty. If they care for the physical processes of this world, they do so for pragmatic reasons, not out of any sense that they are thereby somehow honoring and relating to God. In this truncated view, except for a rescue mission and preserving those who have been rescued, God has abandoned this world. There is no sense of any direct connection with the life of God through "creation." This view does not abandon the body and the material world; it simply sees them as largely irrelevant or incidental to the life of God and of creation.

As I have encountered people who hold to this view, I have found Christians who take an extremely utilitarian approach to life. They do not see its beauty or its glory, only its "usefulness." And this usefulness is a very drab, typically joyless approach to the world. They cannot see this world as God's creation. They see it as a burden that must be endured while we await the return of Christ. They usually articulate a "spiritual life," but it too remains drab, and its joy is almost entirely postponed until some future glory. When they bring redemption into their theology and lives, it is a redemption that promises something for the future but nothing for the present. *Redemption* is reduced almost entirely to the knowledge that they are sinners, that God forgives them, and that one day they will be changed. In this distortion of the trinitarian grammar of creation, we can see that it also grows out of or leads to a loss of the dialectic of creation and redemption.

To correct this loss of the Spirit in the trinitarian grammar of creation and to guard against the dangers to which it exposes the church, we must recover the work of the Spirit in creation. Many in the Christian tradition fear that we will fall into pantheism or panentheism if we too closely identity God with creation. These fears and traps may be avoided by a robust trinitarian account of creation. In such an account, the distinctness of God from creation is maintained by the work of the Father and the ascension of the Son.[31]

As we recover the work of the Spirit, we must recognize that the work of the Spirit in giving life to the world is not a generic giving that tends toward a blending and homogenization. Rather, the gift of life from the Spirit particularizes life in all its various manifestations. We see this not only in life itself but also in the gifts of the Spirit to followers of Christ. All of Paul's teaching about the work of the Spirit in the church reflects the particularity of the Spirit's work in the overarching oneness of the body of Christ (1 Cor. 12; Eph. 4).

This reflects what we learn about life from the doctrine of the trinity. God is Life not because the Father, the Son, and the Spirit blend together into a generic divinity, but because in their particularity they give themselves to one another and in so doing fully live their particular identities as Father, Son, and Holy Spirit. If we add to this our understanding of the dialectic of the kingdom through the work of Christ, we must realize that the telos of this dialectic is not an undifferentiated blob of oneness, but the reconciliation of all things in Christ so that all things that are rightly aligned with God will enjoy fully and eternally the life that is proper to each in its particularity. As the world in which we live is claimed as creation by the Father, the Son, and the Spirit, the drabness of the world is filled with color, and those colors are not homogenized into monochrome oneness but brought together into the polychrome beauty of creation that reflects the polychrome beauty of the Father, the Son, and the Spirit.

31. To this point I have not included the ascension with the incarnation, the crucifixion, and the resurrection in my recitation of the work of the Son because its relevance would have had to be explained before it became relevant to my exposition. Now I may note that the ascension establishes the rule of Jesus Christ over the world so that it is continually sustained and constituted as creation by the power of the risen Lord through the presence of the Holy Spirit. The ascent of Christ and the descent of the Spirit together make possible this rule. See Farrow, *Ascension and Ecclesia* and *Ascension Theology*; Dawson, *Jesus Ascended*.

Father, _____, Spirit. Imagine people who hear the "good news" of Jesus Christ according to the distorted grammar and economy that omits the Spirit. Imagine that they live much of their lives under the impression that this distortion is the good news, take it or leave it. Some take it; some leave it. Many people live their entire lives with this tragic (mis)understanding of the "good news" of Jesus Christ. But sometimes people begin to sense that something is not right with this grammar. They see goodness and beauty in the world that they cannot place in this distorted story.[32] Some who come to this realization find their way to a more complete trinitarian account of creation—and redemption—that corrects this distorted grammar and economy.

However, it is often the case that people believe that this distortion is the only way to tell the story of Christ. When they can no longer make sense of their world through this story, they look elsewhere. In such a search they are likely to end up with an account of the world that makes some sense of its beauty and goodness, but then they find it difficult to give an account of the world's need for redemption. They react against the distorted and shriveled gospel that has no place for the Spirit as the one who gives life to the world through the work of Christ by the will of the Father. In this reaction, they abandon the notion that the world is in need of redemption. Instead, they see the world simply as a blessing and gift sustained by the life of the Spirit. So they give themselves to romantic views of nature and a spirituality that does not require the reconciliation of the world to God.[33] Because the work of Christ exposes the fallenness and evil of this world, one who affirms its goodness and beauty may overreact by discarding Christ and his work.

Whether people come to this position through an early rejection of faulty proclamation of the gospel or through a long journey from a faulty view of the gospel to a celebration of the goodness and beauty of the universe, they run the danger of exchanging one faulty trinitarian grammar of creation for another. In reaction against the misrepresentation of Christ as one who rescues us from an evil world and the neglect of the Spirit's sustaining and completing work, they swing to a misrepresentation of the Spirit as one who simply opens our eyes and connects us to the beauty and goodness of the universe.

---

32. Circumstances vary around the world. We must guard against thinking that goodness and beauty are more obvious and prevalent in affluent settings. The testimony of many who live and follow Christ in less affluent environments is that the goodness and beauty of the world is more prevalent and celebrated there than in affluent settings. In these more challenging circumstances—where food, water, and shelter are not so readily available—there is a greater recognition of this world as "creation" and a greater appreciation of it. In affluent environments, the world is often just that: the world that we have made and that we control. It is seen not as a good and beautiful creation but as a useful and achievable world.

33. I find this in the works of Thomas Berry and Matthew Fox.

This view discards or denies the work of Christ in creation and thus denies that conformity to Christ is the way of life in this world that aligns with God's work of creation. When we add in the dialectic of the kingdom, we see that this distorted trinitarian grammar teaches that we are alienated from God as Creator simply because we do not see, appreciate, and live in light of the goodness and beauty of creation.

According to this misrepresentation of the good news, we simply need the Spirit to open our eyes and ears to the beauty and goodness of the world. There may be a small role for a reductionist account of Jesus as the one who teaches us how to live in the Spirit and see beauty and goodness, but this is no longer the good news that declares God's love for the world in its brokenness and the sending of Jesus Christ to bear that brokenness and bring forgiveness, healing, and the promise of the new creation. The Spirit is no longer the sustainer of life through the work of Christ and the one who brings that work to completion. Now the "good news" is that the world is not broken; we have simply been blinded to the world's goodness and beauty by the primitive, superstitious, obsolete belief that we are sinners whose sin must be atoned for in order for us to be reconciled to the Creator and restored to life. Since the Spirit's work is no longer connected to Christ and the dialectic of the kingdom, the Spirit now simply opens us to the realities and possibilities present in this world that we have not previously seen.

The purpose of our lives according to this view is simply the work that we do to recover the sense of beauty and goodness of this world and enter into it.[34] Among other things, we may pursue or enter into this way of life through various disciplines and practices that are most easily identified today as "new age" and by changing the language that we use (Mother Earth, Gaia, body of God). Many of the disciplines and practices that are advised by this view *seem* to be good ways of recovering the goodness and beauty of this world. We must remember that through God's creating work, this is a good and beautiful creation. So the attraction of this "good news" is grounded in a partial representation of proper trinitarian grammar and the dialectic of the kingdom. But because this view has dropped the agency of Christ from creation (and thus also dropped redemption), the practice and disciplines that it teaches

34. This seems to me to be the "aesthetic life" exposed by Kierkegaard, *Either/Or*, and by MacIntyre, *After Virtue*, 24–25, 39–41, 73–74. MacIntyre does not approve of Kierkegaard's overall project and places Kierkegaard's presentation of the aesthete in a different narrative from his own by reading Kierkegaard in light of Kant and arguing that Kierkegaard's project centers radically on choice. I read Kierkegaard differently. It is an interesting question to consider whether MacIntyre's later move to Thomas might change his reading of Kierkegaard. (In *After Virtue*, MacIntyre is still seeing everything within a particular Aristotelian light.)

take us on a different journey to a different end from the new creation by the Father, the Son, and the Spirit.[35]

We must take care to sustain or recover the agency of the Spirit in the work of creation, but we must always do so through a full trinitarian grammar of creation. We must recognize that during modernity some parts of the church drifted away from the work of the Spirit in creation. Other parts of the church actively abandoned any account of the Spirit's work in creation. As a result, in more recent times some have abandoned the church altogether, and many have regarded the church and Christianity as detrimental to caring for this world. In our concern to identify and correct these errors, we must not be reactionary and simply deny the agency of the Son in creation. Rather, in our desire to correct the mistaken grammar of creation and recover the Spirit's agency in creation, we must regain a full trinitarian grammar of creation that continues to include the agency of the Son in the work of redemption.

_____, _____, **Spirit.** At first this error may not look very different from the previous error. But it is still another step removed from full trinitarian grammar—to such an extent that it really cannot claim any resemblance to Christianity. Those who intentionally and persistently teach and live in light of this construal of the world must acknowledge that they have moved far beyond the good news of Jesus Christ. In Western culture, this exclusive reliance on the Spirit is often a further reaction against Christianity's relative neglect of the agency of the Spirit in creation. This neglect leads to a drab, mechanical view of the world that eventually loses plausibility. A common response is to swing to another extreme by turning to the "Spirit" exclusively.

However, in focusing solely on the Spirit, we collapse all the agency of "creation" into the work of one center of agency, one solitary god. When this happens, we do not really have "creation," a world that trusts an agency outside itself for its life. In this instance, the world must have within itself the power of its own existence, life, sustenance, meaning, and end. When these things are sought within the world system itself, the "Spirit" is often identified as the source or at least the name of this cluster of power. But at this point, the "Spirit" is not the Holy Spirit who lives in union and exchange of life with the Father and the Son and completes the work of the Father and the Son. In this view, the "Spirit" becomes simply an aspect of the world. This solitary "Spirit" has no source of life outside itself. How, then, can it sustain a world that has no life outside itself? The "Spirit" is identified with the world, so one cannot appeal to it as the source of life or to the world as the source of its own life.

35. Although I will not argue it here, I see this approach in the work of Gustafson, *Sense of the Divine*, and McFague, *Body of God*.

Yes, of course, there is something rather than nothing, so there is life. But what does "life" mean in this case? It really becomes sheer, meaningless existence glossed over by an appeal to goodness and beauty that we cannot explain.

One of the tragedies of the theological neglect of creation in the church, and of bad trinitarian grammar in our teaching and life, is that we fail to bear witness to the glorious goodness and beauty of God's creating and redeeming work. This failure leaves the world floundering to explain itself to itself. This floundering is evident in the attempts to recover heterodox and heretical strands of Christianity such as gnosticism, as well as the turn to Westernized Hinduism and Buddhism. One critical task for followers of Jesus Christ today is to recover a robust, mature doctrine of creation guided by trinitarian grammar and the dialectic of the kingdom so that we might also recover faithful life in and witness to the good news of Jesus Christ.

As we pursue this task, we will always relate the work of the Spirit to the work of the Father and the Son. We will also relate the character of the Spirit to the Father and the Son. At times, we may be tempted by a romantic notion of the Spirit as a counter to a (mis)perception of the remoteness of the Father and the judgment of the Son in his death on the cross. To resist this romantic temptation, we must recover the trinitarian grammar, which teaches us that in the economy of creation and redemption, the Spirit is doing the will of the Father through the work of the Son. The Spirit's loving embrace and giving of life to the world that redeems creation is the work of the Father, the Son, and the Spirit and reveals the character of the Father, the Son, and the Spirit.

Father, _____, _____. At the opposite extreme from a unitarianism of the Spirit is a unitarianism of the Father as Creator. In this view, the one God who is known as Father creates the world, sets the rules for its life, and lets it go its own way, directed by the rules and ordering intrinsic to it as created by the Father. This approach has a place for Jesus of Nazareth, but not as God with the Father and the Spirit, nor as an agent of the work of creation. Rather, in this view Jesus typically becomes the one human who perfectly exemplifies the way to live according to the "laws" of the order created by the Father. Some of what Jesus taught can be retained and affirmed by this unitarianism of the Father, but in doing so this view must also stop short of believing and affirming the purpose and identity that Jesus declared as the telos of his way of life, his person, and his work.

Those who follow this unitarianism of the Father can affirm that Jesus came to do the will of the Father, but they must understand that will as simply a revelation of the order of the world as created by God; they cannot affirm the "will of the Father" as the death of Jesus Christ for the redemption of the world. Nor can they understand the "will of the Father" as a seamless activity that is one with Jesus's identity as the Son. And, according to this view, the life of following Christ would be within reach of everyone's natural ability as a human created by God, enlivened and guided by the example of Christ. In other words, for this view "sin" is simply our ignorance of the way that we are to live or our willful decision not to live according to God's moral order. This ignorance and willfulness can be corrected simply by our own reception of the knowledge of life demonstrated by Jesus and a willingness to live in accordance with it.

In this view, God's grace is a much reduced reality that may be seen in God creating the world and establishing a moral order that may be lived by humans if we have the right knowledge and will. There is no sense of the world having gone wrong or being broken. Rather, humans need some correction and direction, and that is achieved by humankind itself. God's grace is reduced to God's willingness to empower Jesus to live a life fully in line with the order of creation.

In this nontrinitarian view, our human calling is simply to live by the moral order created by God and demonstrated to us by Jesus of Nazareth, who is unique in his having lived in perfect accord with God's created order. Since he is a human who has done so, doing so also lies within our capability. This view is realistic in its acknowledgment that Jesus alone has done this. The hope of the rest of humankind is to live close to the way of life that Jesus lived, so that we may flourish. Typically, this view teaches the immortality of the soul as a property possessed by all humans. Our blessedness after death depends on our good moral character, not on the forgiveness and righteousness that we receive through Jesus Christ.

The Spirit, according to this unitarianism of the Father, is typically reduced to the afterglow of Jesus's impact on us. We are so impressed and even overwhelmed by the example of Jesus that his spirit—his energy, trust, courage, everything that marks his character and way of being in the world—reshapes our lives so that we reflect this spirit. In this teaching, the spirit is not one of the three persons who is God. Rather, the "spirit" is merely an aspect of our way of being in the world. Thus, there is no Spirit who is the agent of the completion of creation and God's ongoing presence sustaining and guiding the world to the new creation.

The view that I have just described has been taught in some form at various times in the church and is often identified by the label "deism." This view has a strong sense of "creation" as an originating act of God, who established the natural and moral order of the universe but then set it free to run on its own without continuing dependence on God. In other words, the universe has an original but not a continual dependence on God. Usually this view includes belief in life after death, not in the new creation but in a disembodied, spiritual continuation of human souls, who were given immortality in the original creation. By denying any continuing relationship between God and the universe for the sustaining, renewing, or redeeming of the universe, deism guards itself against certain kinds of scientific and historical criticism. But it does so by reducing God and the universe to minimalist concepts. Furthermore, it is defenseless against the scientific arguments that attack notions of design and deny any moral order in the universe.

This unitarianism of the Father as Creator does not always result in a fully developed intellectual position such as deism. People who hold this view have often slipped into this way of thinking and living without considering it carefully. When people say that God has abandoned us, they may very well be reflecting something like this view. Such a person may be saying, "Yes, I believe in God and I believe that a Supreme Being had to create this world. But science, history, and my own experience and observations of this world prevent me from thinking that God has anything to do with us today. He must have created the universe and forgotten about it at some point. The stories of the Bible may be comforting for some, but I think that they are just wishful thinking by people like me who were hoping for something better."

This is very close to what Job wrestles with in the midst of his own suffering.[36] What God offers Job is not an answer to the problem of evil or an explanation for Job's suffering. Instead God confronts and ultimately comforts Job with God's ongoing intimate involvement with the world as God's creation. God's sustaining of creation promises the redemption of creation. That redemption is exemplified in the restoration of Job's life. What is true for Job will be true for creation.

To correct this faulty trinitarian grammar that practices a unitarianism of the Father, we must avoid reactionary mistakes. For example, we must not abandon the grammar of the Father as the originator or initiator of creation. In our reaction against the extreme that regards the originating work of the Father as the only work of "creation," we may be tempted to abandon that affirmation. Sometimes theologians have argued along these lines by urging us to give up any talk of the transcendence of God. Their reasons for so arguing

36. See Burrell, *Deconstructing Theodicy: Why Job Has Nothing to Say to the Puzzle of Suffering.* I take the book of Job to be a display of the limits of our understanding and wisdom. In other words, it does not answer the question of why there is evil and suffering. To do so would be an immoral act. It would be making evil into something other than evil. If we could actually make sense of evil, it would no longer be evil. The story of Christ tells us that there is real evil in the universe and that God in Christ has defeated evil but not yet destroyed it. Living in between the times, we live toward the new creation.

are many; a frequently given one is the deleterious effects of an (over)emphasis on God's distance from the world.[37] But we correct an overemphasis on God's transcendence and its effects not by abandoning the originating role of the Father and transcendence but by recovering a full, robust trinitarian economy of creation and dialectic of the kingdom that does not collapse God's identity into the universe.

The role of the Father is to envision and initiate the work of creation that is accomplished by the Son and completed by the Spirit. Apart from this trinitarian grammar and economy, we may develop mistaken images of the Father as aloof, distant, remote, and uninvolved. But when we see, think, live, and witness the work of creation as the work of one God—Father, Son, and Spirit—we may then be enraptured by the fullness of the Father's love and creation as the gift of life.

_____, Son, _____. This error in the trinitarian grammar of creation may begin in deeply pious, committed communities of discipleship that focus profoundly on Jesus. Over time, such a community may drift into locating all of God's work in Christ. The community ends up, practically speaking, with a Son who is not sent by the Father and whose work is not continued and extended by the Spirit. In this development, then, the community no longer has an account of the gospel in which the Father, the Son, and the Spirit work together in creating and redeeming.

At this point, the dialectic of creation and redemption unravels. If there is any doctrine of "creation" here, it will take one of two forms. One form is that the world of matter is simply an evil thing in which we have been trapped. This material world owes its existence to a "creator" who made something inferior and evil, not good, in its origin. (Below I identify this teaching, in its more developed instances, as gnosticism.) "The Son" teaches us how to live so as to escape this material world. Jesus is not really human; he is a spiritual being who takes on the appearance of flesh in order to reveal to us the way to escape our miserable, evil material existence. Our true humanity is spirit; our predicament is not that we are sinners in need of redemption but that we are spirit beings trapped in a material world. Likewise, the material world is not the work of the good God, nor is its predicament that it has come under the rule of an alien force that is the enemy of life. Rather, the material world is the work of an incompetent, perhaps evil god. The material world is not part of God's good creation that is under the rule of sin and in need of God's

37. Sallie McFague is a theologian who has contributed to an increasing awareness of the devastation of creation and the need for more attention to the doctrine of creation. However, I think that her work tends toward this reactionary mistake. See her *Body of God*. Even more problematic is Kaufman, *In the Beginning—Creativity*.

redemptive work based on God's love for what God creates. Rather, the material world is a world detested by the god who is the spirit-being revealed in Jesus so that we might gain the knowledge that will free us from our entrapment in the material world.

The other direction that people take with creation if they are rooted solely in "the Son" (who, remember, cannot really be the Son without the Father) is to think and live as if this universe were merely a testing ground for our discipleship to Jesus. This is similar to the false teaching I identified in chapter 4, which treats creation as a "stage set" for the working out of our salvation. Here, however, error has been added to error by denying the Father and the Spirit. When someone has only the Son, Jesus becomes the sole creator who now identifies with his creation to restore it. But in this view, how does Jesus retain any sovereignty over the world? How is it that he has the power of life in himself alone? We are now back to the irrationality of thinking that a unitary, solitary god provides both life for that which is not god and the means by which to make sense of the existence of something rather than nothing. Even if we simply grant the existence of something based on our perception that something does actually exist and then posit the existence of a unitary, solitary god incarnate and revealed in Jesus Christ, we have a very different account of what this world is as "creation." And that account is much weaker and less sensible than a trinitarian account.

Conclusion

We do not have an absolute proof or undeniable case against any of these trinitarian errors. This is not because there are different ways to make sense of this world as creation. There is only one way to make sense of life and this world as creation: through the trinitarian grammar and economy revealed by God in Christ and received by God's people gathered as the disciple community by the power of the Spirit. Rather, we have no such proof against these false accounts because the creation is the work of one God—Father, Son, and Spirit—who gives life freely. As the work of the Father, this world belongs to God. As the work of the Spirit, this world is sustained in freedom from being God. As the work of the Son, this world is shaped to be conformed to the image of the Son. As the work of the Spirit draws us into Christ so that we may have life forever through the love of the Father, we are free to be other than what God made us to be. That is the gift of the Father, the Son, and the Spirit because the only way to live is to live in free relationships in which being fully alive comes by fully giving to the other.

6

Remapping the Doctrine of Creation

Although the title of this chapter promises something like a doctrine of creation, it would be a mistake to think that we are only now approaching the doctrine. All our work to this point has already been engaged with the doctrine of creation. It has been important to identify and ponder the context within which we think *creation*. What that word means in everyday use differs from age to age and place to place. Words come with a history and are used in communities of meaning. (Think very simply of the difference between saying *football* in the United States and saying *football* in most other English-speaking countries.) So we must be reflective, not naive, in our development of the doctrine of creation in our geographical and cultural places and times. At the same time, this understanding of place is not preliminary to doing theology but rather is already the process of doing theology. Ironically, our present circumstances make it difficult to identify our place, precisely because we do not have a robust, mature doctrine of creation. We are like adventurers who are lost because they do not have a map or other knowledge of the terrain. In the midst of not knowing where we are, we are trying to draw a map that situates us.

In addition to understanding the place where we are seeking faithfully to recover a fuller understanding of God's cosmos, I have also been concerned with recovering the broad theological guidance that we must draw from and submit to in order to remap our doctrine of creation. Before we could begin the work of this chapter, we had to be equipped for the territory that we are entering by establishing the dialectic of the kingdom and the trinitarian grammar and economy of creation. To continue the adventurer's analogy, we not only have to understand the territory that we are entering; we must also have the right equipment for it. We must not be naive day hikers who set off up a mountain on a clear morning not realizing that mountain weather can change quickly and drastically. The dialectic of the kingdom and the grammar of the trinity are essential equipment for any exercise of faithfulness to the Father, the Son, and the Holy Spirit.

With all of that in mind and ready to use, we will consider many of the dimensions that have traditionally been a part of the doctrine of creation. Those we do not consider here will be considered in the following chapters. Because my intention is to remap the doctrine of creation in continuity with the work that we have already done, I will not always use familiar headings for developing a doctrine of creation. But I will identify somewhere along the way which traditional phrases or words I am remapping in this doctrine of creation. So, for example, although there is no heading for *creatio ex nihilo* (creation from nothing) in this chapter, I treat the concerns represented by *creatio ex nihilo* in several places in the chapter.

Gift

In our times, we often experience the cosmos as a burden.[1] We are weighed down by economic, health, and environmental woes. For those of us in the West, we seem to have passed through a time of expansion and prosperity. It is dangerous to try to read the times that we are presently in—hindsight seems to be so much clearer and accurate—but there are evidences of a growing malaise in our culture.

As we identify this malaise, however, we must not approach our context fatalistically, as if our circumstances determine our understanding of life in this world. As Christians, we must always sustain lives guided by the dialectic of the kingdom. This guidance enables us, even frees us, to see the gift of creation-being-redeemed. In some circumstances, we may find reason to think of this cosmos as a gift simply in itself, without reference to God's creative and redeeming work. But that disposition is impossible to maintain without severely restricting the scope of one's sensibilities to a narrow slice of life. If we are to give an account of creation as a gift, an account that can encompass

1. The question of "can a gift be given" has become a lively topic at a very high level of intellectual engagement. My exposition here is informed by that discussion, but my concern is slightly different. For a representative entry in the theological discussion, see Milbank, "Can a Gift Be Given?"

all of life, we can do so only on the basis of the dialectic of the kingdom and trinitarian grammar.

Creation is a gift, not a burden, because creation is the substance of God's redemptive work that leads to the new creation. The new creation is the work of God incarnate, whose body is crucified, whose body is raised from the dead, whose Spirit in us and in the world is the guarantor of the new creation. This new creation comprises all things of this world that are reconciled to God through Christ. In this promise and hope, which we see being enacted daily in the upholding of the universe and in the transformation of life in conformity to Christ, we perceive that what we experience now as a burden will one day be revealed as a gift through the redemptive work of the Father, the Son, and the Spirit. Yes, even the hard, impossible, nonsensical parts of life may become gifts through the redemption of creation.

This creation is a gift also through the trinitarian economy of God's creative activity. The one God—Father, Son, and Spirit—is Life. God does not need to do something outside God in order to be alive. Moreover, God lives in relationship without beginning and end. God has no need of something outside God in order to be in relationship. Because of God's trinitarian life, God creates not out of a need for life or relationship but simply as the gift of life and relationship. In other words, creation as the work of God is a gift because that work gives to the cosmos the overflowing joy of being alive and in relationship with the Father, the Son, and the Spirit, whose own life together is one of eternal, overflowing, ecstatic love. No greater gift can be given. No other could give this gift than the one Creator—Father, Son, and Spirit.

At this point we can return to the dialectic of the kingdom and recognize that the gift of creation means that redemption is likewise a gift. Because God was not bound to create the cosmos but did so freely (recall that God's love does not compel God to create, but rather that in freely creating God creates a cosmos that expresses and reflects God's own triune life of love), so God freely redeems the world in love. This dialectic, then, guards us from the error of supposing that God freely creates but is bound to redeem. To the contrary, God both creates and redeems in freedom. This freedom is fully established in the encounter between God and Moses, when God declares, "I AM WHO I AM" (Exod. 3:14).

Creation and redemption are the activities of God with us, in and through which we are given life with God in love. The obvious corollary of creation as gift of God is creation received by humans. We must be very careful to safeguard the joyous truth of the gift-reception dynamic on two fronts. First, we must be very careful of the language of cocreation that seeks to place humans in partnership with God in creation. Although the theological tradition

"Behold"

of Thomas Aquinas has a carefully guarded account of humans as "cocreators," most use of the phrase today elevates the work of cocreation into a symmetrical relationship between God and humans. To do this is to attempt the impossible: to eradicate the dialectic of the kingdom and the trinitarian grammar of creation (and redemption). That is, this particular language of cocreator seeks to insert us into the trinitarian economy as agents. The language of cocreation used in this way mistakes a subtle distinction: we are caught up into God's life by the trinitarian dialectic of the kingdom, but we do not thereby ascend to partnership with God. We are participants in God's work of creation and redemption but are never partners.

This language of cocreation seems to offer us greater freedom and a more substantial role, but in the end it dooms us to bondage and failure: it is the repeat of the original temptation to become like God (Gen. 3:5). To fall into that temptation and aspire to be like God is to reject our humanity, which is the only life given to us. To seek to be cocreators is to turn the gift of creation into a task. To see creation as the human task is to take upon ourselves something that we cannot accomplish. When we take the task of creation upon ourselves as humans, even in putative partnership with God, the consequence is death, not life.[2]

The second front on which we must guard the gift-reception dynamic is in the continual cultivation of the spirit and practice of receptivity. The culture in which we live and our awareness of the difficulties that we face on our planet very quickly drive us to frantic action that seeks to "save the planet" and "solve the problems." As difficult as it is for us to grasp in our context, these actions, which seem so obvious and necessary, are the opposite of what we need when we look at creation as a gift. We will later see that we do have a calling from God to protect and cultivate life, but that calling must be understood and practiced within the context of creation as a gift. To see that creation is a gift and to act in accordance with that vision does not free us from responsibility for life on this planet, as some Christians seem to suppose. Rather, creation

2. I have written about the language of "cocreation" in unequivocal terms. Although I consider the use of the concept of "cocreation" and "cocreators" inherently and unavoidably problematic, I do not know that everyone who uses the terminology falls into the errors that I have identified. For example, if someone uses the language of "cocreation" to refer to "culture-making," that is a misappropriation of the terminology. The making of culture is a profound human engagement with the world and with creation, but it does not make us "cocreators." It is better to speak of our being "subcreators," following the guidance of Dorothy Sayers, J. R. R. Tolkien, and C. S. Lewis. See also Levenson, *Creation and the Persistence of Evil*, 117, where he endorses the "coregency of God and humanity" and asserts that "the priority of God and the lateness of the creation of human beings make the term 'cocreator' or 'partner in creation' inaccurate."

as a gift opens up the possibility that we can act in accordance with life as God creates and redeems it, not in accordance with a false vision of life as something that we create and control.[3]

Blessing

To receive creation as a gift means that we are dependent but not that we are passive. God blesses all of God's work of creation and in that blessing calls us to life as participants in God's work. To confess God's work as "creation" is to recognize it as a blessing. That is, blessing is intrinsic to the meaning of creation. In Genesis only humans are blessed by being directly addressed by God and given work to do: "God blessed them and said to them, 'Be fruitful and increase in number; fill the earth and subdue it. Rule over the fish in the sea and the birds in the sky and over every living creature that moves on the ground'" (Gen. 1:28). We will later consider at length Genesis 1–3. Here my interest is in understanding the context of this "blessing."

Just as the teaching that creation is a gift runs counter to so much of our experience and observation of life, so also does the declaration that creation is a blessing. Some humans live in circumstances where the things that make for long and flourishing lives are readily abundant. But many more humans live in circumstances that make life short and troublesome, often brutal. To declare that creation is a blessing is once again to locate creation in the dialectic of the kingdom and the trinitarian economy of the Father, the Son, and the Holy Spirit.

Creation is God's act of blessing because in creating, God gives work and the resources for work to humans. We often think of work as a curse and a burden. We cannot wait for times when we do not have to "work," whether that is the end of a "workday" or a "workweek," a vacation, retirement, or winning a lottery. But to think of work in this way may be mistaken in two ways. First, it narrows our understanding of work. Second, it locates the meaning of "work" not in creation but in the world, in this case as all that does not know God's love and acknowledge God's life-giving rule.

When we locate work within God's creation, we can see from the beginning that it is tied to blessing. Indeed, in Genesis 1 the work that God gives us to do is the very meaning of God's blessing. To be human creatures in God's creation is to be blessed by being given work and the resources for that work. When we are told in Genesis 3 that sin has made the labor of the woman and

3. For further development of this observation, see chap. 12, "Blessed Are the Meek."

the man burdensome, this does not eradicate the good gift of work. Rather, the pronouncements of God in Genesis 3 tell us that the end (purpose) of work—to enact and extend God's blessing—has been taken over by another end. That alien usurper of work ends in death, not life; curse, not blessing. When God's work reclaims the world as creation, then the true, life-giving end of work has been reclaimed by its rightful ruler. Then work becomes participation in life. And in that participation, we once again discover creation as blessing.

Creation is a blessing because God's creation is the proper home of humankind and the context for human work and flourishing. To recognize creation as a blessing is to reject dreams of another world. That "other world" for which we may dream is already given to us in the dialectic of the kingdom that allows creation to be creation and redemption to be redemption as God brings these works to fulfillment in the new creation. The new creation is not a cosmos other than creation; it is creation fulfilled—its end realized through the redemptive work of God. Again, in John's vision God says not, "I am making all new things," but "I am making all things new" (Rev. 21:5 NRSV).

The celebration in Scripture of God's abundant provision for life is a response to this conviction that creation is a blessing. In this light, worship is the fullest enactment and extension of God's blessing. It is "the work of the people" that enacts our conviction that creation is a blessing that gives to us the setting and resources for living. In worship, we are most fully alive. But we must not draw a firm line between the work of worship and other work that we do. We must distinguish between worship work and other work, but we must not separate them or put them in opposition to each other. Although there is clearly a difference—the Sabbath command reveals this—worship work and other work together make it possible for us to enjoy God's blessing in creation. Without that "other work," Sabbath work would not be possible: life is sustained by that "other work." At the same time, Sabbath work teaches us that our other work is also the gift of God, which we return to God in our acts of praise, thanksgiving, lament, and repentance.

We must be especially careful of the Sabbath command(s) here. The command to keep the Sabbath differs in Exodus 20:8–11 and Deuteronomy 5:12–15. These commands tell us to cease from our labor. But that very labor is the fulfillment of the blessing of Genesis 1:28–31. So is our labor actually set against our worship work? Not at all. The command to cease our labor does not make it a bad thing or even a second-rate thing. Rather, keeping the Sabbath by ceasing from our labor celebrates our "other work" and fills it with meaning because in our worship we bring all the fruit of our other work before God. This is true quite simply because we bring our lives before God. And work is the blessing that enacts and extends the life that God gives in creation.

When we keep the Sabbath and come before God in the work of the people (*liturgy*), we engage in a practice that teaches us the blessing of creation. We learn to relax and to be unanxious about our lives and the planet. In true worship, we surrender our deeply held but false belief that life depends on us. We also surrender the fear that the struggle to survive—to get what we need for life, hold on to it, increase it, and pass it on to our progeny—is the deepest reality of this cosmos. Everything about proper worship is directed toward teaching us that creation is a blessing.[4]

It is a measure of our faulty, weak doctrine of creation that worship is seldom directed toward this end. More often, worship leaves us with only the teaching that the struggle for survival is the deepest reality of this cosmos, that God in Christ helps us in this struggle, and that when the struggle is over, we will be rewarded with a better life in heaven. This faulty practice of worship leaves the world in place and interprets life within the context of the world and its distorted end rather than celebrating the new creation and orienting all of life to that end.

The biblical term for worship that directs us to false, faulty ends is "idolatry." Without a robust, mature doctrine of creation to guide our worship, we are susceptible to many idols, idols that today typically come in the guise of ideologies cloaked in religious, spiritual, and biblical language. This is one of the consequences of the theological neglect of the doctrine of creation and our failure to follow the dialectic of the kingdom. If we present the gospel as redemption apart from creation, as a spiritual rescue operation that merely directs our discipleship to an inner disposition or an entirely future state of affairs, then we leave a vacuum in our lives that other ideologies rush in to fill. That is, apart from robust, mature teaching on the fullness of God's creative work and the dialectic of creation and redemption, we have few resources for discipling many dimensions of life—economic, political, medical, and more. We may identify or argue about the inner disposition toward these matters that disciples of Jesus Christ should have, but we offer very thin, weak guidance about the actual reality of God's work in those spheres. Our worship, then, becomes idolatrous because it is directed by and serves ends other than the one end of creation, which is the new creation.

4. Among the many recent books on the Sabbath, see Wirzba, *Living the Sabbath*, and Dawn, *Keeping the Sabbath Wholly*. The best books on worship that deepen our understanding of creation are Schmemann, *For the Life of the World*, and Kavanagh, *On Liturgical Theology*, esp. part 1, "Liturgy and the World."

We engage in idolatrous worship when we allow this world to set the context of our worship. In this approach to worship, we think of it as a way to recharge our batteries, cope with life, teach us how to make our way in this life and prosper. These ways of thinking make us vulnerable to ideologies, programs, and gods that promise us help for life in this world. But all of this simply leaves this world and its rulers in charge of our lives. This "worship" serves merely to occupy us until death takes our lives.

In contrast to this idolatrous worship, true worship brings us into another story: the story of the redemption of creation. In this story, we are made fit for another reality, the reality of life. This reality is present even now in the midst of death. Thus, worship is not an escape from this world but rather a call into another story that encompasses the cosmos. This conviction provides the dynamic for so much of the teaching of the Bible about life in this world but not of this world, about losing our lives in order to find them, about the life of discipleship that goes against the grain of this world but "with the grain of the universe."[5] These things are difficult to sustain unless we regularly enter into the story that gives them their meaning and truth and life. True worship is the practice that brings us into the blessing of creation that makes it possible for us to live by "creation" in a rebellious world because in worship we live into the reality of the redemption of creation.[6]

A proper grasp of creation as an act of blessing frees us from ideological necessity and temptation. We no longer need to control this cosmos when we know that its purpose and end—life—is given to us by God's blessing. It is crucial to recognize that blessing is the mark of creation in relationship to the Father, the Son, and the Holy Spirit; their relationships of perfect, complete, eternal self-giving and receiving, which is Life, the blessed life of God. From that blessed life, God pronounces blessing on that to which God gives life. With this confidence, that the telos of creation is grounded and guaranteed not in this world but in the blessed life of God, we are freed from the frantic pursuit of control.[7] Again, Sabbath names the practice that teaches and extends the reality of the blessedness of knowing that God's blessing rests on creation; we need not fear.

At the same time, to know the blessing of creation also frees us from the desire to escape. This is the other side of our frantic pursuit of control. If we do not know the blessing of creation, if we think that "creation" is a burden

5. This phrase is the title of the published Gifford lectures by Stanley Hauerwas, *With the Grain of the Universe*. Hauerwas takes the phrase from John Howard Yoder, "Armaments and Eschatology," 58.

6. This is why my book concludes with a chapter on worship.

7. See MacIntyre, *After Virtue*, chaps. 7–8; Wilson, *Living Faithfully*, 43–45.

and a curse, then one temptation is to seek to control the world, to bring it under our rule. But if for various reasons we conclude that such a project is not possible due to unpredictability, human limitations, complexity, and the like, then our impulse will be to escape the curse and burden of this world.

This escapism is often obvious in Christian teaching about salvation that reduces salvation to the promise of another world. "Just hold on; this world won't last." One thing that makes this imperative and promise so powerful is the partial truth that it contains. God is making "another world": the new creation. But that promised world is made from this creation. The world is a burden and under a curse, but creation is under a blessing and a gift. And that work of creation is the work that we enter into by faith in Christ today. That is the place where eternal life is lived even now because it is already participating in the dialectic of the kingdom that ends in the new creation. The promise of the gospel is not escape from creation but the redemption of the world as God's creation. The promise of the gospel is also the blessing of creation that we know and enter into now by life in Christ through the Spirit. "In this world you will have trouble," Jesus says, "But take heart! I have overcome the world" (John 16:33).

Finally, to know creation as a blessing is to know the proper place of beauty in life. If the universe is a curse and a burden and not blessed creation, then beauty is an anomaly in the universe. Beauty becomes a means of coping with the burden and curse, finding a bright spot amid all the ugliness. Beauty in this case merely helps us go on in a cursed and burdensome world. It relieves momentarily the pain and trouble of life; it breaks through the darkness for a time; it provides a refuge in the midst of death and destruction. But in this view, beauty is not a sign of the blessing of creation; it is rather an anomaly in an otherwise meaningless, cursed world.

When Christian teaching fails to connect beauty to the blessing of creation, an alternative account of beauty may develop. In some cases, beauty is appropriated and affirmed as a tool for witness to the gospel. The mistake here is subtle: rather than celebrating beauty as an aspect of the blessing of creation and thus an essential part of the good news of creation and its redemption, beauty becomes merely instrumental to Christian witness. This instrumental use of *beauty* actually empties things of their beauty and subtly reintroduces the anxiety rooted in a failure to recognize creation as a blessing. This anxiety means that we tend to judge everything by its usefulness for life, however we may measure that.

In an effort to correct this mistaken approach to beauty, some teachers may advance an argument for "useless beauty"—that is, to view beauty for its own sake. That proposal may help us, but it needs to be taken further so that beauty is rooted in a recovery of the dialectic of the kingdom and a trinitarian economy. All that is good, true, and beautiful has a place in God's creation. But it is also true that what is good, true, and beautiful may be fully known and celebrated only when we are able to see it in the blessing of God on creation. The good, true, and beautiful have no reality apart from the work of the Father, the Son, and the Spirit in the redemption of creation.

These last two assertions play on both the being of beauty and the knowing of beauty. We may assert that beauty has being, that it exists, only through the work of the Father, the Son, and the Spirit. But is it possible for us to know and appreciate beauty apart from knowing the Father, the Son, and the Spirit and apart from acknowledging the Triune God as the source of beauty? We seem to confront this possibility when we encounter great works of beauty that are not the work of those who know the Father, the Son, and the Spirit. But if we believe that beauty is inseparable from creation and that beauty is an aspect of the blessing of creation, then any claim to knowing and appreciating beauty must be located within our belief and participation in the work and life of the Father, the Son, and the Spirit. What we encounter in the work of many is the gracious blessing of God in the beauty of creation that exists in dependence on God. But because it is God's gift, it may not be known explicitly as the work of God's redemption of creation. At the same time, that beauty is incomplete until we locate it within the telos of creation.

The telos of beauty is to participate in and bear testimony to the blessing of creation. We do not understand or practice this fully, but for that very reason we need God's gracious presence to place us on the journey to understanding that end (among many others) and guide us to its completion in the new creation. For those who refuse to participate in this journey and be guided by the God whose beauty blesses creation, beauty then becomes simply another source of ideologies and idols that bring their followers to a very different end. (This is why the Nazis, for example, could famously enjoy the "beauty" of Mozart, Beethoven, Wagner, and also do evil. What we call "aesthetic sensibility" or taste, when captive to a false end, merely serves death.) When we properly locate beauty in the telos of the new creation, we have been led to understand that the beauty of God's blessing in creation is the cruciform beauty of the dialectic of the kingdom and the trinitarian grammar of creation.[8]

The cases of work and beauty lead us into deeper understanding of the blessing of creation. When we understand that the Father, the Son, and the Spirit initiate, sustain, uphold, redeem, and complete creation in the new creation, we are prepared to recognize, receive, and participate in the blessing

---

8. I am indebted to Tora Klassen for reminding me of this.

of creation. We are taken from the cursed "world" to the blessed creation. We are taken from death to life.

Life

In our study of the work of the one Creator—Father, Son, and Spirit—we explored the relationships of the Father, the Son, and the Spirit as Life. This God—"I AM"—simply *is* Life. God's name declares that to us; the doctrine of the trinity provides the conceptual-linguistic tools necessary to contemplate this eternal blessedness; the confession of one God—Father, Son, and Spirit—directs and empowers our worship. This God, the only God, is Life, the Living One, I AM.

In creating, I AM gives life to that which is not God. This life is a gift and a blessing. This gift and this blessing are also life: not God's life, not God as Life, but the life of creation given by the One who lives as Father, Son, and Holy Spirit. The life of creation is not "triune"; only God is triune. But the life of creation is given by the God who is triune. Therefore, the life of creation is determined and shaped by the God who lives because this one God is triune. The language here is difficult. How do we say that the one God who is Father, Son, and Spirit is the only possibility for life? It is really the other way around: only the God who is Father, Son, and Spirit can live, can be Life. All other gods are (lifeless) idols.

At first it may seem trivial to say that creation is life. Is not "life" simply a definition of creation? How could we have a creation that is not alive? But when we confess creation as the work of the Father, the Son, and the Spirit, the assertion of creation as life invites us into more profound and revealing reflection. The assertion that creation is life is an invitation into a mystery that deepens both our understanding of God and creation and our living-in-relationship.

Although the life of creation is not identical to the life of God, it does reflect the reality of the life of the Triune God. The life of creation is not identical to the life of God because creation is dependent on God—it does not have life in itself as God does. Creation is, well, creation, not Creator. In the same way that creation is a gift and a blessing of the Father, the Son, and the Holy Spirit, so also is creation life, in dependence on God. We could easily use the term *life* to reflect on and teach the whole range of Christian convictions about creation. But for our own instruction and living, some differentiation brings greater clarity and understanding to our human thinking and living. We have already considered two aspects of created life: gift and blessing. Here, under the actual category of "life," we will consider how creation reflects the life of the God who creates.

Just as God the Father, the Son, and the Holy Spirit live in continual self-giving and self-receiving, so also do all created things live—things in heaven and on earth, visible and invisible. At the present time, this giving and receiving in order to be living has been upended in the world, which is in rebellion against God's rule and God's way of life. The world is now ruled not by giving and receiving but by taking and keeping. The word for taking and keeping is *death*. When we refuse the process of giving and receiving that is life, then we short-circuit the process of life so that all that remains is death. This dynamic of death inextricably implicates the refusal to recognize God's creation as a gift and a blessing.

One may rightly understand the first humans taking of the fruit of the tree of the knowledge of good and evil in this light. "When the woman saw that the fruit of the tree was good for food and pleasing to the eye, and also desirable for gaining wisdom, she took some and ate it" (Gen. 3:6). The key to understanding this act is that "she took it." She did not believe that God had given and would continue to give all that was needed for blessing and life. She turned from receiving life to taking it; in so doing she turned from life to death. This dynamic of refusing gift and blessing, and instead taking and keeping, which leads to death, is very well established and "natural," now that we are lost in our sin. We may sense our lostness and imagine that death is not right. But we see death and life clearly only when our eyes are opened by the apocalyptic intervention that is the incarnation, crucifixion, and resurrection of Jesus Christ: "In him was life, and the life was the light of all people" (John 1:4 NRSV).[9]

To believe what is revealed of death and life in Jesus Christ is to enter already into life and receive the gift and blessing of creation. When we enter into this reality, we are returning to God's work of creation in which giving and receiving is life. This life, which is the only way of true life, turns this upside-down world right side up. But because this world is upside down, it rejects the way of life revealed in Jesus Christ. This rejection is vividly displayed in Jesus's own story. Throughout John 10–17, we receive from Jesus his teaching about the reciprocity of life. He lays down his life and takes it up again because his life is rooted in relationship with the Father (John 10, especially vv. 15–18, 29,

---

9. I use *apocalyptic* here to remind us of the shocking, world-shattering revelation of Jesus Christ to a world that assumes the rule of death and the undeniable "reality" of the way the world is, always has been, and always will be. Only the life of Israel could prepare us for the shock of actuality in Jesus the Messiah. Then and now, we manage too often to evade even that preparation for the gospel of life.

37–38). He gives his life to others because the Father has given him all things: "Jesus, knowing that the Father had given all things into his hands, and that he had come from God and was going to God. . . ." (John 13:3 NRSV).

This dynamic of life in contrast to the dynamic of death calls us to give up ourselves in order to receive ourselves:

> Then he said to them all: "Whoever wants to be my disciple must deny themselves and take up their cross daily and follow me. For whoever wants to save their life will lose it, but whoever loses their life for me will save it. What good is it for someone to gain the whole world, and yet lose or forfeit their very self?" (Luke 9:23–25)

Now we are in a position to see that the very form of Christian discipleship is itself deeply intertwined with the very life of creation. We are saved from the bondage of death, which is served by taking and keeping, and freed to be bound to life by giving and receiving. This salvation and freedom is the shape of discipleship in which we give up our death-bound lives, joined to Christ crucified, and receive our life-bound lives, joined to Christ risen.

Thus, the doctrine of creation provides insight and greater depth for the life of discipleship in which we lay down our lives for others and receive our lives back from God so that we may give them once again to others.[10] This is the very shape of creation. But we must also recognize that such life is opposed by death and by a world in rebellion against God's gift and blessing. It is hard to live a faithful life of Christian discipleship—giving and receiving—in a world enslaved by taking and keeping. Jesus tells us that we will have trouble in this world. But he also tells us that he has overcome the world. This world sought to take Christ's life and, at a deeper level, sought to force him into betraying life by taking and keeping his own life. But Jesus, the incarnate Son, remained faithful to his life with the Father and the Spirit and trusted that the gift of his life for the sin of the world would have its end in his receiving it back from the Father in the power of the Spirit. In the life of the Father, the Son, and the Spirit, giving and receiving overpowers the world's taking and keeping. We are assured that what is true for Christ is true for his followers as well: "And if the Spirit of him who raised Jesus from the dead is living in you, he who

10. On a draft of this manuscript, Ian Campbell wrote: "So in 2 Corinthians 1, where the context is one of trouble (even death if the whole letter is taken into account), Paul turns such things to the giving of life (comfort and meaning in suffering) because he himself is giving/passing on the life that he has received from God. Indeed he maintains that the purpose of his suffering is *so that* life and growth can occur amidst suffering. This is all the more remarkable because, as the whole of 2 Corinthians points out, the greater the perceived attack on human life unto death, the greater the triumph of life for those who are in Christ. Death, where is thy sting?"

raised Christ from the dead will also give life to your mortal bodies because of his Spirit who lives in you" (Rom. 8:11).[11]

Having learned the necessity of giving and receiving for life by the apocalyptic coming of Christ, we may now consider more closely what it means to affirm creation as life. In the first place, to affirm creation as life is to deny that life may be found somewhere else. When we say that life can be found only in creation, we are also reaffirming the dialectic of the kingdom and the trinitarian grammar of creation. We are not using *creation* with some vague, general meaning; we are saying, rather, that life can be found nowhere else but in this cosmos as creation. Given the freedom of the cosmos, we may try to construct life and live by some other means, but all other so-called ways of life are in the end ways of death. This is why Jesus testifies, "I am the way and the truth and the life. No one comes to the Father except through me" (John 14:6).

This affirmation and denial also teaches us that we should remove from our vocabulary the language of "lifestyle" or "lifestyle options" and be very careful when we talk about "*ways* of life." This language implies that life is a kind of given for humanity and that we are free to choose how we "live." But I am arguing that there is only one way to life: through Jesus Christ, who is the redemption of creation. All other so-called lifestyles are really "death-styles"; that is how serious all of this is. Because we have not fully developed our teaching on creation, we have become confused about the life of creation and taken it to mean that we can choose among many different ways of life. When we begin to recover a robust, mature understanding of creation and its life, we must do some very hard thinking and then repent—change our thinking about life.

To affirm creation as life is also to commit ourselves to the grace-sustained discipline that enables us to see past the way that this upside-down, death-bound world goes about the everyday. To understand life as I have described it here is to acknowledge that everything has been changed. As Paul says, "Therefore, if anyone is in Christ, the new creation has come" (2 Cor. 5:17). And so begins the lifelong journey of learning to see everything new and to live "new lives" in the creation that is being redeemed for the new creation. These are matters of life and death, as God repeatedly declares in Scripture. Yet because of our weak and often nonexistent attention to the doctrine of creation, we have consistently deflected these warnings and tried to continue business as usual with the world. At our better moments, we have taught that our responsibility as followers of Christ is to try to make things better, improve people's lives, and tell them that something new has been promised

---

11. We will consider this very important biblical passage at greater length in chap. 7.

to us if we believe. But even that falls short of the life of creation. We have often failed to grasp in any significant measure that the coming of Jesus Christ claims this world as creation and calls us now to live in and bear witness to the redemption of creation for the new creation. We often reduce the declaration of newness in Christ to a personal reality and in so doing deny its cosmic import. We interpret the lordship of Christ to mean that he now has control of the power centers of this world and will direct them toward a better end.

But that falls short of what the coming of Jesus Christ means for this world and for creation. Rather, the coming of Christ means that Life has been revealed in the midst of death, that death and all its servants have been conquered, and that the life of creation has been shown to be the willingness to give one's life to God only to receive it back through being in Christ. This giving and receiving is not a scheme devised by God to see how serious we are about following Christ; it is not a test of our commitment and our willingness to obey. Rather, giving up the old life that is ruled by death simply is the way to life. The various disciplines and regimes that we pursue and serve in our attempt to manage our way in this world presume the final reality of death, not the abundant, inexhaustible reality of creation as life. Most of our Christian attempts to participate in this world through Christian ethics, political activity, social action, and the like presume the fixedness of these arrangements, their presumption about this world, and the final reality of death. Thus, even Christian activism often leaves unquestioned the world's illusions and impotence in the face of death that the apocalypse of Christ exposes to humiliation, making "a public spectacle of them" (Col. 2:15). Tragically, even after Christ's humiliation of these powers, we who claim to follow Christ have often fallen into various ways of covering their shame and restoring their honor by submitting to the lie that they reign over life.

This coming of Christ is of such importance that we cannot really identify it in comparative terms. It is not most important, most crucial, most significant; the coming of Christ is incomparable. It is the new creation. We often glide right over this declaration and miss its utterly unprecedented, unexpected, unimaginable, unbelievable, unachievable reality apart from God. The word that best describes this reality is *apocalyptic*. Unfortunately, *apocalyptic* has been co-opted by Christian pulp novels, date setters, doomsayers, ideologues, and crazies.[12] But the term confronts us with the incomparable reality of the

12. Perhaps we should watch for just such occasions in history and know that when a term is taken over and discredited, it is likely because the term could reveal so much and teach so much. See Keller, *God and Power*; Northcott, *Angel Directs the Storm*. Both offer good critiques of the abusive use of *apocalyptic*. Northcott is concerned also with the recovery of a proper apocalyptic. Recently, some theologians have begun to revive a more mature understanding of

new creation in Christ.[13] In the midst of a world ruled by death, in which the imagining of any other world seems so unrealistic, in which belief in another reality seems foolish, the coming of Christ to redeem creation is *apocalyptic*. That is, it reveals something that comes to be and comes to be known *only* by that coming.[14] This new wine cannot be contained in old wineskins.

To enjoy and bear witness to the life of creation that is given to us in Christ, we must be "born again" by the power of God. Being born again is not a special category of Christian or an entry into a place of privilege. Rather, being born again is entry into the life of creation in which we give our lives because we have received them from God and know that our lives are guaranteed by the presence of the Spirit, who gives life to our mortal bodies (see Rom. 8:11). To claim to be "born again" is to commit ourselves to laying down our lives for others as Christ did. (We must be careful here to learn well the story of Jesus in company with others so that giving up our lives for others is Christlike and not ideologically driven or suicidal.)

It may seem at this point that the exposition has veered away from the doctrine of creation. But it is precisely this type of reflection that actually recovers the doctrine of creation in its fullness as part of the dialectic of the kingdom and the trinitarian economy. The life that God gives in creation is not different in shape from the life that God gives in redemption. God's life and the life that God gives to creation is giving and receiving. When we take and keep, we are not living but dying. When we die and are raised in Christ, we have life given to us on the other side of sin. Only then are we alive to God and alive in creation.

Now, having developed our understanding of life in its apocalyptic manifestation—our life with God in Christ—we may extend that understanding

---

apocalyptic. Unfortunately, some of the discussions have entailed fine distinctions and polemics that distract from the important work of retrieval that is also going on. See Martyn, *Galatians* and *Theological Issues in the Letters of Paul*; Kerr, *Christ, History and Apocalyptic*. Kerr's work, while lively and challenging, overreaches in its attempt to establish its uniqueness and significance. Still, it has contributed to opening up this important discussion. For a brilliant exposition of "The Apocalyptic Pastor" that grounds this retrieval in biblical and pastoral work, see Peterson, *Contemplative Pastor*, 39–49, and *Reversed Thunder*. Dawn, *Unfettered Hope*, makes "apocalyptic" live in everyday lives as we seek to be freed from our enslavement to the world and freed for life in the kingdom.

13. There has been a resurgence of attention to healthy apocalyptic thinking through the work of J. Louis Martyn, Douglas Harink, Christopher Morse, and Nathan Kerr. My reflections on this resurgence and adoption of apocalyptic thinking will appear in an essay "On the Aesthetics of the Kingdom: *Eschatos* and *Apocalypsis*" in a forthcoming Festschrift.

14. *Apocalyptic* comes from the Greek word that is translated "revelation." Thus, the last book of the Bible may be titled "the book of Revelation" or "the Apocalypse," with "of John" sometimes attached. In chap. 7, we will see the importance of this book for the doctrine of creation.

of life throughout creation. Everywhere in creation all forms of creation are sustained by giving and receiving. It begins with God, as God gives from God's own life for the life of creation. We Christians confess that there is only one place of aliveness: the one God—Father, Son, and Spirit. In doing so, we also confess that if the cosmos is alive, then that life must come from God. Before God initiates creation, there is "nothing." This "nothingness" has no life. It is God who brings life where there was only nothing. What is this nothing? Since there is now something and since we are now alive, there is no way for us to conceive actual nothingness or the absence of life outside the triune life of God. How is there anything in addition to the triune life of God?[15]

In light of our trinitarian description of life, we must acknowledge that all creation lives by giving and receiving. Right now, this supposed giving and receiving appears more like taking and keeping: animal predation, human conflict, perpetual violence—all are marks of this world.[16] Is there a way to reconceive this taking and keeping as a disordering of the receiving and giving that I argue is the life of creation? Can we see in the taking of life the very reversal of the way that the giving of life sustains and fulfills the life of the giver so that the giver does not lose life but rather finds it? Can this be true of all creation?

That is exactly the image of the new creation revealed to the prophets and John, the seer of Revelation:

> "The wolf and the lamb will feed together,
>   and the lion will eat straw like the ox,
>   and dust will be the serpent's food.
> They will neither harm nor destroy
>   on all my holy mountain,"
>   says the LORD.
>
> Isaiah 65:25

And I heard a loud voice from the throne saying, "Look! God's dwelling place is now among the people, and he will dwell with them. They will be his people, and God himself will be with them and be their God. 'He will wipe every tear from their eyes. There will be no more death' or mourning or crying or pain, for the old order of things has passed away." (Rev. 21:3–4; cf. Isa. 25:8)

The promises of these scenes is unimaginable in the present world: life is sustained by the taking of life, is it not? Is not death necessary to the continuation

---

15. See the reflections on this mystery in Barth, *Church Dogmatics* III/3, 289–368; Moltmann, *God in Creation*, 86–93.

16. This exposition could raise the question of the place of death in creation prior to the fall and in the new creation. See chap. 8 for a consideration of this question.

of life? No. No. A thousand times: No. What the life of the Triune God reveals to us and what the Triune Creator gives us is life through giving and receiving, not taking and keeping. What a wonderful future to imagine and delight in. It is truly apocalyptic in revealing to us a future that is not an extension of the way this world functions. And it is christologically apocalyptic because it takes seriously the new creation revealed in Christ's death and resurrection.

Imagine for a time one possible alternative to this apocalyptic vision of the new creation. (Again, I use the term *apocalyptic* to signal the severe interruption of the [dis]order of this world envisioned and proclaimed by God's prophets and seers.) What if the news is that this world in all its brokenness, violence, and death is eternal? Intriguingly, just such a life is what vampire myths proclaim: the curse of eternal life that depends on taking the life of others. Perhaps the popularity of these stories in print and on film indicates the longing for eternal life that can be conceived not as eternal life but only as a living death.

Let us take one more step in understanding that this apocalyptic vision of the new creation is not the denial of creation but its redemption. Without the dialectic of the kingdom and the trinitarian grammar of creation, the apocalyptic visions of Scripture threaten to undo life.[17] Indeed, that seems often to be the case with apocalyptic accounts of the "end of the world."[18] In these accounts, the apocalyptic visions of the disruption and destruction of the order of sin and death are taken to be the destruction of creation as well. But properly understood, the apocalyptic visions of Scripture are the defeat and destruction of sin and death and all evil things so that life may take hold of creation—or better so that creation may come to life once again. Or in more powerful imagery, the apocalyptic visions see the burning away of the impurities, the fire that consumes all that does not belong in God's good creation. What survives this conflagration is all that is proper to God's good creation—all that is good and true and beautiful by the one criterion, the apocalyptic event, the coming of Jesus Christ.[19]

---

17. Too much has been made of the passage in 2 Pet. 3:10–13. This passage is read against the rest of Scripture when it is read as an anticipation of the dissolution and eradication of the created order. It is read in congruence with the rest of Scripture when it is read as an assaying, a testing of all things by God to determine what of this world fits the new creation and what does not. This passage describes God's judgment of good and evil, not God's destruction of the created order. See Bouma-Prediger, *For the Beauty of the Earth*, 76–77; Harink, *1 & 2 Peter*, 181–85; Moo, "Continuity, Discontinuity, and Hope."

18. See the works by Keller and Northcott cited above.

19. See Hartt, *Christian Critique of American Culture*, 119: "The criterion of all Christian witness, and therefore of every judgment of the world, is not so much a life as a living presence, and an everlasting actuality. To be Christian is to surrender one's life to the interpretation of the Holy Spirit whose text is Jesus Christ. The Christian is not a mere passive object in this process. He too is subject. He is an interpreter as well as an interpretation, he is speaker as well

Telos

What the apocalyptic visions of Scripture portray for us, along with other biblical passages and our theological reflection, is the telos of creation in the new creation. This teleology is an essential mark of God's creation. *Telos* and *teleology* simply mean the purpose or end that is appropriate to a thing. So we may say that the telos of a hammer is to pound on something, such as a nail, a dent, a concrete block. The telos of a hammer is not to saw a board in two or to drive in a screw. Or imagine trying to beat an egg with a butter knife or serve soup with a fork. We understand the telos of many things in our everyday lives and take them for granted.

When we reflect on the doctrine of creation, we must not only inquire about the telos of creation; we must also recover the very notion of telos. This need is rooted in the history that I have briefly identified and assumed as background and context for this doctrine of creation.[20] That history and background are the theological retreat from the doctrine of creation that began about three hundred years ago with the rise of science. At that time, as I have suggested, teachers of the church became convinced that they could not compete with the explanatory power of the sciences and their ability to control "nature." The very turn from "creation" to "nature" is itself a part of this process.

As a result of this retreat, accounts of the cosmos were left to the sciences. Theology confined itself to accounting for the inner life of people or for the history of salvation, a specific current within the larger river of history, a current visible only to those with special vision called "eyes of faith."[21] In this way, as I have suggested, theology sought to protect its account of the gospel from "the acids of criticism." But in so doing, theology abandoned accounts of the full gospel of Jesus Christ, such as the one that I seek to develop here. At the same time, theology also surrendered accounts of the cosmos to the sciences. The cosmos was no longer "creation"; it was now "nature."

When the cosmos became nature it was approached as something reliable and dependable, so that experimental sciences could be developed, their hypotheses tested, and the results believed. But as the sciences developed, they had no need for an account of the telos of what they were studying. Thus, as the sciences developed and theology retreated, arguments about teleology

---

as word. He must know what to speak about Jesus Christ before he knows what to say about the good and evil of this world."

20. For accounts of the loss of telos, see MacIntyre, *After Virtue*; Wilson, *Living Faithfully*.

21. There is some truth in both of these notions. The mistake is made when the gospel is reduced to one or both of them. To be faithful to the gospel, these notions must be set within the public reality of God's redemption of creation.

quietly ended. This development is quite understandable since theology ceased to confront the sciences with the claims entailed by the redemption of creation. I suspect that theology abandoned "creation" because theology had already severed the connection between creation and redemption. Therefore, theology had no functioning teleological account of creation from which to challenge the shedding of teleology by the sciences. From the side of the sciences, being bound to a telos would rob humans and the world of the account of "freedom" that both underwrites and is underwritten by modernity.[22]

However, freedom in the modern sense is simply destined for failure.[23] If Christians had a robust, mature theological conversation about creation, this inevitable failure would already and always be evident to us. The putative freedom of modernity is the delusory belief that I create my own self and that human society should be organized to maximize my freedom to create myself. But as we can see in the context of the dialectic of the kingdom and a trinitarian grammar of creation, this modern belief leads only to death. The lie that I can create myself is my undoing.

The recovery of the telos of creation in the new creation is also the recovery of God's work of creation and redemption that is life. For what (telos) is creation made? Creation is made for life. This recognition may also help us solve one of the conundrums in the history of theology. Does God create for God's glory or for the fulfillment of humankind? The answer, as with so many such questions, is yes. God creates for both. Although this may seem obvious, it has not been easy to arrive at such an answer. But if we recognize that life is the telos of creation and that life rooted in the Father, the Son, and the Spirit is not a zero-sum game, then we may see that in the new creation, both God and all creation are glorified in ways appropriate to each. God is glorified by giving life to the cosmos. The cosmos is glorified by receiving life as God's creation and returning it to God in praise and obedient trust.

Brokenness

Several times in this chapter, we have briefly considered our rejection of creation as gift, our experience of creation as burden, our loss of life, and our denial of creation's telos. It is time now to focus on these issues. As we do

22. See Blumenberg, *Legitimacy of the Modern Age*, although his focus is political thought, not the "sciences." Gillespie, *Theological Origins of Modernity*, exposes modernity's covert quest for a new metaphysics or theology that is directly implicated in the loss of "creation."

23. We are at a point in the history of our culture where this is becoming clear. See the powerful narrative analyses of MacIntyre, *After Virtue*; Taylor, *Sources of the Self* and *Secular Age*.

so, however, I begin with a warning that this discussion is not quite properly placed in this book and could contribute to perpetuating a theological error.

Neither sin nor evil, neither disobedience nor unbelief, neither taking nor keeping, neither violence nor death, have a rightful place in God's creation.[24] Thus, when I discuss these things in this chapter, I am doing so to argue that when we restate creation according to the dialectic of the kingdom and the trinitarian economy of creation, these things are really "anticreation." That is, sin, unbelief, taking, violence, and the like are not part of creation but are part of the doctrine of creation in the same way that sin is not part of our salvation but is part of the doctrine of salvation.

When we view these anticreation pseudopowers in this light, we can see that they deny the dialectic of the kingdom and the grammar of creation. In denying the dialectic of the kingdom, these forces of anticreation deny the redemption of the world. They lie to us by posing as "the way the world works" and imposing on us a "realism" that is a tissue of lies built into a facade masquerading as the inevitable, unavoidable, unassailable limit to our vision and constraint on our action. In so doing, these forces insinuate themselves as the only possible telos of the world. We adapt our vision and actions to their lies and adopt various means of coping with the death toward which they draw us, with religion, entertainment, and technology being three dominant ways of drugging ourselves in our enslavement to the false telos of the world. They are pseudopowers because they have been defeated and publicly humiliated by the death of Christ; they are now under the rule of Christ for the redemption of creation.

Alternatively, these powers (when their illusory power is exposed and their plausibility collapses) leave us with . . . nothing. In other words, when these gods fail us, we may conclude that there are no gods and that there is no meaning in the world. No matter how we try to cloak or reinterpret this conviction, it is at its hollow center the denial of life. When this happens, our enslavement to religion, entertainment, and technology deepens and devours our lives even more gleefully.

At this point, we have in place the elements for reflection on what it means to say that these anticreation forces are the distortion and denial of the telos of creation. In the history of theology, we have typically interpreted the present rule of these forces, especially identified as sin and death, as the result of the fall from the perfection of the original creation. This teaching produces many different tangles for theology. A different understanding of the source

---

24. In Rom. 8:37–39, Paul tells us that none of this brokenness can overcome God's telos for creation.

and nature of sin and death, one that is teleological in its logic, enables us to avoid or dissolve many of these tangled knots.

One key to understanding our present situation and God's work of redemption and creation that "ends" in the new creation is to understand that sin and death are not the result of the fall away from an original perfection. Rather, sin and death are the consequence and evidence of the turn away from, resistance to, and rebellion against the telos of creation. In other words, the fall is a rejection of God's purpose for life. It is best understood not as a corruption of the original but as the disruption and deflection of the completion of creation in eternal life, which is the new creation. One way of expressing this is to say that in its beginning creation was teleologically perfect, not originally perfect. In other words, God made the cosmos perfectly suited for the fulfillment of its purpose in Jesus Christ. This is not a proclamation of the imperfection of creation but a recasting of what "the perfection of creation" means.

In this view, God created precisely the cosmos that God intended to create, a cosmos that would by God's work become the new creation by virtue of God's love for the cosmos and the cosmic response to God's love. In this view, if we had not turned from the telos of creation, God would have brought about the new creation by the incarnation of God the Son and the perfection of creation in God's life. But the death of the Son of God would have been unnecessary. The telos of creation would have simply been worked out in an unbroken relationship with the one Creator—Father, Son, and Spirit. In this case, we would not have to recognize and maintain "the dialectic of the kingdom" in creation and redemption. Rather, the work of creation would have been completed by the assumption of creation by the incarnation of God the Son so that we would also share in the life of the Father and the Spirit. In this particular economy of creation, the roles of the Father, the Son, and the Spirit would have been differentiated roles as they are in redemption. However, creation would not be redeemed or "restored," but rather completed.

But that is speculation about something that did not happen—about a "counterfactual." Given the "fall" from the telos of creation, in order to become the new creation the cosmos requires the interweaving of God's work of creation and redemption. To further develop this understanding, we also need the trinitarian grammar of creation. If we think about the fall as teleological rather than original, then redemption and restoration also have a teleological orientation. In this case, redemption reclaims the world as creation and realigns it with its journey toward the realization of its telos in the new creation. The fall into sin has put the cosmos on a path to death and destruction—thus it is not "creation" but "world." Redemption removes the world from this dysteleological path and places it back on the teleological path of creation. In other words, redemption does not return the world to an original state. Rather, redemption returns the world to its telos. Likewise, restoration does not restore the original state of creation but rather restores created things to their purpose and points toward the completion of all creation in its telos: the new creation. Thus, the restoration of sight to the blind, hearing to the deaf, freedom to the captive, and forgiveness to the sinner are signs and promises of the fulfillment of the telos of creation.[25]

In the dysteleological situation of destruction and death, the gospel of creation and redemption may shine ever more brightly, its aroma restoring our appetite for life, and its beauty enchanting us more delightfully. When we encounter the news that the telos of this world is the new creation through God's work of creation and redemption, we may be stirred from our drugged stupor and awakened to the blessing, gift, and life of creation so that we may begin to live now what is ours for eternity through the Father, the Son, and the Spirit. Believing that message and living it in this world are possible only by the work of the Father, the Son, and the Spirit.[26]

Peace

Although peace pervades the good news of Jesus Christ both in anticipation of his coming in the Tanak and in the narration of his coming in the Gospels, Acts, Epistles, and Apocalypse, the concept of peace has seldom been a

25. I am indebted to a breakfast conversation with Cam Tucker for reminding me of this. Here we may also recall John 9, where the disciples wanted to know the origin of the man's blindness, but Jesus redescribes the situation teleologically. The "works of God" (John 9:3) point us toward the dialectic of the kingdom.

26. Here I am paraphrasing Julian Hartt, who writes:

"God is our judge and our redeemer. The unreality systems created by man threaten to throttle man's created possibility, or at the least to disfigure it. When therefore God speaks as present with us in Christ, our essential being stirs in drugged sleep and begins the struggle to welcome its true Lord. In this sense the essence of man is struggle, conflict, tension: man is an *agon*, a momentous contention with God. The end of the contention is disclosed in Jesus Christ: that we might become, in the whole circuit of our life, and in the vital center, what we are in the creative seeing of God. 'Be transformed' is the imperative of the righteous God communicated in Jesus Christ. The essential struggle is the work to free 'the original plan of creation,' the created possibility, from the dead weight of character and institution produced to block or distort the full realization of the creative spirit. Victory in this struggle is impossible without the power of God. The name of Jesus Christ is also Immanuel: God with us." (Hartt, *Christian Critique of American Culture*, 87).

Hartt's reference to the original *plan* (my emphasis) and "the created possibility" are indications that he is thinking teleologically about creation.

focus of studies of biblical theology.[27] Rather than examine reasons for this neglect, I am concerned here with recovering the biblical teaching of peace and placing it within the context of the doctrine of creation. Apart from the historic peace churches such as the Mennonites and the Quakers, Christians tend to think about *peace* as "peace of mind": no more worries about our relationship with God or our eternal destiny. I will not discount that aspect, but it must be subordinate to an expansive understanding of cosmic peace in order for "peace of mind" to be more than a therapeutic attempt to cope with the condition of this world.

We seldom develop in any detail an account of peace that engages the entire cosmos by recognizing that the gospel of "peace" is good news for all creation. This good news for all creation is not merely that humans are free from anxiety and fear and therefore possibly less likely to harm others. Rather, the good news of peace for all creation is the good news that God in Christ is bringing the world to the wholeness of life that will be enjoyed forever in the new creation. This work of peace, of wholeness, of the weaving together of created things, is the redemption of creation. Therefore, we who believe and live in Christ have peace of mind not because we know that we are okay with God, but because we know that the entire cosmos is being made "okay" with God through Christ. The peace of Christ is so much more than my peace of mind. It is cosmic in its scope. The peace of creation is secured in Christ, so that nothing in all the world should be able to disturb the peaceableness of Christ's followers.

But given our reflections on creation, we can go one step further than is usually taken in accounts of peace grounded in Scripture and the proclamation of the gospel. If we grasp the meaning of creation as gift and blessing, if we understand the life and telos of creation, then the peace that Christ brings and the peacemaking to which his followers are called is not an idealistic, starry-eyed, irresponsible dream or a public policy for the reduction of violence; rather, peace is the very shape of the life of creation.[28] The God of creation and redemption is also the God of peace. Willard Swartley points out that the appellation "God of peace" occurs frequently in the Gospels and the Epistles, while the appellation "God of reconciliation" does not occur.[29] Yet we have

27. Willard Swartley has given an account of this neglect and contributed a significant work to the recovery of the centrality of peace for NT theology and ethics. In doing so, he attends briefly to the OT teaching. We need a study of the OT equivalent to Swartley's. The one major drawback to Swartley's otherwise commendable study is his neglect of the doctrine of creation in his exposition of the covenant of peace. See Swartley, *Covenant of Peace*. See also Hays, *Moral Vision of the New Testament*, 317–46.

28. This is what John Howard Yoder means by his testimony that "people who bear crosses are working with the grain of the universe." See Yoder, "Armaments and Eschatology," 58.

29. Swartley, *Covenant of Peace*, 190–91; see also 5–8.

many more studies of reconciliation than of peace. The peace of God is not a political or ideological program doomed to failure in its confrontation with a realistic appraisal of this world and the rule of death. Rather, the peace of God is the very heartbeat of the cosmos created and redeemed by the Father, the Son, and the Spirit, for whom peace is also the shape of Life.[30]

We have seen that conflict—taking and keeping—marks this world. But it does not mark creation. At times in the past I have been willing to acknowledge that "peace" and peacemaking are not "politically realistic." I have also been willing at times to grant the term "Christian realism" to Reinhold Niebuhr and his heirs, as long as I could claim "biblical realism" or "gospel realism" for the call to living in Jesus's way of peace.[31] But in working on this doctrine of creation, I have come to realize that although "political realism" and "Christian realism" help identify historical examples, neither is truly realistic.

Realistically, the God of peace is the ruler of the universe. The peace that the one God—Father, Son, and Spirit—establishes and calls all creation into is the final and ultimate realism. This peace is "the most real world."[32] All other claims to rule and to determine the limits of our action are lies. These powers have been defeated and publicly humiliated. They have not yet been destroyed, for that brings the end of this world and the fulfillment of the new creation. God the Father determines when that will come to be. In this time, when we follow the way of peace, resisting and refusing the claim of this world to be the constraining and determining fact in our thinking and acting, we are living "with the grain of the universe." It is in this faithfulness that followers of Christ bear witness to creation. We are right to hear and obey the commission to be witnesses to Christ, but we must leave behind the immature conviction that this witness can be fulfilled by our witness solely to "redemption." When we are mature in our convictions and living, we bear witness to the gift, blessing, life, and telos of creation redeemed.

More theological insight may flow from this account of the peace of creation. For example, we could develop a Christian account of justice rooted

30. One of the weaknesses of many types of Christian "pacifism" is the almost exclusive connection between peace and God's work of redemption. This leaves open the possibility of asserting another realm of God's work—"creation"—in which peace is not a reality. This is the door through which most accounts of "Christian realism" enter the church. One of my claims in this book is that when we properly live by the dialectic of the kingdom, there is no gap between creation and redemption. Rather, the gap is between world and kingdom. Since the church lives in both the world and the kingdom, the church also displays this peace gap. When the church confesses this gap as sin, it fulfills the mission of the church to bear witness to the kingdom.

31. For a recent statement by an evangelical in the Niebuhrian tradition of "Christian realism," see Stackhouse, *Making the Best of It*.

32. I have taken the description "most real world" from Peterson, *Contemplative Pastor*, 27.

in a recognition that the life of creation flows and flourishes as created things are lined up properly in relation to God and one another. *Justice* and *justification* simply name the right alignment of the world with God through the redemption of creation. Justice and justification—and the judgment of God that discerns these and enacts them—are necessary for life. We may even say that God sustains this world by establishing justice through Jesus Christ.

Those things in the world that work against life and for death must be properly lined up in relation to God. In this aligning, they are judged to be against life and therefore condemned. Those things that work against death and for life must also be properly lined up in relation to God. In this aligning, God judges them to be conducive to life. Followers of Christ are called to bear witness to this justice not by enacting it ourselves but by seeking to learn what God's justice looks like—that is, what is conducive to life as created by God, to discern its presence in our world, and to bear witness to it. (If this seems too high an aspiration for the church, recall Jesus's words, "Whatever you bind on earth. . . . " [Matt. 16:19].)

The telos of justice is not revenge or simply the righting of wrongs. Rather, the telos of justice is the life of creation in the new creation. For the new creation to be the proper end of creation and redemption, and for God to be justified in patiently sustaining this world and redeeming creation in the new creation, the things of this world must be rightly aligned with God. God's justice does not offer us an opportunity to do things over. Nor does God's justice set aside the very real consequences of rebellion against the telos of creation. Only God's justice in Christ can take the evil of this world seriously, deal with it appropriately, and bring the world through the redemption of creation to the new creation.

Following from this very brief suggestion about justice, we may then see that *reconciliation* is God's act of aligning all things in their proper relationship to God through Christ's cross. This reconciliation is part of the redemption of creation that ends in the new creation. In the cross, evil is exposed as evil and in this is rightly aligned with God. In the cross, giving and receiving in love is revealed as life and in this is rightly aligned with God. To use an image that we should not press too far, in the cross, the world's account with God is reconciled: debts are revealed, accounted for, and settled; creation is revealed as gift and blessing, and its life and telos made manifest in Jesus. In this way, the reconciliation of all things (Col. 1) means not the salvation of all things but rather the redemption of creation ending in the new creation through "all things" being aligned in their proper relationship to God. In this reconciliation, some things will be "rightly aligned" with

"Growing Together"

God by being judged evil. Other things will be "rightly aligned" with God by being judged good.[33]

Finally, we may think of righteousness in terms of the peace of creation. By placing righteousness in the context of the peace of creation, we may see that righteousness identifies part of the condition necessary to the peace of creation. *Righteousness* identifies the way for humans that is rightly aligned with the peace of creation and thus is the way of life, not death. Righteousness, then, is not some extraordinary way of living that somehow acquires special favor from God because it is extraordinary. Rather, righteousness simply is "right living" in creation. It is living "with the grain of the universe." This realization helps us see that life is neither a reward for an achievement nor something added to those who have the characteristic of "righteousness." Rather, life and righteousness are intrinsic to each other. To be righteous is to live rightly. To live rightly is to live forever because living rightly is only possible for those who have died to this world and its way of death and have been raised to Christ and the way that is life.

Conclusion

In this chapter, I have sought to restate the doctrine of creation in light of our cultural circumstances as analyzed in part 1 and in light of the theological guidance I established in the first two chapters of part 2. This chapter is not intended as a full account of a doctrine of creation; many aspects have not been discussed here. Some of the aspects not covered here may be found in previous and succeeding chapters.

There is much work to be done to reclaim the significance and import of the doctrine of creation for the whole of Christian theology and the life and witness of God's people. When the doctrine of creation is mostly absent from our theology and account of the gospel, the joyful reality of God's redemptive work is muted. Our words and our lives resemble the good news of the redemption of creation, but it is as if we could describe the reality of redemption only in the basic sentences and limited vocabulary of a "first book for readers."

See Jane run. See John run. See Jane and John run. See the red ball. See Jane throw the ball to John.

---

33. See Rev. 21–22, though we must not think that God's judgment is entirely suspended until the "final judgment." Throughout the course of Scripture, the Spirit guides those who speak for God in judgment, and the Spirit continues to guide God's people today.

See God make. See God judge. See God care. See Jesus come. See Jesus save. See the Spirit work. See people believe. Wait for the end. Hope for heaven.

When we gain a more mature and robust doctrine of creation guided by the dialectic of the kingdom and trinitarian grammar, our words and lives participate in and witness to the overwhelming splendor of life as blessing and gift, whose brokenness is being healed, whose destiny is the new creation, an everlasting ecstasy that we cannot bear in this age but will be the all-encompassing reality of the age to come, which is already among us and in which we live by the work of Christ through the power of the Spirit. This is the reality that the doctrine of creation adds to our proclamation of the gospel.

7

Rereading Scripture

As I was in the midst of writing this book, I described it to someone as a "doctrine of creation." The immediate response was, "Oh, so it's a book on Genesis 1–2?" By now you know that this is not a book on Genesis 1–2. You may, however, have been wondering about the place of Scripture in this doctrine of creation and its "biblical basis." So here we are now, finally arriving at a consideration of biblical teaching on the doctrine of creation.

A proper understanding of theology and the Bible should help us see, however, that we are not just now, finally, arriving at the biblical teaching. Instead, we should recognize that biblical teaching has been with us from the beginning. If we have properly submitted ourselves to the teaching of Scripture and allowed ourselves to be formed and transformed so that the world cannot press us into its mold, then from the beginning we have been engaged with the biblical teaching on the doctrine of creation.[1]

Nevertheless, although we should always be engaged with the Scripture to which we have submitted ourselves, there is also at the heart of the disciple community the necessity of engaging the biblical text directly because it is here that the Father, the Son, and the Holy Spirit continue to reveal themselves to us, catch us up into the redemption of creation, and teach us the new creation.

---

1. See J. B. Phillips translation of Rom. 12:1–2: "Don't let the world around you squeeze you into its own mould, but let God re-make you so that your whole attitude of mind is changed," Phillips, *The New Testament in Modern English for Schools*. Intriguingly, there is a clear echo of the doctrine of creation in the previous verse, where Paul urges us to give God our bodies, "as a living sacrifice."

This direct engagement with Scripture is best understood as a particular practice of theological commentary. After many years of relative neglect, theological commentary is once again being practiced by theologians and biblical scholars. But the meaning and practice of theological commentary is widely contested.[2] Without trying to adjudicate this contest, I will set forth what I mean by the practice of theological commentary.

Theological Commentary

The aim of theological commentary is to learn to see God's work in the world, hear God's voice, and live as God intends us to live in the redemption of creation. We do this by submitting ourselves to the vision and voice of God as taught by the Holy Spirit through Scripture in the disciple community. This theological commentary does not simply seek a theological layer on top of textual, grammatical, historical, cultural, literary, and social layers of analysis. It does not seek merely to draw a doctrinal lesson as the final step in exegesis, nor does it aim only to add an application to observation. This work of theological commentary is not the drawing of inference from what it meant for the biblical authors to what it means for us today. Rather, the theological commentary that I practice here seeks to be drawn into and to draw others into the good news of the redemption of creation that is narrated and witnessed in Scripture by the work of the Holy Spirit.

To draw us into creation-being-redeemed, *theological* commentary seeks to correct, clarify, and enlarge our vision—to stimulate, even *create* an imagination that sees God's work of redemption of creation. This creation of imagination is not the work of teaching us to see something that is not there but rather the work of teaching us to see truly what has been there all along—God is redeeming creation. But our seeing has been tutored by a world that does not know how to see God truly and that has invented—fantasized—many ways of seeing God and ourselves. As a result, the way we are taught to see the world is a lie and an illusion. Our vision problem is not just an inability to focus properly, nor is it nearsightedness or farsightedness, nor is it any number of other less common optic pathologies; no, our vision problem is God-blindness. The work of theological commentary is to participate in the

2. The following represent a range of practices by Bible scholars and theologians: Green and Turner, *Between Two Horizons* and the Two Horizons New Testament Commentary series; Vanhoozer et al., *Dictionary for Theological Interpretation of the Bible*; Treier, *Introducing Theological Interpretation of Scripture*; the Brazos Theological Commentary on the Bible series, ed. R. Reno; and the Belief: A Theological Commentary on the Bible series, ed. W. Placher and A. Pauw.

work of God that removes this blindness and to learn from Scripture how to see the redemption of creation.

Our task in theological commentary, then, is to apprentice ourselves to Scripture and learn how God has redeemed creation in justice and mercy in various places and times so that we today may know and celebrate that continuing irruption of God's kingdom.[3] But to say that our knowledge of God is culturally situated in various times and places is not to say that our knowledge of God is culturally constructed. In addition to culture, another agency is at work: the Triune God. It is the work of God that presses upon us, irrupts into our midst, and sweeps us into the glorious creating-redeeming work of God the Father, the Son, and the Holy Spirit.[4]

At this point, we have arrived at the heart of theological commentary. As we enter the mysteries of the trinitarian life of God, theological commentary is nothing more or less than a celebration of and a witness to our entry into that life. Our entry is the beginning of the fulfillment of our life as humans, created and redeemed by God. We participate in God's life, but as humans, not as gods. The life that we participate in never belongs to us; we belong to it. We may say in relation to theological commentary that as God's life apprehends us, we become people who in turn apprehend that life so that we may bear witness to it. That is the task of theological commentary—a narrative account of God's friendship with us in God's work of creation and redemption.

The life of the one God—Father, Son, and Spirit—is the reality in which Scripture lives. Thus, all fitting theological commentary on Scripture is trinitarian. It cannot be otherwise, because it is in and by the life of the Triune God that Scripture participates in and witnesses to God's work of redeeming creation. Thus, if theological commentary is learning to see and participate in God's work, then theological commentary is inescapably trinitarian. Even prior to the coming of Jesus and the confessions of the early church, we are engaged by the Triune God. It is therefore no anachronism to read Scripture from the beginning as a narration of the actions of the Father, the Son, and the Holy Spirit. This is what it means in part to read according to the rule of faith: not to find the rule of faith hidden somewhere at some level in the text, but to read the text knowing that the Father, the Son, and the Spirit call the text into being, sustain it as Scripture, and through Scripture call us to life in God's redemption of creation.

In hearing God's call to see and participate in the redemption of creation, we practice theological commentary in light of the resurrection of "this Jesus,

---

3. Waltke, *Old Testament Theology*, esp. 144–47. My one concern with Waltke's wise and illuminating exposition of the irruption of the kingdom of God is that he tends to treat it as a concept that shapes the text rather than a reality in which the text participates and to which it witnesses.

4. Hütter, *Suffering Divine Things*.

"Psalm 46"

whom [we] crucified" (Acts 2:36). In the continuing power of his resurrection by the work of the Holy Spirit, this same Jesus lives in us and we in him. God's creative-redemptive work continues today. So our study of Scripture and our submission to its teaching must not be a means of "bringing the text to life today" or "transporting us back to a time when God was at work among us" or "helping us hold on until Christ returns and God works among us once again." May it never be so! God is alive and acting today to redeem God's creation. Our study of Scripture for the purpose of theological commentary is to learn from the teaching of Scripture through the powerful presence of the Holy Spirit how today to see God's work, hear God's voice, and participate in the life given by God's creative-redemptive work.

On Creation

In this chapter, then, I will engage in "theological commentary" on God's work of creation.[5] We will be directly engaged with biblical texts for two purposes. One purpose is to uncover and tell the biblical story of creation interwoven with redemption, so that we may see this work of God in actuality today, enter into it as disciples of Jesus Christ, and bear witness to it so that others are invited into life. A second purpose is to test the exposition and argument that I have presented to this point to see if it is congruent with a direct reading of Scripture. As I noted above, we have been engaged with Scripture from the beginning, but now it is time to test our engagement to see if it is true. We may think of this on analogy with the "test" or "assay" that miners submit for "proving up" their claim. Does it contain gold? If so, what quality? And in what potential concentration? What about our work to this point? Have we struck gold?

As I work out these purposes and engage directly with the biblical texts, I will not claim that my engagement yields *the* meaning, the one and only meaning, of a particular text. We have been trained by modernity and our conflicts with modernity about the truth of the gospel to expect, seek, and claim precise and certain meaning for biblical texts. But such expectation is a product of a particular culture and history. It is not necessary to the biblical text. By the work of the Holy Spirit, Scripture is alive to teach us new things about God's work in the world, to remind us of things we have forgotten, and

---

5. For extended textual commentary focused on "creation texts" in addition to works cited below, see Brown, *Seven Pillars of Creation*, and T. Longman, "What Genesis 1–2 Teaches (and What It Doesn't)." These works became available to me after I had drafted this chapter. I find numerous resonances between them and my commentary.

to breathe life into us. Scripture is not fragile or rigid; it is filled with light and life. So as I comment on the texts, I will not argue that my commentary identifies the one and only meaning of the text.[6] Rather, I will seek to indwell the texts so that we can learn to see creation more fully and faithfully.

The texts that we will consider here are not the only texts that could engage the doctrine of creation. Nor do they simply cover the same ground that we have covered in previous chapters, except from a biblical perspective. Rather, these texts complement much of my previous exposition, fill in considerable detail, and extend the exposition. At its best, theological work aspires to a complex interweaving of biblical, historical, doctrinal, and pastoral wisdom.

Finally, as I engage these texts I will read them in an order that may be unexpected. I will read the biblical texts "from back to front" or "from end to beginning." That is, since Jesus is Alpha and Omega, beginning and end, I will begin at the end, at the telos of creation in the new creation. In so doing, I will not be distorting the biblical narrative because we now know that the story is about Christ from the very beginning. In other words, since we have now been told the end and the meaning of the whole story that was established "before the creation of the world" (Eph. 1:4), we may and perhaps should read the story from that perspective. This is like discovering on the last page of a mystery novel who committed the murder so that everything then makes sense. The very best mysteries make us want to reread the story so that we can catch all the things that we did not notice the first time.[7]

The story of God's work of creation and redemption is far more exciting and complex than any mystery, so we will begin at the "end" and read the story from that perspective. But remember, we are not really reading from back to front because God's work of redeeming creation had already begun in Israel when it received God's revelation, told it, and eventually wrote it down as Scripture in Genesis 1. Indeed, as Ephesians 1 tells us, the story begins before creation. One final note may help in understanding this approach. Genesis 1–2 has received so much attention and been such a battleground that we develop a better understanding of creation if we do not start in Genesis with all the questions, suspicions, accusations, weapons, and conflicts that boil over soon after we turn to these texts.

---

6. Fowl, *Engaging Scripture*, is helpful here, esp. 32–61. Also instructive are the various arguments and demonstrations in Ford and Stanton, *Reading Texts, Seeking Wisdom*. Finally, see the very careful and astute arguments in Bockmuehl, *Seeing the Word*, esp. his criticism of Fowl, 117n20. Most important to me is to recognize that Scripture is caught up in the continuing actuality of God's redemption of creation and that the Holy Spirit, as Author of Scripture, comes to us today through the continuing actuality of the disciple community to teach us to see and participate in that actuality.

7. See the delightful essay by Steinmetz, "Uncovering a Second Narrative."

My approach here is anticipated and exposited powerfully by N. T. Wright in *Surprised by Hope*:

> The Bible as a whole thus does what it does best when read from the perspective of new creation. And it is designed not only to tell us *about* that work of new creation, as though from a detached perspective, not only to provide us with true information about God's fresh, resurrection life, but also to *foster* that work of new creation in the churches, groups, and individuals who read it, who allow it to shape their lives. The Bible is thus the *story of* creation and new creation, and it is itself, through the continuing work of the Spirit who inspired it, an *instrument of* creation in human lives and communities.[8]

God's work of creation is for life. God's work for life will inevitably meet with conflict in a world ruled by death. Our Christian witness must always be for life and the superabundance of that life as given by the one God—Father, Son, and Spirit. We must not be anxious; to be anxious and fearful is to betray the very truth of creation: an almighty, just, merciful God who is Life is bringing creation through redemption into the new creation. In that knowledge and reality, we live today in faith, hope, and love. May we be drawn more fully into that reality as we read these biblical texts.

Behold I Am Making All Things New: Revelation 21–22

> Then I saw "a new heaven and a new earth," for the first heaven and the first earth had passed away, and there was no longer any sea. I saw the Holy City, the new Jerusalem, coming down out of heaven from God, prepared as a bride beautifully dressed for her husband. And I heard a loud voice from the throne saying, "Look! God's dwelling place is now among the people, and he will dwell with them. They will be his people, and God himself will be with them and be their God. 'He will wipe every tear from their eyes. There will be no more death' or mourning or crying or pain, for the old order of things has passed away."
>
> He who was seated on the throne said, "I am making everything new!" Then he said, "Write this down, for these words are trustworthy and true."
>
> He said to me: "It is done. I am the Alpha and the Omega, the Beginning and the End. To the thirsty I will give water without cost from the spring of the water of life. Those who are victorious will inherit all this, and I will be their God and they will be my children. But the cowardly, the unbelieving, the vile, the murderers, the sexually immoral, those who practice magic arts, the idolaters and all liars—they will be consigned to the fiery lake of burning sulfur. This is the second death." (Rev. 21:1–8)

8. N. T. Wright, *Surprised by Hope*, 282. Emphasis added.

After teaching first-year undergraduates for a few years in my first full-time teaching position, I discovered that I could set myself up to be accused of heresy if I presented the teaching of Revelation 21–22 without reference to these chapters. I would do this by telling the students that believers in Christ would not spend eternity in heaven freed from our bodies and from life on earth. They would be very quick to tell me that what I was teaching them was absolutely contrary to the good news that they had heard and believed. Indeed, if I drew them out just a bit, they would tell me that what I was telling them was not good news but bad news. Their bodies were the source of guilt and shame, and this world was a terrible burden that had to be endured for a short time in order to receive the benefits of an eternity in heaven as spirit beings with the invisible God.

Once I had drawn out all their concerns, objections, and (frequently) accusations, I would ask them what Jesus meant when he taught us to pray "Your kingdom come, your will be done on earth as it is in heaven." I would press them about the meaning of the incarnation, which we had studied at some length earlier in the semester. I would remind them of the heresy of gnosticism, which teaches that all matter is evil by virtue of being matter, and spirit is good simply by virtue of being spirit. I would ask them why so many Christians are passionate about the physical resurrection of Jesus. Gradually they would begin to open up to what I had declared about our future lives.

Then we would turn to Revelation 21–22, where John sees a new heaven and a new earth, a new Jerusalem coming down out of heaven, and hears a voice saying, "Look! God's dwelling place is now among the people, and he will dwell with them. They will be his people, and God himself will be with them and be their God" (Rev. 21:3). On the basis of this text, then, we would begin to explore the telos of creation and redemption in the new creation.

In these two chapters of Revelation, John receives a vision of the end of all things. The entire book is written for the encouragement of God's people in the midst of history to assure them that the story in which they are caught up has meaning, participates in life, and "ends" in life with God for eternity. In this final vision of Revelation 21–22, we are also assured that this end is the fulfillment of God's work of creation through the redemption accomplished by the Alpha and Omega.[9]

As we reflect on these images, we should be grasped by them so that their promise illumines our present realities. In Revelation 21, the first heaven and earth "pass away"; they are not destroyed, judged, cast into the abyss or the

---

9. For what follows, see generally Gorman, *Reading Revelation Responsibly*, 160–75; Mangina, *Revelation*, 237–55; Minear, *Christians and the New Creation*, *I Saw a New Earth*, esp. chap. 7, and "Cosmology of the Apocalypse"; Carroll, "Creation and Apocalypse," and references there; Caird, *Revelation of St. John the Divine*, 261–301.

lake of fire as are Babylon and the enemies of God in the previous chapters (Rev. 18–20). We are told rather that "the old order of things has passed away" (Rev. 21:4). Although we use "pass away" to refer to death, this passing away is more the complete transformation of the old. God does not make "all new things." Rather, God makes "all things new" (Rev. 21:5 KJV).

In this newness, God's creation is seen in its full reality. Creation—heaven (in this case the stars, planets, galaxies, as we know them) and earth—is seen in all its goodness as its telos is realized through the one who is the "Alpha and the Omega." In a comment that needs to be more widely known, G. B Caird observes:

> The end is not an event but a person. In much that has been written during the last thirty years on the subject of eschatology the debate has turned on the nature of the *eschaton*, the final event, and whether this *eschaton* can be properly said to have entered history in the person of Jesus Christ. But the word *eschaton* (neut.) does not occur in the New Testament. John knows only of the *eschatos* (masc.), a person who is both **the beginning and the end.**[10]

As creation comes to its telos in the *eschatos*, Jesus Christ, the whole life and order of creation is aligned with God. It is only through the coming of God the Son that this work can be done, with all that is evil and contrary to life being expelled and all that is good and conducive to life being welcomed. When this happens, God dwells with us on earth just as the Word became flesh and "dwelled among us" (John 1:14; the same Greek word, *skēnē*, is used). The new creation is realized only through the redemption of creation. We learn the deep significance of this reality from the vision of Jesus as "the Lamb," an image that unavoidably and powerfully recalls the sacrifice of Christ for the redemption of creation (Rev. 21:9, 14, 22, 23, 27; 22:1–3; see Rev. 5–6; Exod. 12:3, 13).

In this new creation, the gift of creation is made evident. The heavenly city, the new Jerusalem, comes down from heaven. This is striking because we do not readily think of creation in relation to the built environment.[11] And when we think of "city," we think of human work, not God's work. In this image, then, we are shown that God redeems what we have done with this world and incorporates it into the new creation as God's gift to us.

The same vision of gift is extended into blessing by John's declaration that

> the city does not need the sun or the moon to shine on it, for the glory of God gives it light, and the Lamb is its lamp. The nations will walk by its light, and

---

10. Caird, *Revelation of St. John the Divine*, 266, emphasis in original.
11. For a striking and illuminating exception, see Gorringe, *Theology of the Built Environment*.

the kings of the earth will bring their splendor into it. On no day will its gates ever be shut, for there will be no night there. The glory and honor of the nations will be brought into it. Nothing impure will ever enter it. (Rev. 21:23–27a)

This vision may surprise us with the declaration that what is good, true, and beautiful in human culture has a place in the new creation.[12] By God's blessing and judgment, the culture that we form from what God gives us in this world may become part of the new creation.

Further vision of God's blessing in the telos of creation is set before us by the declaration that "'he will wipe every tear from their eyes. There will be no more death' or mourning or crying or pain, for the old order of things has passed away" (Rev. 21:4). This declaration envisions a removal of the effects of the curse that comes from our turning away from the telos of creation. However, it does so not by restoring childbirth and labor to their original state but by putting an end to the suffering brought about by the fall from our telos. The new creation is not a second creation or a simple restoration of the first heaven and earth; it is the redemption of creation for its telos that takes place in Jesus Christ. The "blessedness" of the beatitudes is now fulfilled in the new creation.

This telos is also the fulfillment of the life of creation. The one who makes this possible, the Alpha and Omega, says, "I am the Living One; I was dead, and now look, I am alive for ever and ever! And I hold the keys of death and Hades" (Rev. 1:17–18). By becoming flesh and dwelling with us to death and rising to life, and by dwelling with us in the new creation, the Word embraces us and draws us into Life, the one God—Father, Son, and Holy Spirit. All that is not embraced and drawn into Life is cast away. This is the second death of all that is not creation.

The final image in this vision that we will consider is the tree of life in the midst of the city:

Then the angel showed me the river of the water of life, as clear as crystal, flowing from the throne of God and of the Lamb down the middle of the great street of the city. On each side of the river stood the tree of life, bearing twelve crops of fruit, yielding its fruit every month. And the leaves of the tree are for the healing of the nations. (Rev. 22:1–2; see 21:6; 22:14, 17, 19)

This image of the tree of life draws immediately from Genesis but once again sets it in the new creation; the tree of the knowledge of good and evil is

---

12. See Mouw, *When the Kings Come Marching In*. See below for further commentary on the teaching of Isaiah from which John draws much of his imagery.

conspicuously absent. Since God judges and allows no evil in the new creation, there will be no opportunity to know good and evil.[13] This purification is accomplished by the Lamb of God who bears the sin of the world so that the peoples may be healed and creation brought to its fulfillment.

Sustaining All Things: Hebrews 1:1–3

> In the past God spoke to our ancestors through the prophets at many times and in various ways, but in these last days he has spoken to us by his Son, whom he appointed heir of all things, and through whom also he made the universe. The Son is the radiance of God's glory and the exact representation of his being, sustaining all things by his powerful word. After he had provided purification for sins, he sat down at the right hand of the Majesty in heaven. (Heb. 1:1–3)

The letter (or sermon) to the Hebrews offers a rhetorical and conceptual world very different from the other New Testament letters. Its cosmology has been much studied and debated by students of the New Testament.[14] For a period of time, many New Testament scholars located the thought world of Hebrews in the "hellenization of Christianity," regarding the teaching of Hebrews as a sign that Greek culture had come to dominate the presentation of the gospel. Recent studies, however, have persuasively argued that the letter to the Hebrews is filled with references to and echoes of the Tanak.

The first verses of Hebrews echo Psalm 2; such echoes of the Psalms reverberate throughout the book. In these few verses, we have an anticipation of the entire book. The superiority of Jesus Christ is celebrated in many ways, but the center is his sacrifice for the forgiveness of sin. This sacrifice is an inextricable part of his role as heir of "all things." In order for the Son to inherit all things, those things must be purified for life with God. Since he has accomplished that purification, he can also sustain all things by his word. That is, God is justified in sustaining the life of a rebellious, dysteleological world because God has acted to make the universe into a temple fit for the dwelling of God and redeemed humankind.

13. See below on the temptation to know good and evil in Gen. 2.

14. See McDonough, *Christ as Creator*, 192–211; Laansma, "Cosmology of Hebrews" and "Hidden Stories in Hebrews." The former essay by Laansma is largely a historical survey; the latter is more focused theologically. Of significant help is Schenck, *Cosmology and Eschatology in Hebrews*. The gaps that he identifies in the "narrative world" of Hebrews invite us into the mystery that he also uncovers in his study: "Christ stands as the true *end* of the creation and thus as its beginning purpose and direction, the very ground upon which the heavens and the earth were founded" (184). At the center of the cosmology and eschatology of Hebrews is the sacrifice of this same Christ.

The word often translated "universe" (v. 2) is the Greek word *aiōniou*, which is the plural form of the word usually translated "age." Here then, properly, is the confession that it is through the Son that God has made "the ages." This fits better with the rest of the teaching of Hebrews in which this age is passing away and will be shaken, but the age that is coming cannot be shaken. This unshakable age is set before us in the image of the universe as God's temple, in which purification for sins has been accomplished. Because the purification of the sins of this age has taken place in this cosmos, it is now fitting for God to take up residence in the cosmos as the temple of God, where eternal life will be directed in worship to the one God, who made that sacrifice.

As we hear the entire message of Hebrews unfolding from these verses, we learn once again that creation is God's gift, which through redemption will come to its telos in the new creation. We also learn something deeper about the identity of Christ as the one for whom creation is made. He is the heir to this world, but to inherit it is also to die for its redemption. Creation, redemption, and the new creation find their reality, their life in the sacrifice of the Son of God.

Reconciling All Things: Colossians 1:15–20

> The Son is the image of the invisible God, the firstborn over all creation. For in him all things were created: things in heaven and on earth, visible and invisible, whether thrones or powers or rulers or authorities; all things have been created through him and for him. He is before all things, and in him all things hold together. And he is the head of the body, the church; he is the beginning and the firstborn from among the dead, so that in everything he might have the supremacy. For God was pleased to have all his fullness dwell in him, and through him to reconcile to himself all things, whether things on earth or things in heaven, by making peace through his blood, shed on the cross. (Col. 1:15–20)

In this crucial and memorable passage, Paul compresses many dazzling truths regarding Christ and creation. It is as if this passage were a barge in the harbor from which a fireworks display would be launched. But even that image is too transitory and entertaining. Rather, this passage is like a brilliant overture that introduces the themes of a great, unending symphony.

In this passage, Christ is preeminent in creation and redemption:

> The hymn moves from creation through redemption, speaking of them separately but offering praise for God's work that begins in creation and anticipates the final reconciliation of all things. In its structure, it sets creation and redemption

parallel to each other. Each has its focal point in Christ, who is the firstborn, agent, and goal of both creation and new creation. Because Christ is the agent of creation, he is also the agent of the re-creation of the world. Here, then, in confessional terms and the language of praise we find testimony to the great drama of God's creation of the world and the promise of its final redemption. The God who made the world in Christ will redeem it through Christ, for God has not abandoned the cosmos and its inhabitants.[15]

When we read how Paul communicates this cosmic reality to the Colossians, we learn something very significant about creation and redemption. This letter reveals the concerns of the Colossians and Paul's declaration of the good news of Jesus Christ in relation to their concerns; we find that the redemption of creation and the reconciliation of all things in Christ are related to "the principalities" and "powers" (Col. 1:16 KJV; 2:8–15, 20). Apart from these passages where the language clearly refers to principalities, powers, and forces, several other passages in this short letter also refer to these realities without using this specific language. Scholars have vigorously debated the meaning of these terms.[16] Without having to be absolutely precise and certain, we may recognize that Paul uses these terms to refer to anything that may contest the claim of Christ as Lord, reject his supremacy over creation, and deny his work of reconciliation. In other words, these principalities and powers are anything in this world that claims to give a better, truer account of reality and how to live than does Christ.[17]

Therefore, the relationship between Christ as Creator and Christ as Redeemer is critical. The "way" of Christ's redemption is also the "way" of creation. In seeing that these two ways are really one, our eyes are opened to the lies and impotence of the principalities and powers. We discover that because Christ made all things, including these principalities and powers, his redemption also restores them to their proper place in creation. Politics, race, gender, class, and many other things are realigned with their created purpose through the reconciliation accomplished by Christ's cross. They are not erased but rather aligned properly in our lives when they are aligned properly in relation to God.[18]

15. Thompson, *Colossians and Philemon*, 28.

16. The scholarly debate may be followed in the various commentaries and in Berkhof, *Christ and the Powers*; Caird, *Principalities and Powers*.

17. For studies that are each illuminating, in different ways, see Yoder, *Politics of Jesus*, 134–61; Wink, *Naming the Powers*, *Unmasking the Powers*, and *Engaging the Powers*; Dawn, *Powers, Weakness, and the Tabernacling of God* and *Unfettered Hope*; Gorringe, "Principalities and Powers."

18. This understanding turns right side up the politics of identity so that identity becomes the very possibility of, the grounds for, and the site of reconciliation among our differences. It also overturns the postmodern tendency to erase the person in pursuit of a horrible misconstrual

The redemption of this world makes the world once again God's creation by making it gift and blessing, the place of life that finds its telos in peace.

Another striking and essential element in this work of creation and redemption is that in the middle of these words about Christ's relation to God and creation, we also read that "he is the head of the body, the church" (Col. 1:18). Here we have a profound connection that we have not considered before. One sign, perhaps *the* sign, of the redemption of creation is the church. This may seem to be an astonishing claim. But if we understand that the redemption of creation is accomplished in part by exposing all the ways that this world binds us to lies, to dysteleology, and to death, then the existence of a people who confess disbelief in those claims is a sign of the redemption that makes this world creation and finds its telos in the new creation. There God's people live forever in praise of the one God—Father, Son, and Spirit.

Thus, the people of God seek to live without illusion, to be people of the truth—that is, people who live with the grain of the universe as revealed in Jesus Christ. We also reject the dysteleological fate of the world and commit our lives to practices of grace that bear witness to the telos of the new creation by welcoming the stranger, serving the poor, forgiving the enemy, loving our neighbors. We are not bound by the lies of the fallen principalities and powers that alienate us from ourselves and one another. Finally, we are a people who do not fear death or live our lives as if death were the final word. Death is the last enemy to be destroyed, but we know that it has been publicly humiliated and disarmed by Christ. So we seek to witness to and walk in the way of the redemption of creation, which is life.

This way can be very hard to embrace for those who are doing well and are well regarded by the world's way. When the way of the world applies labels to us or when we "self-identify" (what a deadly phrase!) in terms that give us status in the world and apparent access to the powers of this world, we may have great difficulty recognizing and confessing the supremacy of Christ. James Alison reminds us that "people who are of no importance in the order of the world are especially suited to becoming signs of the New Creation."[19] Alison follows this reminder with the warning that we must not succumb to the temptation to turn these "signs of new creation" into a force in the age that is passing away. We are called not to reorder the world but to live in the new creation that is a whole new reality not bound to or constrained by the old order of things. God comes in Christ not to reorder the world but to

---

of a way to peace. It is precisely in our identity as persons that we participate in the cessation of power conflicts.

19. Alison, *Joy of Being Wrong*, 210. I am indebted to Isaac Villegas for reminding me of this passage in Alison.

redeem it in the new creation. The people of God live now as the sign of that new creation.

All this comes together when Paul announces that the reconciling work of God in Christ is the work of "making peace through his blood, shed on the cross" (Col. 1:20). Thus, the work of reconciliation is not the full completion of the redemption of creation because reconciliation merely brings two or more parties back together. Making peace, in the sense of making whole, is the healing of creation that culminates in the new creation. Once again, Alison illuminates this reality: "The creative self-giving up to death (because unmoved by death) in the midst of human violence, forgiving that violence, *is* what divine creation looks like in the midst of the creation-shot-through-with-vanity in which we live."[20]

This takes us one more step into seeing God's work today through Paul's teaching. If the church is the sign of the supremacy of Christ, the reconciliation of all things, and the making of peace, then the life of the church bears witness to these things. We may bear witness to these things by God's blessing on our faithfulness; we may also bear witness to these things by God's judgment on our unfaithfulness. In either case, the vision of Christ and creation in Colossians gives us the telos and direction of the life of the church. We are to witness to the supremacy of Christ over all other powers by letting none of those other powers determine our relationships with one another. We must recognize other members of Christ's body not by what these other powers, such as race, class, gender, nationality, or politics tell us, but by the reconciliation of all things through "the blood of his cross."[21] Paul's celebration of the supremacy of Christ and God's reconciling work calls the church to bear witness to "the making of peace."

These practices of the church reveal the good news about creation. In the history of the church's teaching, we have often missed the inextricable interweaving of the great redemption that we have in Christ with the healing of the world so that it is once again *creation*, the gift and blessing of God that is life and finds its telos in the new creation. The rest of Colossians fills this in. Paul asserts that this good news "has been proclaimed to every creature under heaven" (Col. 1:23; "every creature" embraces all living creatures, not just humankind). He tells us that Christ is "the hope of glory" (Col. 1:27). He works to "present everyone fully mature in Christ" (Col. 1:28; "mature" translates the Greek word *teleion*: "perfect," "complete"—that is, "being

---

20. Ibid., 208.

21. We have many wonderful narratives of reconciliation today. For contemporary, wide-ranging studies and stories of reconciliation, see the Resources for Reconciliation series of books by IVP cosponsored with the Duke Center for Reconciliation.

brought to one's full and proper *telos*"). We learn that Christ is the one "in whom are hidden all the treasures of wisdom and knowledge" (Col. 2:3). Paul encourages us to recognize and live free of "human rules" that simply bind us to the present order of things, the principalities that Christ has humiliated and defeated (Col. 2:16–23). He then instructs us in how to live according to our citizenship in "the kingdom of light" and of the Son God loves. (The kingdom images are found in 1:12–13; the instructions are found in 3:1–4:6.)

Is the church part of the good news for "every creature under heaven"? Do we live in hope of financial security, political stability, smooth careers, health, and wealth? Or do we live in Christ, the hope of glory? Do we understand our full maturity to be rooted in our life in creation-being-redeemed? Do we know that Christ is the fount of wisdom and knowledge, or do we get taken in by "fine-sounding arguments" that perpetuate the way of the world? (Col. 2:4). Are our lives directed and even controlled by "human rules" taught us almost every moment of the day and inscribed in "just the way things are"? Do we think that our "heavenly life" awaits us in the future, or do we recognize its presence in our current relationships and Paul's warnings and exhortations?

Do we really know that in Christ we "have put on the new self, which is being renewed in knowledge in the image of its Creator"? (Col. 3:10). In this newness and knowledge, in this image, we are no longer subject to the rulers of this age and to the identity markers of this world that alienate us from one another, from the world, and from God. We are no longer imprisoned by the labels that seek to control so much of our lives. In Christ, we are one. This is the redemption of creation in which the church lives and to which the church bears witness.[22]

Creation Waits in Eager Expectation: Romans 8

> I consider that our present sufferings are not worth comparing with the glory that will be revealed in us. For the creation waits in eager expectation for the children of God to be revealed. For the creation was subjected to frustration, not by its own choice, but by the will of the one who subjected it, in hope that the creation itself will be liberated from its bondage to decay and brought into the freedom and glory of the children of God.
>
> We know that the whole creation has been groaning as in the pains of child-birth right up to the present time. Not only so, but we ourselves, who have the firstfruits of the Spirit, groan inwardly as we wait eagerly for our adoption to

---

22. Although he is more cautious about applying the language of the new creation to this passage, Richard Bauckham offers an illuminating account of this passage in *Greening Paul*, 87–115.

sonship, the redemption of our bodies. For in this hope we were saved. But hope that is seen is no hope at all. Who hopes for what they already have? But if we hope for what we do not yet have, we wait for it patiently.

In the same way, the Spirit helps us in our weakness. We do not know what we ought to pray for, but the Spirit himself intercedes for us through wordless groans. And he who searches our hearts knows the mind of the Spirit, because the Spirit intercedes for God's people in accordance with the will of God.

And we know that in all things God works for the good of those who love him, who have been called according to his purpose. For those God foreknew he also predestined to be conformed to the image of his Son, that he might be the firstborn among many brothers and sisters. And those he predestined, he also called; those he called, he also justified; those he justified, he also glorified.

What, then, shall we say in response to these things? If God is for us, who can be against us? He who did not spare his own Son, but gave him up for us all—how will he not also, along with him, graciously give us all things? Who will bring any charge against those whom God has chosen? It is God who justifies. Who then is the one who condemns? No one. Christ Jesus who died—more than that, who was raised to life—is at the right hand of God and is also interceding for us. Who shall separate us from the love of Christ? Shall trouble or hardship or persecution or famine or nakedness or danger or sword? As it is written:

> "For your sake we face death all day long;
>   we are considered as sheep to be slaughtered."

No, in all these things we are more than conquerors through him who loved us. For I am convinced that neither death nor life, neither angels nor demons, neither the present nor the future, nor any powers, neither height nor depth, nor anything else in all creation, will be able to separate us from the love of God that is in Christ Jesus our Lord. (Rom. 8:18–39)

This powerful passage occurs in the midst of Paul's great narrative of salvation in Christ.[23] It is often seen as the conclusion to Paul's description of salvation in Romans 1–8, before he turns to the status of Israel in Romans 9–11, then to practical matters in 12–16. But if we are to recover the centrality of the doctrine of creation and understand the church as the sign of God's redemption of creation and the telos of the new creation, then this passage is pivotal to Paul's narrative and deeply revealing of creation-redemption-new creation, not as a three-stage process or a three-act drama, but as three ways of identifying the actuality of God's work.

---

23. For a superb account of this passage, see J. Kirk, "Resurrection and New Creation: Romans 8:12–39," in Kirk, *Unlocking Romans*, 132–60; see also E. Adams, "Paul's Story of God and Creation: The Story of How God Fulfills His Purposes in Creation," cited in Kirk, *Unlocking Romans*, 143n41; R. Bauckham in *Greening Paul*, 63–85.

In this passage, Paul teaches us that the Spirit is the one in the trinitarian economy who brings creation to its telos through redemption. When we suffer in the present world and see the suffering throughout the world, we may be inclined to doubt the good news of the redemption of creation in Christ. But if, through the good news, we have come to believe in Christ and receive the Holy Spirit, then we are seeing and experiencing the first fruits (v. 23) of the redemption of creation. Even though our bodies are wasting away outwardly and thus seeming to confirm the power of death in this world, the Spirit is renewing us so that we may look forward not to an escape from our bodies but to the fulfillment of bodily life by sharing in Christ's resurrection and his glory. As Paul Barnett argues,

> We must reject the idea of a non-material "heaven." From early times in Christian history believers began to think that "heaven" was "up there," inhabited by disembodied souls in white gowns seated on clouds playing harps. This vision owes more to Greek philosophy than to the Bible's vision of the kingdom of God. That kingdom is ahead of us at the end of history, not above us in the clouds. It is not dis-embodied but re-embodied. . . .
>
> The creation awaits its redemption but so "also we ourselves" await redemption, that is, of our body. Redemption in both creation and humanity is not "spiritual" but physical, as "the redemption of our body" shows.[24]

The verses that precede this passage in Romans recall for us two characteristics of creation that we have already considered: life and peace (Rom. 8:6) and righteousness (v. 10). The passage itself reveals the fundamental problem with the present order of the world: "creation was subjected to frustration" (v. 20) and is still so. This language describes the failure of something or someone to realize its proper telos. Its aim, its purpose, its goal is frustrated:

> The simplest and most straightforward interpretation would seem to be to take *mataiotes* [the Greek word translated "frustration"] here in the word's basic sense as denoting the ineffectiveness of that which does not attain its goal . . . , and to understand Paul's meaning to be that the sub-human creation has been subjected to the frustration of not being able properly to fulfil the purpose of its existence, God having appointed that without man it should not be made perfect. We may think of the whole magnificent theatre of the universe together with all its splendid properties and all the chorus of sub-human life, created to glorify God but unable to do so fully, so long as man the chief actor in the drama of God's praise fails to contribute his rational part.[25]

24. Barnett, *Romans*, 194, 196.
25. Cranfield, *Critical and Exegetical Commentary*, 413–14.

In that frustration, the world is dysteleological. For Paul, this seems primarily to be centered in the failure of humankind to be aligned with God's purpose. If humankind is not aligned with the telos of creation, then all creation is frustrated. Thus, the justification of humankind understood as the right alignment of humankind with God's telos for creation means also the freeing of all creation from its frustration.

In light of this, we must keep in balance two truths by emphasizing both equally. One truth is that creation is God's good gift to us. The second is that creation will not be redeemed until the work of the Spirit is completed in the return of Christ, the glorification of humankind with Christ, and the new creation.[26] Since the present order of things is incapable of fulfilling its telos, we cannot expect to make the world right by our actions. Humans cannot do the work of creation. At the same time, however, God through Jesus Christ "justifies" sinners. That is, those who believe in Christ are justified, aligned with the telos of creation, so that our lives bear witness to the final justification, which is the redemption of the world in the new creation.

As Paul describes the role of the Spirit, we also learn more about what it means for the Spirit to be the one who completes this work. We may understand the suffering of the Father who sends the Son and the suffering of the Son as he dies for the sins of the world. Now we understand the suffering of the Spirit: as the Spirit fills us and gives life to creation, the Spirit also groans as the Spirit labors to sustain the world, bring the world to its rightful state as creation, and through redemption bring it to its telos, the new creation.[27]

Once we know that the presence of the Spirit is the sign of the presence of the power of Christ's resurrection and of our present participation in the future hope of glory, we may see how the rest of the chapter follows from this certainty about the redemption of creation. Because through Christ and the Spirit, God is redeeming creation and we are participants, everything that

26. See Barnett, *Romans*, 191–98, for an accessible exposition of these realities.

27. The recent book by Macchia, *Justified in the Spirit*, fills in the work of the Spirit to some extent, but the doctrine of creation is less prominent than the subtitle seems to promise. Bergmann, *Creation Set Free*, offers some helpful reflections (312–21), but his commitment to a theology of correlation leads him to search through the theological tradition for resources that may be useful to "the present ecological crisis," so that a particular construal of context sets the parameters for any doctrine of creation. At this point, theology becomes a utilitarian enterprise. Likewise, Wallace, *Fragments of the Spirit*, takes theology to be a purely rhetorical practice (19) that once again searches the Christian tradition for language that is useful for addressing a present problem. Wallace seems not to hesitate as he abandons trinitarian theology and gives no attention to the gospel of Jesus Christ. Very few studies of the Holy Spirit combine orthodox, trinitarian theology with significant reflection on the Spirit's work in creation. One outstanding exception is Pinnock, *Flame of Love*, 49–77, and the references in chap. 5. Another helpful account, though brief, is Schweizer, *Holy Spirit*, 108–11.

happens to us will be brought into alignment with that telos. Likewise, since our participation in Christ by the Spirit is participation in the right ordering of the world, nothing in the world can separate us from the love that redeems creation. It is not merely that the power of Christ and the Spirit is greater than the powers of the world. Rather, it is also that the power of the resurrection of Christ and the presence of the Holy Spirit realign the powers of the world so that the end (telos) they serve is not the kingdom of death and darkness but that of life and light, the kingdom of God's Son.

All Things Were Made by Him: John 1:1–18

In the beginning was the Word, and the Word was with God, and the Word was God. He was with God in the beginning. Through him all things were made; without him nothing was made that has been made. In him was life, and that life was the light of all mankind. The light shines in the darkness, and the darkness has not overcome it.

There was a man sent from God whose name was John. He came as a witness to testify concerning that light, so that through him all might believe. He himself was not the light; he came only as a witness to the light.

The true light that gives light to everyone was coming into the world. He was in the world, and though the world was made through him, the world did not recognize him. He came to that which was his own, but his own did not receive him. Yet to all who did receive him, to those who believed in his name, he gave the right to become children of God—children born not of natural descent, nor of human decision or a husband's will, but born of God.

The Word became flesh and made his dwelling among us. We have seen his glory, the glory of the one and only Son, who came from the Father, full of grace and truth.

(John testified concerning him. He cried out, saying, "This is the one I spoke about when I said, 'He who comes after me has surpassed me because he was before me.'") Out of his fullness we have all received grace in place of grace already given. For the law was given through Moses; grace and truth came through Jesus Christ. No one has ever seen God, but the one and only Son, who is himself God and is in closest relationship with the Father, has made him known. (John 1:1–18)

Like the other texts that we have engaged, this passage is jammed with rich teaching about "the Word made flesh." In my consideration of this text, I will focus on four aspects: the indications of a trinitarian economy, the dialectic of the kingdom, the images used for the Word, and the Word made flesh. Again, my intention is to allow this Scripture to test my doctrine of creation and flesh it out. In doing so, I hope to encourage readers to be more attentive to the doctrine of creation in their reading of Scripture.

In the first verses of this gospel, John provides us with a hint of the doctrine of the trinity. The Word is both God and with God. These statements identify the Word with God and indicate a differentiation of God and the Word (else the Word could not be *with* God). Although this is certainly not a full doctrine of the trinity, it is one of those statements, along with verse 18, that contribute to the development of the doctrine of the trinity. In John's unfolding of the story of Jesus Christ, it is fitting that the Father and the Son are in view here, but also that the Spirit becomes an actor in the story only a few verses later.

This identification and differentiation of God and the Word is crucial to the doctrine of creation. If there were no differentiation of God's identity as Creator, then one of several conclusions would follow. One would be that John is simply wrong in what he declares here. He is either confused or mistaken. But when as followers of Christ we reject this option and submit to the teaching of Scripture, we learn something essential from John's testimony. If there were only one lone creator god, then there would be only two options available in the relationship between God and the world. One option would require that the creator god remain aloof in order to remain creator and sustain what the god had made. The other option would be to identify the god with the world made by this one lone god and thus become one with creation. In neither case could there be a way for this lone creator god to be both creator and redeemer.

In other words, the identification of the Word with God and the differentiation of the Word and God are essential to the declaration that the "Word made flesh" is good news. In our contemplation of the trinitarian grammar of creation, we learned this same lesson about the Father and the Son. Although the Spirit is not yet part of John's telling of the story of Jesus, John introduces the Spirit's role very soon. And in a later passage in John, Jesus indicates the role of the Spirit, saying,

> Very truly I tell you, it is for your good that I am going away. Unless I go away, the Advocate will not come to you; but if I go, I will send him to you. When he comes, he will prove the world to be in the wrong about sin and righteousness and judgment: about sin, because people do not believe in me; about righteousness, because I am going to the Father, where you can see me no longer; and about judgment, because the prince of this world now stands condemned. (John 16:7–11)

This work of the Spirit in the world testifies to the Spirit's role in sustaining the world and in bringing the world into the work of creation so that its telos may be completed in the new creation.

This work of the Spirit is necessary because of the world's turn from its proper telos, which is Jesus Christ, the one whose blood makes reconciliation and peace into reality as we saw in Colossians 1. This Jesus Christ, who is the Word made flesh, comes to the world that he creates, and the world does not receive him. Once again, the gift of creation is rejected. The freedom in which God creates is reflected in the freedom of the world that God creates. Our freedom is the freedom not to choose our own way of life but rather to choose between life and death. In that freedom, we disbelieve, and in our unbelief we choose the kingdom of darkness and death.

So the Creator-Word comes to us as light and life. In this characteristic imagery, John confronts the very center of the realities of this world: darkness and death. But this world, under the rule of death, does not recognize its true life and light. The interplay of "glory" in John's gospel gives us guidance about the coming of the Word, who is neither recognized nor received by the very world whose life comes from him and goes toward him. In these opening verses, John tells us that "we have seen his glory, the glory of the one and only Son, who came from the Father, full of grace and truth" (John 1:14). This glorious one is rejected, but in that rejection, which is fully displayed in his crucifixion, the glory of God shines ever brighter. Jesus prays,

> Father, the hour has come. Glorify your Son, that your Son may glorify you. For you granted him authority over all people that he might give eternal life to all those you have given him. Now this is eternal life: that they know you, the only true God, and Jesus Christ, whom you have sent. I have brought you glory on earth by finishing the work you gave me to do. And now, Father, glorify me in your presence with the glory I had with you before the world began. (John 17:1–5)

This prayer, just before the Word made flesh is crucified, reveals to us the true glory of the one God—Father, Son, and Spirit—who is Creator: in creating this world God gives God's life to and for the world. Creation and redemption are united in God's love for the world.

This gift of life, than which there is no greater gift, comes to its full revelation in "the Word . . . made flesh" (John 1:14 KJV). Here the life of creation and the life of God come together in a union deeper than any other except for the union of the Father, the Son, and the Spirit. Indeed, this union of Word and flesh is possible only because of the Son's relationships to the Father and the Spirit. Apart from these relationships, either the Word would be wholly consumed by the flesh or the flesh would wholly consume the Word. In this mystery of Word-made-flesh, neither consumes the life of the other; instead, each gives life to the other and then together to the whole cosmos.

However, this giving of life is not symmetrical. The Word is the agent of creation and thus the source of the life of the flesh. Therefore, the life that the flesh gives the Word is the life that can die for the sin of the world. In the gospel's recounting of the testimony of John the Baptist, the Word-made-flesh is "the Lamb of God, who takes away the sin of the world" (John 1:29). This mortal life is the gift of the flesh to the Word. But since this mortal life has its origins in creation, it too ultimately is God's gift to the world, which God then "receives" in the Word-made-flesh, for the redemption of the world.

The Fullness of Earth Is God's Glory: Isaiah

> Holy, Holy, Holy is I AM, the Almighty;
> the whole earth is full of God's glory.
> Isaiah 6:3[28]

The book of Isaiah represents a turning point in the doctrine of creation, especially in this great theologian's understanding of God as Creator and Redeemer. Genesis 1–3 certainly introduces the claim of God as Creator, and many psalms (such as 19 and 104) proclaim and praise God's work of creation. But Isaiah receives and explores God's work as Creator with depth and breadth like no other section of the Tanak. To this Isaiah adds the interweaving of redemption, so much so that much of what I have written in this book could be recast as a running theological commentary on Isaiah.

Here I will explore two aspects of Isaiah's teaching and note several others along the way. As I do so, I will take the book as a canonical whole, recognizing that we may be instructed by comparing the various sections of the book but also by placing these sections within what I take to be a deliberate canonizing of Isaiah as one book.[29]

Isaiah 6:3 may stand as a summary for most, perhaps all, of the teaching of Isaiah. Isaiah's vision is a "heavenly" vision. He is taken from his mundane, everyday life into the inner sanctum of God's life. In this vision, God's holiness overwhelms in every way. Yet the earth is also kept in view. This binocular vision sustains the prophecies of Isaiah throughout the book. It may very well be imagined as the anticipation of and foundation for Jesus's teaching of prayer: "Your kingdom come, your will be done, on earth as it is in heaven" (Matt. 6:10).

It is also in this vision and the testimony of the heavenly beings that I AM is confessed to be "Almighty." The term translated "almighty" (Heb., *Sabaoth*) has its origins in military terminology. *Sabaoth* (translated "hosts," as in "Lord of hosts" in earlier versions) denotes an army prepared to do battle or engaged

---

28. My translation, following the suggestion of Waltke, *Old Testament Theology*, 10–12, 359–69.
29. See Childs, *Isaiah* and *Struggle to Understand Isaiah*; Wilken, *Isaiah*.

in battle. So even this vision of the heavenly holiness of I AM does not set aside the work that God must do in the world that belongs to God as creation.

At the same time that Isaiah reports the heavenly vision, he also confesses an earthly reality: "the whole earth is full of God's glory." This confession unfolds later in Isaiah, especially in chapters 40–66, where the visions of Isaiah portray a world that is fully realized as God's creation through the redemptive work of God in Israel:

> This is what God, I AM says—
> the Creator of the heavens, who stretches them out,
>   who spreads out the earth with all that springs from it,
>   who gives breath to its people,
>   and life to those who walk on it:
> "I, I AM, have called you in righteousness;
>   I will take hold of your hand.
> I will keep you and will make you
>   to be a covenant for the people
>   and a light for the Gentiles,
> to open eyes that are blind,
>   to free captives from prison
>   and to release from the dungeon those who sit in darkness.
>
> "I am I AM; that is my name!
>   I will not yield my glory to another
>   or my praise to idols.
> See, the former things have taken place,
>   and new things I declare;
> before they spring into being
>   I announce them to you."
>
> Sing to I AM a new song,
>   his praise from the ends of the earth,
> you who go down to the sea, and all that is in it,
>   you islands, and all who live in them.
> Let the wilderness and its towns raise their voices;
>   let the settlements where Kedar lives rejoice.
> Let the people of Sela sing for joy;
>   let them shout from the mountaintops.
> Let them give glory to I AM
>   and proclaim his praise in the islands.
> I AM will march out like a champion,
>   like a warrior he will stir up his zeal;
> with a shout he will raise the battle cry
>   and will triumph over his enemies.

"For a long time I have kept silent,
  I have been quiet and held myself back.
But now, like a woman in childbirth,
  I cry out, I gasp and pant.
I will lay waste the mountains and hills
  and dry up all their vegetation;
I will turn rivers into islands
  and dry up the pools.
I will lead the blind by ways they have not known,
  along unfamiliar paths I will guide them;
I will turn the darkness into light before them
  and make the rough places smooth.
These are the things I will do;
  I will not forsake them.
But those who trust in idols,
  who say to images, 'You are our gods,'
will be turned back in utter shame."
                    Isaiah 42:5–17 (NIV slightly altered)

This lengthy passage represents the major themes of Isaiah's visions of the whole earth full of God's glory. In these visions, Isaiah sees the new creation coming to be as the whole earth is healed and its telos fulfilled.[30] The striking centerpiece of these visions is the servant of I AM, through whose sacrifice and self-giving creation is redeemed. Here the "Lord of Hosts" does battle with the evil of this world by exposing its lies and rejecting its claims and structures that try to teach us that life is sustained by taking and keeping. It is also striking that these visions foresee and foretell the new creation that goes beyond simply the restoration of the conditions of God's first work of creation. This new creation simply does not work the way that this world works. Wolves and lambs lie down together, and children play by the venomous snake's hole. The high and mighty are brought down and the lowly and weak lifted up. The way of the world is shown not to be the way of creation.[31] These visions of God's redemption of creation reach their fullest expression in John's visions in Revelation, where Isaiah's visions culminate in John's privilege of knowing that this promise is fulfilled in Jesus of Nazareth.

This vision of the fulfillment of God's purposes for creation in Christ may be delightfully represented by the recent proposal of H. G. M. Williamson

30. See the exploration of Isaiah's vision of new creation in Brown, *Seven Pillars of Creation*, 197–220.

31. For fitting commentary on later passages in Isaiah that declare this redemption, see Hanson, *Isaiah 40–66*, 241–52; Blenkinsopp, *Isaiah 56–66*, 279–317.

that the better translation of the second part of Isaiah 6:3 is "the fullness of the earth is the glory of God."[32] Williamson gives a number of reasons for his proposal and certainly establishes the credibility of such a translation in the context of Isaiah's proclamation. If we follow Williamson, then the text sheds further light on the doctrine of creation. In this reading of Isaiah's vision, Isaiah turns his readers from locating the glory of God in military might or a particular people to relocating it in the fullness of the earth—we may say the fulfillment of earth's telos, the completion of creation in the new creation. The visions and proclamations of Isaiah that follow become an unfolding of this confession. Such an understanding returns us to the trinitarian economy of creation in which the glory of God and the fulfillment of creation diminishes neither. Such a vision fulfills both by drawing on the wellspring of the life of creation in the one God—Father, Son, and Spirit—who is Life: I AM.

Fear of *I AM* Is the Beginning of Wisdom: Proverbs, Job, Ecclesiastes

> By wisdom I AM laid the earth's foundations,
> by understanding he set the heavens in place;
> by his knowledge the watery depths were divided,
> and the clouds let drop the dew.
> Proverbs 3:19–21 (NIV slightly altered)

The book of Proverbs teaches us that wisdom has a dual relationship with creation: as the ordering of creation and as the way that humans enter into and participate in that ordering, which is life.[33]

First, Proverbs teaches us that wisdom is the eternal and righteous ordering of creation by I AM for the life of the world. In the passage above, wisdom is the instrument by which God creates.[34] As a consequence of God's instru-

---

32. Williamson, *Holy, Holy, Holy*.

33. These wisdom books are central to the recent magisterial work of Kelsey, *Eccentric Existence*. Although Kelsey's focus is theological anthropology, his work also develops a theology of creation. At most points, our books complement each other. I place a greater emphasis on the redemption of creation as the context for wisdom than does Kelsey. I believe that wisdom guides us into life in the created order that is made present to us through God's work of redemption. In *The Lamb of God*, the Orthodox theologian Sergius Bulgakov makes "sophiology" the center of his Christology and of the theological basis for ecological concern and action. See the critical discussion of Bulgakov in Jenkins, *Ecologies of Grace*, 207–24.

34. A number of scholars go further than this and argue that wisdom is an agent of creation. In spite of the many scholars who hold this view, it seems to me an obvious misreading of the text. However, my presentation here does not depend on whether one accepts or rejects the teaching that wisdom is an agent of creation. What really matters is that however it comes

mental use of wisdom in creating, wisdom also becomes the ordering of the world toward its telos. At this point, the telos is not entirely in focus, though it is clear in Proverbs that in some way the telos is life.

In Proverbs 8, the relationship between wisdom and creation is once again celebrated:

> I AM brought me forth as the first of his works,
>> before his deeds of old;
> I was formed long ages ago,
>> at the very beginning, when the world came to be.
> When there were no oceans, I was given birth,
>> when there were no springs overflowing with water;
> before the mountains were settled in place,
>> before the hills, I was given birth,
> before he made the world or its fields
>> or any of the dust of the earth.
> I was there when he set the heavens in place,
>> when he marked out the horizon on the face of the deep,
> when he established the clouds above
>> and fixed securely the fountains of the deep,
> when he gave the sea its boundary
>> so the waters would not overstep his command,
> and when he marked out the foundations of the earth.
>> Then I was constantly at his side.
> I was filled with delight day after day,
>> rejoicing always in his presence,
> rejoicing in his whole world
>> and delighting in humankind.
>
>   Proverbs 8:22–31 TNIV (slightly altered)

Although this passage falls short of portraying wisdom as the agent of creation, we must not let that detract from the glorious, joyful portrayal of wisdom in the work of creation.[35] This joyful, playful depiction of wisdom also sets before us a joyful, playful depiction of creation. There is no agony here, no burden, no dysteleology. Through the presence of wisdom and our participation in it, we enjoy life as God created it.

One of the ways that Proverbs most memorably portrays this is in its depiction of wisdom as "a tree of life" (Prov. 3:18; see the same image used for

---

to be, wisdom is the righteous ordering of creation for life. For support for my position, see Waltke, *Book of Proverbs*, chaps. 1–15, 406–23, esp. 417–20; and Longman, *Proverbs*, 203–13.

35. For a delightful account of Wisdom playing in creation, see Brown, *Seven Pillars of Creation*, 161–76.

various aspects of wisdom in 11:30; 13:12; 15:4). The image of the tree of life occurs in only two other places in Scripture: Genesis 2 and Revelation 22. In its use in Proverbs, we are being taught that wisdom brings us into the ordering of creation that is life.

The second relationship between wisdom and creation is the recognition and exhortation to enter into the ordering of wisdom so that we ourselves become wise. Wisdom, then, not only characterizes God's work of creation; wisdom also characterizes those who follow the way of wisdom in the world:

> My [beloved], if you accept my words
> > and store up my commands within you,
> turning your ear to wisdom
> > and applying your heart to understanding—
> indeed, if you call out for insight
> > and cry aloud for understanding,
> and if you look for it as for silver
> > and search for it as for hidden treasure,
> then you will understand the fear of I AM
> > and find the knowledge of God.
> For I AM gives wisdom;
> > from his mouth come knowledge and understanding.
> He holds success in store for the upright,
> > he is a shield to those whose walk is blameless,
> for he guards the course of the just
> > and protects the way of his faithful ones.
> > > > Proverbs 2:1–8 (NIV slightly altered)

At first reading, the book of Proverbs may appear to be superficial and very ordinary. But there is a profundity in its teaching that becomes evident to those who desire wisdom, who are willing to "cry aloud" and "search for it as for hidden treasure." In the midst of what seems to be everyday routine and just the way things are, there are two competing ways, one leading to death and one leading to life.

When this stark contrast between life and death apprehends us, we begin a journey that leads us deep into the order of God's world. As we journey into God's world as creation, we are also journeying into redemption: we are moving from folly to wisdom, from death to life. The placement of the recurring admonition that "the fear of I AM is the beginning of wisdom" (Prov. 1:7 NIV slightly altered; 9:10; 15:33) is not a veneer of faith laid over pragmatic advice. Rather, this admonition is a warning of the profound—as in life or death—consequences of our response to the teaching of wisdom.

We mistake the nature of created life and the relationship between creation and redemption when we regard the wisdom of Proverbs as trivial, mundane good advice on the order of *Poor Richard's Almanac*, "Dear Abby," or Dr. Phil.[36] It is in the very ordinary, daily journey that we follow either the way of life or the way of death. Yes, this is ordinary, everyday life, but there is nothing trivial about it if we see clearly God's work of redeeming creation. That reality is perceptively described in Proverbs 9. There Wisdom and Folly have built houses and invite "the simple." Wisdom calls to us:

> Come, eat my food
> > and drink the wine I have mixed.
> Leave your simple ways and you will live;
> > walk in the way of insight.
> > > Proverbs 9:5–6

On the other side:

> Folly is an unruly woman;
> > she is simple and knows nothing.
> She sits at the door of her house,
> > on a seat at the highest point of the city,
> calling out to those who pass by,
> > who go straight on their way,
> > "Let all who are simple come to my house!"
> To those who have no sense she says,
> > "Stolen water is sweet;
> > > food eaten in secret is delicious!"
> But little do they know that the dead are there,
> > that her guests are deep in the realm of the dead.
> > > Proverbs 9:13–18

Although there has been significant discussion, debate, and disagreement regarding the teaching on creation in the Wisdom literature of the Old Testament, today a growing body of literature acknowledges the coherence of creation and redemption in wisdom and recognizes that Wisdom literature participates fully in God's covenant with Israel. Some of the earlier controversies were generated by the same separation of creation and redemption that I am seeking to overcome in this book. In Proverbs (and in Job and Ecclesiastes),

---

36. At one point in the twentieth century, there was strong scholarly support for regarding wisdom, and especially Proverbs, as "secular" instruction for living that had little connection with Israel's relationship to God through the covenant, the law, and the prophets. We need not be detained by that error, but we must be on guard against its revival.

there is a clear recognition that this world is not properly aligned with God and with its telos as the work of creation. To live, according to the teaching of wisdom, is not merely to learn the skills of maneuvering through life and avoiding the dangers that are present. Rather, to live is to be carried by God from the way of folly, which is to be in Sheol, to the way of wisdom, which is life with God. In gospel terms, this means that we are transferred from the kingdom of darkness and death to the kingdom of light and life. This is the redemption of creation.[37]

Among other things, the book of Ecclesiastes teaches us that the skills, insights, knowledge, and energy that we acquire must be properly ordered if they are to make us wise and bring us into life. As the "Teacher" (Qohelet), acquires "wisdom," we should read his claims ironically. Nowhere in his story does he tell us that he feared "I AM"—until he reaches the "conclusion" (Eccles. 12:13). In his early descriptions of his accomplishments, there is no hint of wisdom as the gift of God. Wisdom is described as a gift of God only when he comes to 2:26: "To the person who pleases him, God gives wisdom, knowledge, and happiness." There has been no happiness for the Teacher to this point, only emptiness. He has mistaken knowledge, insight, and skills as the means for him to take and keep for himself—the very description of the dysteleology of a world that has turned away from wisdom.[38]

This description of the dysteleological way of folly is a brilliant portrait of an age like ours in which we have an overabundance of knowledge and skills, but little wisdom to teach us the proper telos of such things. We are a foolish age, whose foolishness and emptiness is masked by our apparent ability to get what we want and to control our environment. We have a simulacrum of wisdom but not the reality. If we are properly grasped by the relationship between wisdom and creation, then we will begin the way that is life through the redemption of creation. Thus, the concluding section of Ecclesiastes enjoins us, "Remember your Creator in the days of your youth" (Eccles. 12:1). This admonition warns us that if we stray into the wrong telos in our youth, the way to the right telos is possible only by great effort and God's grace.

37. The relationship between Christ and Wisdom is a lively, tangled scholarly debate. The issues are fascinating at many levels. I have resisted the temptation to enter into the debate here. My brief response is that we need a christological doctrine of creation (see chaps. 4 and 5, and earlier passages in this chapter). We also need a doctrine of creation guided by wisdom. Moreover, both of these—Christology and Wisdom—reveal significant aspects of God's work of redeeming creation. Whether we can say that "Wisdom" in Proverbs 8 is Christ, I am undecided. Such indecision does not change my commitment to Christology and Wisdom in a doctrine of creation. For the debate, see Waltke, *Book of Proverbs*, 406–23; Boersma, *Heavenly Participation*, 141–44; and the especially helpful weighing of the issues and evidence by Treier, *Proverbs & Ecclesiastes*, 44–57.

38. For further development of this insight, see Brown, *Seven Pillars of Creation*, 177–96.

Job teaches us that even if we were grasped by wisdom so that we may be like Job, who is acclaimed as "blameless and upright; he feared God and shunned evil" (Job 1:1), we are not God but human, we are not Creator but creature (Job 38); we may be wise, but we will never know what God knows (Job 42). In Job's suffering and complaining, knowing that he does not know, he turns to God; his friends, knowing that they do know, turn to their own "wisdom." In the end, God affirms Job's speech and condemns the friends' speech. Although the text does not explicitly state this, the subtle teaching of the book is that Job's speech is affirmed because he knows that the only hope of redeeming his life, the only way to make sense of his life is not by his own efforts or his own wisdom, but in God alone.[39]

Once again, this is a powerful lesson for us today. We live so much under the illusion that our knowledge and technology give us the power to understand, explain, and control our world. They do not. God alone is Creator; God alone is wise. We were not present when God began the work of creation; we cannot know creation fully. We are God's creatures, and when we are wise it is by the gift of God.

The cosmos is created in wisdom, the righteous ordering that is the flourishing of life. But this world has fallen into folly, rebelled against the Creator, and wandered onto the path of death. Only by the redemptive work of God may we once again walk in the way of wisdom, which is the life of the world. In Proverbs, Job, and Ecclesiastes, "wisdom" is used to identify the order of living that enables us to participate in God's creation as it is being redeemed. As wisdom enables this participation, it also becomes a trait of those who live as God creates us to live. Wisdom is set over against the disorder of the world, a disorder that leads to death and is named in these books as "folly." Those who walk in this way of death and destruction are foolish. But in a world ruled by death, folly and wisdom are turned upside down. Thus, the cross of Christ, which turns the world right side up by redeeming it as God's creation, appears as foolishness to those who have given their lives to folly. The cross is the climactic call of wisdom to the way of life in God's creation that is redeemed.

I AM Reigns: Psalms

> May the glory of I AM endure forever;
>   may I AM rejoice in his works—

39. Also note the profound reflections on Job 10 in Kelsey, *Eccentric Existence*, chaps. 6 and 7, 242–308, on "living bodies" and "personal bodies." Like my exposition, Kelsey's pays attention to our limitations that are also graced by God.

he who looks at the earth, and it trembles,
   who touches the mountains, and they smoke.

I will sing to I AM all my life;
   I will sing praise to my God as long as I live.
May my meditation be pleasing to him,
   as I rejoice in I AM.
But may sinners vanish from the earth
   and the wicked be no more.

Praise I AM, my soul.

Praise I AM.
          Psalm 104:31–35 (NIV slightly altered)

The psalms celebrate the dialectic of the kingdom more fully and clearly than any other text in the Tanak apart from Isaiah. When the psalms do so, they do not celebrate "nature" and "salvation," as if these were two realms that engage us separately. Rather, the psalms celebrate creation and redemption.[40] The psalms do not portray two books of God that may be read and understood apart from each other. It is better to say that the psalms portray two lenses given by God so that we may see clearly who God is, what God is doing, and thus enter into praise.[41]

This is the center of the psalms: I AM is worthy of praise because I AM is Life and gives life. Our understanding and acknowledgment of the praise that is proper to God is our fulfillment as the humans to whom God gives life through creation and redemption. As we humans give praise, the telos of creation is coming to fruition, and thus all creation joins in praise. This teaching of the psalms runs in a direct line to Romans, where Paul narrates the work of God to create a people of righteousness who are the sign of the new creation. With this narrative in place, Paul turns in Romans 12 to tell us that we are to present our bodies as living sacrifices. Read in light of Romans 9–11, this means the giving up of our identity according to the world so that our true identity may be located in creation and so that we may be one people through redemption. This, he tells us, is our logical worship; it fits our telos. In light of all that Paul has recounted in the previous chapters, worship of God is the fulfillment of our destiny.

40. On this psalm specifically, see Waltke, Houston, and Moore, *Psalms as Christian Worship*, 340–75.
41. I both agree and disagree with John Calvin here. In his *Institutes* I/VI.1, he describes Scripture as the "spectacles" that enable us to see creation clearly and know God as Creator. I agree that we need spectacles, but I relocate the question from one of nature and Scripture to one of creation and redemption. Calvin and I are not far apart, but I suspect that for many Calvinists the distance between us may be short but the chasm deep.

The psalms anticipate this and represent an overflowing banquet for us. With the psalmists, we lament the dysteleology of the world. With the psalmists, we celebrate God's redemption of creation. This redemption and celebration are seen in the extensive and imaginative rehearsal of the glories of God in creation. They are seen also in the psalms that celebrate God's triumph over enemies and God's rescuing and blessing the people of God and the king, God's representative among the people. In most cases, however, the human king of Israel is displaced by the recognition that "I AM reigns."

This phrase captures the teaching of the psalms regarding the dialectic of the kingdom. Whose kingdom is it? I AM's. Who establishes this kingdom? I AM. From whom does this kingdom draw its character? I AM. To whom do we turn for the blessings of this kingdom? I AM.

I AM reigns. In Psalm 104, we read thirty-four verses that celebrate the life of creation. Then we get the surprising last verse:

> Let sinners be consumed from the earth,
> And let the wicked be no more.
>   Psalm 104:35 NRSV

When this verse surprises us, it forcefully reminds us that the biblical vision of creation and redemption knows that the presence of sin and sinners on earth prevents its fulfillment as God's creation. For the psalmist, indeed for any follower of Jesus Christ who delights in the gift, blessing, and beauty of creation, the plea that God would eradicate sin and sinners from the world is wholly interwoven with the longing that this world be brought to fulfillment in the new creation. In other words, the plea for judgment and deliverance from enemies is teleological.

If we have a maturing understanding of the dialectic of creation and redemption, we find no escape from sin and sorrow in "nature" or even "creation." Rather, we will find ourselves learning to sorrow and grieve the distance between the ways of the world and the way of God. We encounter our own spiritual poverty in the face of such overwhelming problems. We recognize that only God can heal the wound of creation, so we restrain our drive to make things right and save the world. We will discover a deeper, more passionate hunger for justice. We are free from the many longings of the world and long for only one thing: the reign of I AM. As we live more fully into the redemption of creation, we will extend mercy to others, recognizing that they are captive to the dysteleology of the world. We will seek the peace that is the healing of the world. And knowing that we are following the way of wisdom, living with the grain of the universe, and entering now into life eternal, we will bless those who turn against us.

All of this is the very life of God's people portrayed in the psalms. Rooted in the reality that I AM reigns, our lives will be caught up in praise and lament, thanksgiving and confession. In all of this, we will know the blessing promised by Psalm 1 and by Jesus in the Beatitudes (Matt. 5:1–11). The work of creation is blessing; the work of redemption is the fulfillment of that blessing in the new creation.

Live Long and Prosper: Deuteronomy

> So be careful to do what I AM your God has commanded you; do not turn aside to the right or to the left. Walk in obedience to all that I AM your God has commanded you, so that you may live and prosper and prolong your days in the land that you will possess. (Deut. 5:32–33 NIV slightly altered)[42]

Deuteronomy teaches a theology of life and death inextricable from the dialectic of the kingdom and our participation in it by obedience to God. This obedience is not a test extrinsic to the blessings of God. It is not a reward or an award for accomplishing the impossible task of faithfulness to God's commands, nor is the command to obey God and live meant to crush our pride and humble us so that we will then be prepared to receive the gifts of God's grace. Rather, the law is God's gift to God's people so that we may know the way to life that is God's redemption of creation.

The way to life—the way to live—was, is, and always will be life in accordance with God's creation. The way of life was, is, and always will be the gift of God. When we turned from that gift and entered the other way, the way of death, we then became a people and a whole world in need of rescue from death. God's creation of Israel—a people who were once not a people—is the way of redemption narrated in the Tanak. But Israel is redeemed as a people for the purpose of the gift of the Messiah Jesus, who is the one from whom, through whom, and to whom are all things.

Therefore, the way of life taught by Deuteronomy is the way of life embodied by Jesus Christ.[43] This is why he can say that the law is summed up in the command to love. As we have seen in chapter 5, the way of life and the way of love are identical when we understand them rooted in the one God—Father, Son, and Spirit—who is Life.

42. It may surprise many people today to know that this phrase comes from Deuteronomy. *Star Trek* has made "live long and prosper" part of popular culture, especially through Leonard Nimoy, who took the phrase from his own Jewish heritage.
43. For an extended reflection on this reality, see Work, *Deuteronomy*.

With this preparation, we may now engage the text of Deuteronomy. The instructions of Deuteronomy guide God's people in the way to live in this world as God's creation. But the instructions of Deuteronomy do not form a blueprint for that way of life, which is simply to be rebuilt from one generation to another. Rather, the instructions of Deuteronomy represent and form a people who are to grow in their understanding of life. The accounts of Israel's history narrate this story in light of Deuteronomy: Where did the people of Israel stray from the path of life? Where did they follow it faithfully? The prophetic books give accounts of those whom God has given to God's people to help them discern where they are going astray and rebelling so that they may return to the path that is life. In all this, Deuteronomy is the key to the way of life that is God's purpose for creation. But we must not lose sight of the reality that for God's purpose for creation to be fulfilled, God calls into existence and forms a people. This is the center of God's redemption of creation because through the calling and instruction of this people God creates a witness to the way of life.

In Deuteronomy and in the prophets, the faithfulness of God's people in the way of life is simply also the way of blessing. That is, to live in the way of life is to enter into the blessing of creation. However, as we have seen in our engagement with other texts, to follow the way of life in a world that follows the way of death does not mean "blessing" as an enjoyment of worldly prosperity or an escape from suffering. Rather, the blessing and prosperity offered by Deuteronomy and the prophets is the promise of life, which is life with I AM in the redemption of creation. In this way, then, by the work of the Holy Spirit, Deuteronomy bears witness to the gospel and the way of Jesus Christ. In other words, its promise of "blessing" is the promise of Christ's crucifixion and resurrection as the redemption of creation and the formation of a people who bear witness to life "with the grain of the universe."

Both Deuteronomy and the prophets teach us that life with I AM has an unbreakable integrity. Just as passages such as Romans 8 teach us that all created things are frustrated in their fulfillment by the sin of humankind, so these teachers in the Tanak portray for us the way that the land and animals, water and crops suffer and are frustrated in their purpose by human sin. Deuteronomy warns repeatedly that the life that Israel is given in the land must not be taken for granted or claimed as human achievement:

> So if you faithfully obey the commands I am giving you today—to love I AM your God and to serve him with all your heart and with all your soul—then I will send rain on your land in its season, both autumn and spring rains, so that you may gather in your grain, new wine and olive oil. I will provide grass in the fields for your cattle, and you will eat and be satisfied.

Be careful, or you will be enticed to turn away and worship other gods and bow down to them. Then I AM's anger will burn against you, and he will shut up the heavens so that it will not rain and the ground will yield no produce, and you will soon perish from the good land I AM is giving you. (Deut. 11:13–17 NIV slightly altered)

Variations on this blessing and warning occur throughout Deuteronomy. For example, God's people are warned not to attribute their wealth to their own power and strength (Deut. 8:10–18), to other "gods" (that is idols: Deut. 8:19–20), or to their own righteousness (Deut. 9). These early warning passages frame the later narratives and laws of the book.

We must be careful not to make the mistake of locating the narratives and laws of Deuteronomy within a narrowly conceived salvation history (Ger., *Heilsgeschichte*) that is a history of "redemption" separate from creation. This is the error of some biblical scholarship in the twentieth century that sought to preserve God's redemptive work while retreating from public claims about the truth of the gospel. That is, it separated the "facts" of history and science from the "values" of Christian faith in order to create a space for Christian faith and salvation in the midst of scientific and historical criticism of the Bible and attacks on the truth of Christianity.[44]

The book of Deuteronomy teaches us that the good news is God's redemption of creation. The life that God promises over against death is the telos of creation realized through redemption. Just as we learned of the church in the New Testament (especially Rom. 8), here in Deuteronomy the life of the people of God is the sign, the witness to the peoples of the earth, that God is redeeming creation. The "redemption" declared and described in Deuteronomy is grounded in creation: life in the land and with one another on the basis of the life that we form from the land.

If we have any doubt about this engagement with Deuteronomy and the firm grounding of redemption in the work of creation, we have only to turn to the prophets. Isaiah, Jeremiah, Ezekiel, and the Twelve (commonly and misleadingly called the "minor prophets") measure Israel's life by the teaching that we find in Deuteronomy.[45] They are called by God to continue the

---

44. For an accessible critique of this privatization and an account of the public gospel, see the work of Newbigin, esp. *Foolishness to the Greeks*. I have plans for a book titled *Foolishness to the Nietzcheans*, which responds to further shifts in Western culture.

45. It would be quite appropriate to have a separate section on the prophets. I have chosen to discuss them here because they really are grounded in the theology of Deuteronomy and God's covenantal promise of life. By placing the prophets in this context, we better understand the dynamic of life and death to which they bear witness and the way that the prophets teach us the dialectic of the kingdom.

proclamation of Deuteronomy that to turn to God is to turn to life and to turn from God is to turn to death. For these prophets, the turn to life is profoundly and concretely rooted in the land. When Israel turns from God, the land is cursed and life begins to fail: food withers on the vine and in the field; soon afterward humans begin to wither. For the prophets, the withering of life is not a disconnected punishment for Israel's disobedience, like a parent taking away car privileges because a teenage son or daughter has neglected schoolwork. Rather, for the prophets the withering of life is tied directly to Israel's disobedience of God, like a teenage son or daughter failing a course due to neglecting schoolwork.[46]

This reality is declared throughout the prophets; because of our neglect of the doctrine of creation and our separation of redemption from creation, we have not had ears to hear this or eyes to see. Among many texts, consider this one:

> Hear the word of I AM, you Israelites,
>   because I AM has a charge to bring
>   against you who live in the land:
> "There is no faithfulness, no love,
>   no acknowledgment of God in the land.
> There is only cursing, lying and murder,
>   stealing and adultery;
> they break all bounds,
>   and bloodshed follows bloodshed.
> Because of this the land dries up,
>   and all who live in it waste away;
> the beasts of the field, the birds in the sky
>   and the fish in the sea are swept away.
>   Hosea 4:1–3 (NIV slightly altered)

For Hosea, the covenant between I AM and Israel is a covenant of life in which material life—life in the land—is inextricably woven together with all other forms of life.[47]

In the unfolding of the dialectic of the kingdom and its climax in Jesus Christ, we learn that this covenant with Israel is for all the peoples of the earth and for all creation. We have already seen how Isaiah learns this and declares it; in Jesus Christ we see how God fulfills that vision of Isaiah. "The land"

46. See Marlow, *Biblical Prophets and Contemporary Environmental Ethics*.
47. Ibid.; Davis, *Scripture, Culture, Agriculture*; C. Wright, *God's People in God's Land* and *Old Testament Ethics for the People of God*; Bouma-Prediger, *For the Beauty of the Earth*; Northcott, *Environment and Christian Ethics*; Waltke, *Old Testament Theology*, chaps. 18–20.

is no longer just one geographically bounded land on the Mediterranean; in the vision of Isaiah, the coming of Christ, the creation of the church, and the vision of John, "the land" is all creation, redeemed by God for life everlasting. When God's people are properly aligned with the life of creation, God's justice and righteousness will be established on earth, and this world will be God's creation, living forever in the wholeness that is the peace of creation.

It Was Very Good: Genesis

> God saw all that he had made, and it was very good. And there was evening, and there was morning—the sixth day.
>
> Thus the heavens and the earth were completed in all their vast array.
>
> By the seventh day God had finished the work he had been doing; so on the seventh day he rested from all his work. Then God blessed the seventh day and made it holy, because on it he rested from all the work of creating that he had done. (Gen. 1:31–2:3)

As I recounted earlier, many people expected this book on creation to be a book about Genesis 1–2.[48] In our culture, that is an unsurprising response. Most of our public conversations about "creation," both in the church and in society, have focused on these chapters and their relationship to "science." That conversation will continue.[49]

In this book, however, I wish to stimulate a different conversation, one that does not focus on how long it took God to make the universe or how long ago God made it. Instead, the conversation (and debate, argument, conflict, and disagreement) that I seek is about the following questions:

- Why is there something rather than nothing?
- Where is this something headed?
- How do we find creation in the midst of the world?
- Why does Scripture teach creation only in relation to redemption?

48. Since this expectation is so prevalent, I should note that I also discuss Gen. 1–2 in chap. 5, where I consider the "brooding" of the Spirit, and in chap. 15, where I discuss the temple imagery and Sabbath structure of Gen. 1–2. Most of the exegetical and interpretive questions regarding Gen. 1–2 have been subsumed under theological interests. For example, the form-function structure of days 1–6 are well discussed in the commentaries. See, for example, Waltke with Fredricks, *Genesis*, 57–58, and Kass, *Beginning of Wisdom*, 31–45. I absorb this exegetical and interpretive recognition of the orderliness of creation in Genesis into my theological account of the order of creation in which we find life through its redemption.

49. For some indication of my thoughts about that conversation, see chap. 8.

- How can we know the One who creates and redeems?
- How can we live in the redemption of creation?
- How can we live in the creation that is being redeemed?
- Is there meaning in this world?
- If so, where do we find that meaning?
- How do we find meaning?
- What meaning do we find?
- How can there be life if there is death?
- What else will we find as we talk together?

To stimulate this conversation, I will here provide a particular reading of Genesis 1–2, then extend it to Genesis 3. I do not intend to replace other readings and debates about Genesis 1–2 (and often Gen. 3).

One of the most illuminating ways to read Genesis 1–2 is to read it in light of other ancient Near Eastern stories of the origins of the world. These stories, however, are not stories of "creation" in the sense that I have been developing the doctrine. Rather, these other origin stories provide a stark contrast to Genesis 1–2 and in so doing also help us see the profound, everlasting reality that we confess as God's work of creation.

Reading Genesis alongside ancient Near Eastern origin stories yields both similarities and differences. Both results are instructive. Among other things, the similarities tell us that the Israelites' confession of creation is not generated by a fantasy world or in isolation from other cultures. They are not inventing some pure language or generating ideas apart from their life in this world. To put it bluntly: they mean for their confession of creation to be a public claim about the world and to challenge other claims about the world.

As instructive as the similarities are, the differences are more significant. For the sake of clarity and space, I will introduce only one comparison here: the Babylonian *Enuma Elish*. This story produces perhaps the starkest contrast; some Egyptian stories of origins, for example, yield much less contrast. I use *Enuma Elish* here not to make the point that Genesis stands starkly over against all other ancient Near Eastern accounts but because this contrast most clearly illuminates what we confess when we confess this world as God's creation.

The *Enuma Elish* (Babylonian, "When on high," the first words of this text) comes to us from some time during the First Babylonian Dynasty (1894–1595 BC) preserved in several similar versions on tablets from around 1000–500 BC. These were discovered and translated by various scholars beginning in the late nineteenth century. The complete text was translated and published by Alexander Heidel of the Oriental Institute of the University of Chicago.[50] This is the most well known and widely cited version of the story. Only a portion of the text concerns us here.

In the *Enuma Elish*, we have the story of many gods who battle with one another over power and social relationships. In this struggle, a few gods are killed. As the conflict between the gods continues, the leader of one gang of gods procreates with another god to produce a son who will be raised to be their great warrior. This warrior-god, Marduk, eventually engages in battle with Tiamat, the great warrior-goddess of another gang that has had the upper hand in previous battles. We pick up the story at this point:

> Tiamat and Marduk, the wisest of gods, advanced against one another;
> They pressed on to single combat, they approached for battle.
> The lord [Marduk] spread out his net and enmeshed her;
> The evil wind following after, he let loose in her face.
> When Tiamat opened her mouth to devour him,
> He drove in the evil wind in order that (she should) not (be able) to
>   close her lips.
> The raging winds filled her belly;
> Her belly became distended, and she opened wide her mouth.
> He shot off an arrow, and it tore her interior;
> It cut through her inward parts, it split (her) heart.
> When he had subdued her, he destroyed her life;
> He cast down her carcass (and) stood upon it.[51]

After Marduk pursues, disarms, and imprisons Tiamat's gang, he returns to the slain carcass:

> The lord [Marduk] trod upon the hinder part of Tiamat,
> And with his unsparing club he split (her) skull.
> He cut the arteries of her blood
> And caused the north wind to carry (it) to out-of-the-way places.
> When his fathers saw (this), they were glad and rejoiced
> (And) sent him dues (and) greeting gifts.
> The lord rested, examining her dead body,
> To divide the abortion (and) create ingenious things (therewith).
> He split her open like a mussel (?) into two parts;
> Half of her he set in place and formed the sky (therewith) as a roof.[52]

50. Heidel, *Babylonian Genesis*.
51. Ibid., 40–41, lines 93–104.
52. Ibid., 42, lines 129–38.

The story continues with the making of other parts of the universe. But when Marduk has completed this work, the only ones available to maintain what he has made are the gods themselves. This disrupts their lives and imposes a burden on them. From praising Marduk, they now murmur against him:

> As Marduk hears the words of the gods,
> His heart prompts (him) to create ingenious things.
> He conveys his idea to Ea,
> Imparting the plan [which] he had conceived in his heart:
> Blood will I form and cause bone to be;
> Then I will set up *lullû*, "Man" shall be his name!
> Yes, I will create *lullû*: Man!
> (Upon him) shall the services of the gods be imposed that they may be
>   at rest.[53]

This proposal is endorsed by Ea, the leader of the gods. So the instigator of the strife, Kingu, is bound and brought before Ea:

> Punishment they inflicted upon [Kingu] by cutting (the arteries of) his
>   blood.
> With his blood they created mankind;
> [Ea] imposed the services of the gods (upon them) and set the gods free.[54]

The world to which this story bears witness is a world ruled ("infested" might be a more accurate word) by many gods who are in constant conflict with one another. It is a world that originates in conflict, violence, and bloodshed. The world of *Enuma Elish* is a world in which only the strong or the unnoticed survive, a world of plots and counterplots, scheming, lying, and betrayal. It is a chaotic world brought into being by an impulsive act that requires further ad hoc response. This world burdens the gods, then humans. The gods want to be left to their own lives and to have as little to do with the heavens and earth as possible.

What a contrast to Genesis 1–2. Here there is one God who acts in an orderly way.[55] The universe is celebrated; it is a place conducive to fertility and

53. Ibid., 46, lines 1–8.
54. Ibid., 47, lines 32–35.
55. There is continuing debate about the presence of chaos in the biblical teaching on creation. That is, is there some indication that God overcame chaos, possibly represented by sea monsters in Job and some psalms, in order to create the world? I agree with Westermann (*Genesis 1–11*, 31) that chaos and struggle are not part of the creation theme. (Westermann is here considering many ancient Near Eastern creation narratives, but the conclusion applies to Genesis.) The images of chaos and struggle in other passages in the Tanak reflect God's struggle with creation, which marks God's work to redeem it. We must not separate redemption and creation.

the flourishing of life. It is marked by harmony and comes to humankind as gift and blessing, not accident and burden. Where the musical accompaniment to the *Enuma Elish* would be cacophony, the musical accompaniment to Genesis 1–2 is Josef Haydn's *Creation*, Aaron Copland's *In the Beginning*, one of Ralph Vaughan Williams compositions (to which I happen to be listening at the moment), or (choose) a Mozart symphony.

Genesis 1–2 portrays a God who creates intentionally, not accidentally, who creates by speaking the world into existence, who creates a world that is orderly, life giving, life sustaining, and peaceful (that is, working together as a harmonious whole). In placing humankind within this world and giving us work to do, God blesses us. We are not created to relieve the gods of the burdens of this world. We are created to enjoy this world and flourish in it through our continuing relationship with the Creator God. This world is, indeed, created "very good."

Such a portrait of the world calls forth a fitting way of life as well. If Genesis is the story of creation, then it calls us to participation in the story by receiving it as God's gift. To do so, we praise and thank God for this gift and submit ourselves to living according to God's design for the universe. Our way of living with the grain of the universe is to be marked not only by praise, thanksgiving, and obedience; it is also to be marked by peace, harmony, joy, and giving. We are to live by trusting God for the sustenance of life.

It is not so with the *Enuma Elish*. Imagine that you are a Babylonian teenager whose family has traveled every year to the capital city for a reenactment of the victory and enthronement of Marduk. (Whether this actually happened in Babylon is a matter of debate. I am not asserting that it did happen, only that imagining that it did illuminates the possible impact of *Enuma Elish* on Babylonian society.) The highlight of the year has been this trip to the capital and the reenactment of the *Enuma Elish*, especially the (re)enthronement of Marduk as the climax of a weeklong orgiastic celebration. What story does *Enuma Elish* call you into? What kind of character does it call you to?

We may well imagine that a Babylonian teenager, indeed any Babylonian, would think that the story of the universe is the story of violence and conflict, scheming and betraying, danger and dying. The character traits that it sets up as ideal are cleverness, ruthlessness, scheming, capacity for violence, skill in identifying potential or real enemies, and the willingness to strike first.

On the other hand, Genesis portrays a creation that is very good and calls us to the way of creation. The way of creation begins and is sustained by

---

Thus, what we think of as God's struggle in history for redemption is also God's struggle for redemption in creation.

giving and receiving. *Enuma Elish* portrays a world that is very bad and calls us to the way of that world: world is destroyed by taking and keeping. In Genesis, the "other" contributes to the flourishing of my life and indeed of all life, whether the other is God, other humans, or other parts of creation. In *Enuma Elish*, the "other" is always a threat to my life and is fundamentally an agent of death, not life.

Now the hard question: Which story do we live in today, Genesis or *Enuma Elish*? Does not our world today look more like *Enuma Elish* than Genesis? Isn't it characterized more by conflict and violence, scheming and betrayal, than by peace and harmony, kindness and love? Do not our lives appear to be shaped more by a world like that narrated by *Enuma Elish* than by Genesis? Don't we seek to protect ourselves from others and gain skills and power that will enable us to survive for a while in a world that is hostile to life? Isn't death rather life the mark of our world?

We must now return to Genesis and add Genesis 3 to the story. For Genesis, the world begins as God's very good creation, then falls away. For *Enuma Elish*, the world was never good. For *Enuma Elish*, the way that the world is today is the way that it always has been and always will be, so we might as well accept that and decide how to make our way in such a world. For Genesis, the way that the world is today is not the way that the world was or will be; therefore, the way that the world is today is only the way that the world *seems* always to be. Through God's redemption this world is once again becoming God's creation in which life, not death, rules.

The people of God who believe this good news of life-not-death are the sign of the redemption of creation, not in our own strength but by the presence of the Spirit, who bears witness to Christ and forms him in us. The people of God (who receive the Genesis story of creation, recognize it as God's truth, proclaim it, and measure their lives by it) bear witness to an immense act of faith in believing that the way that the world seems to be is not the most real world. Rather, the most real world is the redeemed creation to which we bear witness and in which we participate each Christian Sabbath as we enter into God's rest and learn to see and carry that most real world into all our lives.[56]

When we let our engagement with the text of Genesis 1–2 be consumed by arguments about how long it took God to create the world and how long ago God created it, when we direct our energies toward reconciling the teaching of Genesis 1–2 and contemporary sciences, we run the risk (and typically succumb to the risk) of missing the wonderful good news of creation. The good news of Genesis 1–2 is not that God made it in a certain number of

---

56. See Schmemann, *For the Life of the World*.

days, or a certain number of years ago, or by a certain process. Rather, the good news of Genesis is that the universe is God's work of creation, perfectly fit for the flourishing of life. The world ruled by death is an intruder. It is a real, not illusory, world; its claims to permanence and power are illusions. In Genesis, the people of God, living in the world apparently ruled by death, see through the appearance and illusion of the world to creation. Their testimony is rooted in the redemptive work of God that makes them the people of God and transforms their way in the world so that they choose life, not death. This is the good news of Genesis 1–2. It is the good news also of the entire biblical reality that climaxes in Jesus Christ.

The world of Enuma Elish, *in which we seem to be living today, cannot be redeemed. Only the world of Genesis can be redeemed because the Genesis world is created in goodness by the one good Creator—Father, Son, and Spirit.*

Enuma Elish portrays not a "fallen" world. Rather, it is a world that cannot be redeemed because it always has been the way it seems to be. There is nothing to be redeemed. The world of Genesis, into which we are invited to live by faith, is a world that can be redeemed because its telos is life. Death is an intruder—an alien, unnatural power that separates us from God and from one another. Death is the great alienator. Love is the great reconciler. The true ruler of the world is love that reconciles and leads to the new creation. The true ruler of creation, in other words, is Jesus Christ, the Risen One.

I Was Dead and Am Alive Forevermore

On the Lord's Day I was in the Spirit, and I heard behind me a loud voice like a trumpet, which said: "Write on a scroll what you see and send it to the seven churches: to Ephesus, Smyrna, Pergamum, Thyatira, Sardis, Philadelphia and Laodicea."

I turned around to see the voice that was speaking to me. And when I turned I saw seven golden lampstands, and among the lampstands was someone like a son of man, dressed in a robe reaching down to his feet and with a golden sash around his chest. The hair on his head was white like wool, as white as snow, and his eyes were like blazing fire. His feet were like bronze glowing in a furnace, and his voice was like the sound of rushing waters. In his right hand he held seven stars, and coming out of his mouth was a sharp, double-edged sword. His face was like the sun shining in all its brilliance.

When I saw him, I fell at his feet as though dead. Then he placed his right hand on me and said: "Do not be afraid. I am the First and the Last. I am the Living One; I was dead, and now look, I am alive for ever and ever! And I hold the keys of death and Hades." (Rev. 1:10–18)

Jesus's declaration that he is "the first and the last" (Gr., *ho prōtos kai ho eschatos*) reflects the earlier declaration, "'I am the Alpha and the Omega,' says the Lord God, 'who is, and who was, and who is to come, the Almighty'" (Rev. 1:8).

These two declarations together bear witness to the claim of the one God—Father, Son, and Spirit—over all the universe. At this point, we may see that the contrast between Genesis and *Enuma Elish* is rooted in the reality of the God who creates and redeems. The cosmic proclamation (that this *world* is not the way it always has been and always will be) is possible only as the confession of belief that the God of Jesus Christ is the One who is, who was, and who is to come. The gift, blessing, and life of *creation* are not the possession of the universe but the marks of the relationship between the universe and the one Creator and Redeemer—Father, Son, and Spirit.

The declaration of Jesus Christ in verses 17–18 further vivifies this reality. The switch from "Alpha and Omega" to "first and last" (1:8; 1:17) may indicate the direct relationship between the Son and creation. The Son is the one who crafts creation and the one who is incarnate. He is also the one whose death and resurrection justify the sustaining and redeeming of a sinful world by holy God.

Here in this final engagement with Scripture, we must see clearly and vividly that creation—a world in which life that is not God flourishes—is real and actual only because creation is made by the gift of Jesus Christ, the incarnate Son, crucified and risen. This stands in stark contrast to the story of *Enuma Elish*. Apart from Jesus Christ, this universe would be the world described and confessed by *Enuma Elish*. (Remember that the "world" of *Enuma Elish* is not a fallen world.) Conversely, apart from Jesus Christ the universe described and confessed by Genesis simply would not exist, and we would have no way of conceiving it. The confession of "creation" in Genesis looks forward to the coming of the Messiah. He becomes incarnate, knowing that to become human is to submit to death. Yet he sees and lives his life fully in the way of creation. He also sees the world clearly and knows that it is not creation. He refuses the lies and temptation of the world, knowing that by doing so he is also submitting to death at the hands of the world.

Yet death cannot defeat or hold him. He is One with the Father and the Spirit. He is Creator. He is Life. His life is the fulfillment of righteousness, fully aligned with the way of creation. He is risen. His resurrection is the fulfillment of the vision of Genesis and its testimony to "creation" over against *Enuma Elish* and its testimony to "world." Our confession of creation and our way of life find their fulfillment, their meaning and sense-making, their telos, in the resurrection of Jesus Christ.

But for Christ to be risen, he must be crucified. This reality exposes the lies of the world and its way of death. The world that tells us it is the source and way of life kills the one who is life. Our confession of creation and our way of life take place in a world now ruled by death. Christ's crucifixion tells us that God is redeeming *this world*, the one ruled by sin and death. Christ's resurrection tells us that God is redeeming this world *as creation*.

Together, the crucifixion and resurrection of Jesus Christ teach us the way of life in the creation that is being redeemed for the new creation. Discipleship to Jesus Christ is not merely the way of salvation or redemption; it is also the way of creation. When we live the way of creation in a world that is in rebellion against the Creator-Redeemer, we are also following the way of the cross. This is the story of most of the book of Revelation. But the greater story is that when we follow the way of creation, we are also following the way of redemption. The way of creation and redemption is simply the way of life. Therefore, when we believe in Christ and follow the way of discipleship, we are following the way of resurrection, which ends in the new creation.

As we confess creation and live in the way of creation being redeemed for the new creation, we may often be tempted to reduce our confession of creation to something more manageable. We may be tempted to retreat from *this world* as the place of God's redemption of creation and the place where we are to live. Or we may be tempted to find some way of identifying and living as if *this world* were itself redemption. We may seek to save our lives by gaining the world, or at least enough of the world to make us immortal in some way.

The way of creation in this world is the way of the cross. But the way of creation is the way of life, and it cannot be defeated by death. We humans are born into this world and the way of death. That is our story and our dysteleological future if we seek to live apart from Christ. He is the first and the last, our beginning and our end. His life, death, and resurrection are the story of creation redeemed for the new creation. In him, we die to the way of the world and live to the way of creation. In him we have the sure and certain hope of life in the new creation without end.

Part 3

Imagine that our adventurers now have a map for their journey and know the resources and promises that their guide offers to them. They know where they are, what dangers they face, and what territory they will travel through, and they know and trust their guide. Now begins the journey and the everyday work that takes them to their destination. What are the tasks of each day? What equipment is necessary? What character enables them to persist in the journey? What skills and practices do they need?

8

Construing the World

In this chapter, I will construe the world theologically according to the doctrine of creation that I have been developing: the dialectic of the kingdom, the trinitarian economy of creation, the reconsidering of the doctrine of creation, and the rereading of Scripture. Therefore, this chapter is not an attempt to "interpret" the Bible and theology for the world. We may often speak of interpreting theology in light of history or science, where those terms are understood as scholarly fields of inquiry to which theology must respond or even submit. In these instances, we privilege the world, the context, history, and science. In this chapter, I intend to reverse this way of working. I will privilege theology and the Bible and construe the world in light of the doctrine of creation.[1]

We do not have facts that are certain and true, distinct from values that are interpretations that have no claim to truth. Because all things have been made by God and are reconciled to God in Christ, we already have the beginning point for our knowledge of the world. We begin not with humans and what we may know but with God and with God's redemption of creation. From this beginning, we encounter other, competing claims about the world. Some of these claims are covert, smuggled into our culture by assumptions such as the distinction between facts and values. Rather than agreed-on facts and disputed

1. In this construal, I am improving on my suggestion that biblical authority is practiced when we interpret the world. See Wilson, "Toward a New Evangelical Paradigm of Biblical Authority."

interpretations, we have, more radically, different descriptions of the universe and the way of the world. At every point, we are construing the world. These world construals may take many different forms and use varying vocabularies.

Therefore, the doctrine of creation is like every other account of the world in its claim to truth from the beginning. In this chapter, I will construe the world according to the gospel: creation-being-redeemed for the new creation. This is sufficiently different that I will restate it: in this chapter I am not trying to interpret the doctrine of creation for the world; rather I am construing the world as participant in the redemption of creation. In this construal, I do not seek to show how theological claims are supported by the sciences, are compatible with them, or are contrary to them. Such considerations may arise in the course of competing construals of the world, but they are not my aim. Rather my goal is to bear witness to the good news that the one God—Father, Son, and Spirit—engages in the work of creation and redemption to bring this world to the new creation.

My approach in this chapter is subject to at least two serious misunderstandings—the two that are the easiest to fall into and the most dangerous to fruitful conversation.

The first danger is that since my privileging of theology is not a common approach, my presentation could be viewed as special pleading, as an attempt to establish a position that is invulnerable to criticism or disagreement because in the face of such challenges I will simply fall back on a "faith" stance. That is, I will simply say that others disagree with my presentation because they don't have faith, have incomplete faith, or have the wrong faith. In such a response, "faith" is alleged to be either a retreat to the realm of "values" or an epistemological trump card.

Contrary to "faith" as an epistemological trump card or fortress into which I retreat when attacked, I am forced into the public arena by faith in God as Creator and this universe as God's work of creation. To believe in God as Creator and this world as God's work of creation is to make a claim about the world in which everyone lives. This belief is public truth, not private truth. It is a Christian response to revelation, not a subjective invention. "I believe in one God—Father, Son, and Spirit—maker of heaven and earth" cannot be reduced to or transcribed as "I value this world," or "I value a transcendent perspective on this world," or "We should act as if we are answerable to a greater power that created all of this." Rather, "I believe in God the Creator and this universe as God's work of creation" is both a humble and a bold confession. It is humble in its submission to God, to faithfulness to Jesus Christ, and to dependence on the Spirit. It is bold in its claim on a world that does not submit to God, follow Christ, or receive the Spirit.

The second danger is the possibility that since I affirm the doctrine of creation as public truth, any display of that truth must appeal to "truth" and "knowledge" that is publicly acceptable, arrived at by some consensus that reflects the actual convictions of no particular community or tradition. That is, I may arrive at my beliefs privately or on the basis of some particular view of truth and source of knowledge (such as revelation), but when I seek to display those beliefs in public, I must set aside any particular view of truth or source of knowledge and submit to "truth" and "knowledge" as agreed by a consensus arrived at by the "public."[2]

Such an expectation is mistaken. Any "public consensus" is simply another particular view of these things masquerading as a neutral view or a consensus. There is no such thing as a view of truth and knowledge that transcends all particularities and represents a neutral, universal position that can impartially adjudicate among various "particular" accounts of truth and knowledge. All we have are various particular accounts that are sometimes held by large numbers of people or by influential groups and thus appear to be neutral and universal. But they are all contextually dependent and particular.

Therefore, when I begin to construe the world in light of the doctrine of creation, I will be doing so on the basis of truth and knowledge as we know it in Jesus Christ, revealed to us by the Holy Spirit through Scripture and the church. This account does not say to its readers and hearers, "See, what I am showing you is what you've always believed. I'm just using different words and inviting you to a different community. You can believe this without changing your fundamental understanding of truth and way of life." Rather, this account of the world in light of God's work of creation announces that everything must change and that only God can make that change in us. There is a fundamental divide between life and death: outside of God's work of creation and redemption in Christ, there is death; in Christ there is life.

In this chapter, I construe the world according to the dialectic of the kingdom and the trinitarian grammar of creation by considering some of the most recognizable assertions about this world and taking them captive in obedience to Christ (see 2 Cor. 10:3–5). My aim will not be to show that Christian convictions conform to widely affirmed assertions about our world. Nor will I offer a running critique of these assertions. Both approaches would privilege these assertions about the world. In contrast, my intention is to give an account of the world according to the Christian conviction of the doctrine of creation.

2. Newbigin, *Foolishness to the Greeks*, is again helpful here, as is his *Gospel in a Pluralist Society*. See also John Howard Yoder, "But We Do See Jesus: The Particularity of Incarnation and the Universality of Truth," in his *Priestly Kingdom*, 46–62. For a more philosophically oriented account, see the various works of Alasdair MacIntyre.

In light of creation, how should we construe the world in which we live today on the basis of our belief in the Triune God as the redeemer of the world, thus reclaiming it as creation and bringing it to fulfillment in the new creation?[3]

At the conclusion of the previous chapter, I contrasted Genesis with *Enuma Elish*. I acknowledged that the world in which we live today seems more like the world described by *Enuma Elish* than the world described by Genesis. In this chapter, I seek to show why the *Enuma Elish* and other similar accounts of the world seem so persuasive and yet are so mistaken. Most important, I seek to show how the Christian account of creation calls us to life, life that is given only in relationship to the God who is Life.

World Construals

In the rest of this chapter, I will consider several commonplace claims about the world in which we live. Many of these claims arise from within the sciences and are identified with scientists. However, in my consideration here *I will not take any of them to be scientific claims*. At one level, these claims may operate successfully and appropriately within a carefully bounded study of material processes. When taken in this way, these catchphrases represent well-established insight into how the material processes of this world work. In doing so, they give us knowledge that helps us ameliorate the rule of death in this world. For this we should all be grateful.[4]

A Christian doctrine of creation transforms this limited gratitude into limitless praise by declaring to us that the story of this world is not contained in the material processes of this world and the death and destruction that mark those processes. The telos of this world is not contained within the material processes of this world. Rather, it is known only through the apocalyptic teleology accomplished and revealed in Jesus Christ. In him we see and participate in the redemption of creation for the new creation.

In popular culture the catchphrases are detached from their proper place with the sciences and become practical guides to making our way in this world.

3. I take this language and practice of construal from Hartt, *Restless Quest*, 89–90; see also Hartt, *Theological Method and Imagination*, 12–44. For Hartt, "belief in God as Creator and Lord of All" is a "construing belief" that calls us not only to think about the world in a particular way but so also to live according to that construal.

4. For an account of theology and the sciences, I still turn to the older work of Austin Farrer, esp. *God Is Not Dead* (US title; British title: *A Science of God?*) and *Faith and Speculation*. Farrer's work is subtle and allusive. A good brief introduction to this aspect of his work is Hebblethwaite, *Philosophical Theology of Austin Farrer*, chap. 7 (77–93), "God and the World as Known to Science."

They are construals of the world according to a vision of this world. Their construals operate within the limits of the universe as we have it today. In doing so, they are operating as if the world of the *Enuma Elish* is all that has ever been and ever will be. They operate within the horizon of death as telos.[5] These are the catchphrases that I will seek to take captive to Christ and to life in him.

Theology, in faithfulness to the gospel, refuses to accept this world as all that ever has been and ever will be. Grounded in the doctrine of creation, theology construes this world as fallen away from its telos and restored to that telos as creation by the redemptive work of the Father, the Son, and the Spirit. Theology, in faithfulness to the gospel, refuses to accept the rule of death.[6] Grounded in the doctrine of creation, theology acknowledges the reality of death but declares that in Christ death has been defeated and will one day be destroyed so that this world will become the new creation in which life will be sustained forever without death.

If we properly grasp these realities and continue to develop them in conversation, then Christianity and Christian theology have the best opportunity to reaffirm the sciences and their gifts to us in the fallen world. The sciences that arose during the Enlightenment began in Christian faith that provided just these affirmations. In many contexts today, the sciences have been taken captive by the principalities and powers and become one of them. They may be reclaimed by a clearer doctrine of creation and once again be put in their place to serve the Triune Creator and care for the fallen world.

Again, in the context of continuing conflict over the sciences, I want to reaffirm the proper place of the sciences and proper gratitude for them. At their best, they ameliorate life under the rule of death and teach us about this world that is being redeemed. Here we may be instructed by Proverbs 25:2:

> It is the glory of God to conceal a matter;
>   to search out a matter is the glory of kings.

The sciences contribute a great deal to our lives; the doctrine of creation teaches us an even wider and deeper reality that guides us in the Way of Life.

By construing this world as participant in the redemption of creation, we bear witness to God's work of creation and redemption, call followers of

5. I will later suggest that faith in the sciences as a means for gaining control over this world and over death is quickly being replaced by faith in technology as a means of escaping or transcending this world and the rule of death. For a powerful account of the rule of death, see the novels of Walker Percy, esp. *Love in the Ruins* and *The Thanatos Syndrome*.

6. I began to learn the significance of death in our culture from Ellul, *Presence of the Kingdom*; Ellul prophetically sees the rule of death in our culture in relation to what I call *techne*.

Christ into deeper faith and life, and invite those who are not following Christ to believe the good news of God's redemption of creation.

A Clockwork Universe

Among thinkers who have used this phrase over the years and among those who have followed them, "a clockwork universe" is typically used to assert that the universe is a self-contained mechanism that can be studied, explained, and understood without reference to anything other than the mechanism that is being studied. They do not mean to assert that the universe runs perfectly, so they are not necessarily at odds with accusations that if the universe resembles a clock it was made by a "blind watchmaker."[7]

If we take this phrase "a clockwork universe" captive to Christian belief in the work of creation by the Father, the Son, and the Holy Spirit, then we will rightly approach the universe as sustained by God's gracious, merciful, and just care for it.

One of the most cherished gifts I have from my wife is an antique Waltham pocket watch made in 1914. It is a gorgeous thing. I open the back of the watch occasionally to delight in the jeweled movements, the spinning of the master wheel, the sheer, delicate beauty of its construction. But as I write, it is in the shop for repair. In spite of my care for it, some small pieces of lint crept into the works, and the spinning of the wheel eventually spun them into threads and wrapped them around a secondary wheel, jamming the mechanism. I am fortunate to have an "old world" craftsman near my home who delights in the watch almost as much as I. (It is not a gift from his wife, so he cannot delight in it as much as I do.) When he has repaired it, I will once again place it in my pocket and cherish the memory of my wife and her generous and thoughtful gift-giving. Each morning I will wind it and move it forward two minutes, since it loses two minutes each day. Of course, after it is repaired and reset, it may keep the time a bit differently. (Update: I still have to move it forward two minutes each morning.)

The claim that this is a clockwork universe mistakes what it takes to hold this universe together. We may think of it like a clock if we keep the analogy within very carefully guarded bounds. When we do think this way, we must also recognize that the moment-by-moment sustaining of the universe depends on God's continuing relationship. And this relationship is not just that of originator or stem-winder or time-setter. When we think according to the trinitarian economy of creation, we must also recognize that to the extent

7. See a Christian response by MacKay, *Clockwork Image*, and the more recent work by Dawkins, *Blind Watchmaker*.

that we think of the universe on analogy with a clock, we are thinking of a very special, even unique clock.

God is not really related to this universe as a clockmaker is related to a clock that he or she has made. In the latter case, the clockmaker is another object in the same universe as the clock. In the case of creation, God is not an object in the universe alongside other objects, not even alongside other agents. God's action in relation to the universe is unique and cannot be studied like other actions and agency.[8] The agency of God is made flesh in Jesus Christ, but it is simultaneously concealed and revealed in Christ. The incarnation conceals the work of God in the visibility and embodiment of a human; it also reveals the work of God in creation and redemption: "Anyone who has seen me has seen the Father" (John 14:9; see also above, chap. 5).

So once again, we must acknowledge that to the extent that this universe may be described as a clock, it is a unique clock, one sustained by its maker not from the outside but from the Maker's participation in its working and repair.

Such an account takes seriously both the continuing working of the universe and its brokenness. To simply accept "a clockwork universe" without these qualifications is to accept that it is a clock that does not keep good time; indeed when we are confronted with the daily news of drought, famine, disease, and violence we might be inclined to say that if this universe is analogous to a clock, then it is a clock that has quit running but is still accurate twice a day. Such a clock could be studied; the relation of its parts could be analyzed. The manufacture of its case, its crystal, and its works could be known with reasonable certainty. But we would still be missing the knowledge of its proper telos. We might still mistake its purpose in its twice-a-day accuracy: "The purpose of a clock is to be precisely accurate twice a day." These admittedly sharp examples reveal to us the limitations of the "clockwork universe" analogy if that analogy is not finally informed by the trinitarian grammar of creation and the dialectic of the kingdom. Perhaps in more secure, comfortable, and relatively prosperous settings, the universe does seem to tick along like a clock. But in other parts of the world—and even in parts of the more "prosperous" and "developed" world—the clock seems broken.[9]

8. The person to whom I am most indebted for instruction and insight here is Farrer, *Finite and Infinite*; Farrer revises and, according to him, corrects some of the arguments of this work in *Faith and Speculation* (v); see also Farrer's *God Is Not Dead* (US title; British title: *A Science of God?*). See also Tracy, *God, Action, and Embodiment*, which relies on Farrer at many points and develops and revises Farrer at other points. There are more recent discussions of these issues that take the same position, but I learned a lot from these older works, and they continue to be illuminating.

9. This is not to deny the wonderful contributions of the sciences to understanding the universe and often helping to alleviate suffering. Rather, as I will argue in the following paragraphs,

When we construe the world by this dialectic and grammar, we discover that the world is not a clock at all. Construed according to the dialectic of the kingdom and the trinitarian grammar of creation, the world is intended for life. We must not imagine that it is a machine with parts that are mechanically related. It is an organism (something intended for life) dependent on the living One—Father, Son, and Spirit.

A Blind Watchmaker

Once again we confront a disagreement about the story that we are a part of.[10] If the world is meaningless, where do we get the idea that it should have meaning? More basically, where does the very idea of meaning come from? What story makes sense of the language of suffering? If we are simply accidental, temporary collocations of molecules that make up something we call a human with a particular identity that lasts only as long as one's body coheres, then why do we apply the term *suffering* to our lives and others'? Does not the description "suffering" require a story different from the blind watchmaker story in order for the very term to make sense? Again, this is not a disagreement over whether or not there is suffering in the world or what is properly described as suffering. Rather, it is a question about how the very word has meaning for us if this construal of the universe is right.

In spite of these problems, the term "blind watchmaker" should resonate with us. The universe does not seem to work very well. For those of us who believe the biblical witness to creation, the resemblance of this world to the world of *Enuma Elish* should be deeply troubling. At the same time, of course, we must recognize that it does keep going. For the Christian doctrine of creation, this is exactly what we should expect. This world is not the way that God intended and intends it to be. But again this world is not simply the way that things always have been and always will be. The world of the blind watchmaker is a world turned from its proper telos and without hope. It is a world in which we should have no words for *meaning* and *suffering*. Yet we do.

---

my criticism of "the clockwork universe" image reminds us that only redemption restores the universe to its proper working by bringing it back into relationship to God.

10. Dawkins has made the phrase "a blind watchmaker" popular as a title of one of his books. He intends in the book to displace W. Paley's argument from design—the existence of a watch requires a watchmaker, the existence of creation requires a creator—with an argument for evolutionary processes as the "blind" maker of the universe. I take the phrase from Dawkins but do not intend to address his arguments. McGrath and McGrath have already taken care of this in *Dawkins Delusion?* See also McGrath, *Dawkins' God*, chap. 2. My aim here is to show how the doctrine of creation takes this phrase captive and construes the world for faithful Christian discipleship.

For the Christian doctrine of creation, this is not the world of the blind watchmaker. Rather, this is the world of the Father, the Son, and the Spirit, who in the trinitarian economy give life to this universe, bear its brokenness, hold it together, reconcile all things by the bearing of the world's suffering, and are already bringing the world to its proper fulfillment as creation in the new creation. In order to do this, the Father, the Son, and the Spirit see and remember all the suffering and brokenness of the world. Nothing is lost to God. This is the law of the conservation of action and event and character. God knows all things and knows them properly and fully. God's understanding is not lacking, nor are there gaps in God's knowing, understanding, and remembering. We are limited in our knowing, understanding, and remembering because we are in the middle of the story and because we are human. In the middle of reading a well-crafted mystery novel, there are many things that we do not understand, do not understand fully, or even fail to notice. When the end comes, the story "falls into place" and our understanding is less incomplete, though we may still not understand the story as well as the author.

The story of the redemption of creation in which we are participants is a life-and-death story. In God's mercy and love, God has revealed to us the end of the story in Jesus Christ. We cannot know fully where we are in that story nor can we know exactly how the details of our lives and the lives of others fit into that story. What we do know through the good news of Jesus Christ—his life, death, and resurrection—is that this broken, death-ruled world is not the most real world; it is not eternal. This broken, death-ruled world has been redeemed as creation by the one God—Father, Son, and Spirit.

The One who creates and redeems is Life. There is no blind watchmaker but rather an all-seeing, all-knowing God who sustains the universe in its fallenness and keeps it from fully realizing its telos in death—that is, in cessation. The one God who is named I AM redeems creation by acting in love to be just and merciful toward God's world. I AM is not blind to the brokenness and suffering of the universe. The universe continues to be, in its brokenness and suffering, precisely because I AM sees, knows, remembers, and bears the world's suffering. Do we really think that a universe such as this could continue in existence apart from this sure future judgment and justice in mercy? Apart from the God whom we know in Jesus Christ as Creator and Redeemer, how could a universe such as this even come to life?

In light of the Christian doctrine of creation, we should deliberately conflate the material and the moral when we ask such a question. The coming-to-be of the universe must never be simply a question of material conditions; it must always also be a question of the moral conditions for the coming-to-be of such a universe as this.

The suggestion, that if there is a creator of this universe, it must be a blind watchmaker, usually cancels out the moral conditions of the coming-to-be of the universe. The intent of the "blind watchmaker" suggestion is to argue that the very nature of this universe challenges and ultimately defeats the case for belief in a creator and a purposeful creation. But if we are to maintain some sense of morality, then those who deny and oppose belief in God as Creator must provide us with a "cosmodicy."[11] That is, they must now provide an explanation for the moral coming-to-be and conditions of the universe as they describe it.

We do have examples of cosmodicy. Many of Richard Dawkins's books and books by other contemporary atheists represent that project even though they may not be explicit about this aim.[12] But when read as cosmodicies, do these books really offer more persuasive accounts of the world than accounts that arise from the Christian doctrine of creation? Christians believe that the Christian doctrine of creation is the truthful account of the world. The way to bear witness to that truth is by construing the world according to belief in God as Creator (a trinitarian account of creation) and Lord of all (the dialectic of the kingdom).

One final note is absolutely critical. Throughout this section, I have continually appealed to the trinitarian economy and the dialectic of the kingdom. As Christians, we must never fall into the trap of trying to give an account of God as Creator apart from the specificity of the story of the universe that we have been given in the good news of Jesus Christ. When we forget or ignore this and seek to give an account of God as Creator apart from this story and the telos of the universe in the new creation, we enable the skepticism and atheism of our age. More tragically, we fail to bear faithful witness to the good news of Jesus Christ for all creation.

The Selfish Gene

Once again we are indebted to Richard Dawkins for popularizing a memorable turn of phrase.[13] However, there is a critical difference between what Dawkins seems to argue in his book, the impact of his title, and the function of this

11. "Theodicy" (from the Greek for "the justification of God") is the term for accounts that seek to justify belief in God in a world of suffering and death and evils. I am here suggesting that those who do not believe in God need to develop a justification or explanation for the existence of the cosmos. How does a world ruled by death ever come to life?

12. When Dawkins the scientist advances a cosmodicy or arguments against God, he is not writing *as a scientist*, though he may seek to make use of his status as a scientist to persuade us of his arguments.

13. Dawkins, *Selfish Gene*.

book within his overall public presence.[14] Dawkins's critics and his responses generally lead to an admission that assigning "behavioral" characteristics to genes is metaphorical and that genes could also be described—metaphorically—as altruistic. Unfortunately, Dawkins has a public presence as an intellectual apart from his science. Moreover, much of our culture has picked up on a concept of our inherent selfishness as genetically determined and therefore unavoidable and irredeemable.

But we Christians should not move too quickly to deny the selfishness of our "genes." In Scripture and from the beginning of Christian teaching, the mainstream of Christianity has taught some version of original sin and total depravity. Over the centuries, these doctrines have been formulated in different ways from language to language and culture to culture. But in their various formulations, these doctrines have always affirmed that something corrupted human nature in our line of inheritance and that such corruption infects every part of our humanity.

It is important to note that those affirmations are not necessarily tied to any one linguistic and cultural instantiation. Our inheritance of sin is not tied to one particular account of *how* that inheritance takes place. Also important is the recognition that "total depravity" means not that each of us is as depraved as we possibly could be but rather that the effect of our inherited corruption spreads to every aspect of what it means to be human. This formulation of the doctrine of total depravity also means that changing conceptions of the human do not affect the claim of total depravity. In other words, this formulation of total depravity is not affected by whether one believes that humans are made of body and soul; body, soul, and spirit; embodied souls; or some other formula.

Therefore, although we Christians have not previously formulated our doctrine in these terms, we may now claim the language of Dawkins and others to bear witness to the selfish gene. When we recognize how that gene shapes all of human life, the structures we make, the relationships that we engage, and the way that we think, we may even agree on the existence of Selfish Gene.[15] But Christians do not believe that Selfish Gene is sovereign. The selfish gene may explain our behavior and our construction of relationships within the horizon of this world, but it does not rule all reality. Nor does it free us from the bondage, guilt, and impotence of sin.

This construal leaves us without hope in a world ruled by the selfish gene in the face of death. The good news of the redemption of creation is that Selfish

14. See McGrath, *Dawkins' God*, chap. 1.
15. I use the uppercase "Selfish Gene" somewhat playfully to remind us that this incurred self, this general stance of selfishness is a power that rules us apart from Christ's redemption.

Gene has been defeated and our selfish genes may be transformed. As we saw in chapter 7, the human problem is that we are born into the fallen world, inherit original sin, and suffer from total depravity. To be rescued from the fallen world, escape original sin, and be healed of total depravity, we must be born again; not in the trite, popular sense of the phrase but in the profound and impossible-apart-from-God reality of dying and rising with Christ. This dying and rising transfers our citizenship from the kingdom of sin and death to the kingdom of righteousness and life. This latter kingdom is established by Jesus Christ in the redemption of creation that leads to the new creation.

Selfish Gene enslaves us, chains us in a dungeon, and marks us for death. Selfish Gene confines us to the world as it appears to us, the world of *Enuma Elish*, which many take to be the only world that ever has been and ever will be. Rooted in the trinitarian grammar of creation and the dialectic of the kingdom, we know this world to be fallen away from its telos and redeemed by God for the new creation. Selfish Gene is not sovereign: "If anyone is in Christ, new creation" (2 Cor. 5:17, my translation)!

Survival of the Fittest

This is, of course, one of the best-known claims of evolution, especially in its Darwinian expression. This phrase reflects one of the story lines of evolution: the world is a battleground for survival, a life-and-death struggle that only the fittest survive. In popular culture, this story line is received, understood, and lived in many vulgar ways. But underlying all of this is the basic assumption that the way this world is reflects the way it always has been and always will be, as it is demarcated by the final reality of death. In this story line, death makes the world go around. And around. And around.

As an interpretation of the fallen world, I find this story line quite persuasive. Isn't this what Christians would expect of a universe created good and teleologically intended for life, but turned upside down by our rejection of the world as creation? That is, when we reject this world as God's blessing, gift, and life, then it is an entirely reasonable outcome that we know the world as curse, burden, and death.[16] Such a world is indeed a place of struggle, competition, and conflict, where only the fittest survive.[17]

---

16. In anticipation of chap. 9, we may note that much of culture is an attempt to control, suppress, and avoid the world as curse, burden, and death. This is the "worldliness" of culture. But culture may also be an expression of the blessing, gift, and life of creation. Discernment of this difference is a task possible only through the gifts of the Spirit.

17. In some critiques of evolutionary teaching, it is commonplace to argue that "the survival of the fittest" is a tautology—merely stating a definition of who the fittest are. Such criticism,

When Christians think that we have to reject evolution in order to affirm God as Creator, we fall into the error of separating belief in God as Creator and in the doctrine of creation from the trinitarian grammar of creation and the dialectic of the kingdom. When we instead begin our thinking and living in this world by turning for guidance to trinitarian grammar and the dialectic of the kingdom, then we may quite reasonably arrive at the recognition that some form of evolution in the midst of the fallenness of the world follows from our doctrine of creation.[18] I am not saying that Christian belief and theology must conform to the superior account of the world that is generated by accounts of evolution ruled by the survival of the fittest. I am arguing, rather, that the dialectic of the kingdom and the trinitarian grammar of creation provide a superior account of why evolutionary accounts of the world persuasively describe the world in its fallenness but not its telos in the new creation. In other words, Christian belief in creation and redemption may lead us to an expectation that this fallen world will be marked by a certain kind of the survival of the fittest. Moreover, in the sovereign providence of the Father, the Son, and the Spirit, this survival of the fittest will be used by the one God to sustain the life of the fallen world. But we are further led by the Christian doctrine of creation to a larger account of the survival of the fittest.

Thus, "the survival of the fittest" should be recognized as an entirely ap-propriate expectation and description of the way of the fallen world that is uncovered and explained by the sciences, even in the midst of their many debates and disagreements over the exact descriptions and mechanisms of the survival of the fittest. In a fallen world, only the fittest will survive and flourish, whether they do so as individuals or as collectives.

By this time, attentive readers will have picked up on my careful phras-ing: it is in the context of the fallen world that various formulations of "the survival of the fittest" make sense. But for creation, that story line must be placed within a larger story: the story of the redemption of creation. For evolutionary accounts of the world, the survival of the fittest accepts death as the final horizon and limit on our existence. But the good news of Jesus Christ accepts no such horizon and limit. The good news for creation is that the one God—Father, Son, and Spirit—is Life and gives life to this world as creation. The "final horizon" and "limit" is not death but the new creation, which is neither final horizon nor limit, but telos.

---

however, fails to challenge the *explanatory* power of the claim as it is deeply embedded in our cultural practices and ways.

18. I write this fully aware that this is not the typical way that theology engages evolution. I am deliberately changing the course of the discourse. For theological efforts similar to mine, see Moltmann, *Way of Jesus Christ*, VI §3–4; Cunningham, *Darwin's Pious Idea*.

In light of the telos of the new creation, the survival of the fittest takes on a wholly new, almost unimaginable, and for many, really unbelievable meaning. Now the new meaning of survival of the fittest is absorbed into the story of the new creation. Evolutionary accounts of the survival of the fittest depend on an account of the way of the world in which those who fit best also have the best chance of surviving and flourishing. It is likewise for the new creation accounts of the way of the world: those who fit best in this story have the best chance of survival. But, no, that is not quite right. In fact, it is quite wrong when survival of the fittest is put in those terms.

For the new creation accounts, there is only one who is "fit" to survive: Jesus Christ, who in his life and death fits perfectly into creation as God intended it. Since Jesus Christ fit perfectly into creation, death could not defeat him, destroy him, or hold him. The resurrection of Jesus Christ is the vindication of his life and death as the way of life "with the grain of the universe."

The resurrection of Jesus Christ is the greatest display and confirmation of "the survival of the fittest." In other words, is not survival beyond death the greatest feat of survival that possibly could be? This is the story of "survival of the fittest":

- Not the competition, conflict, and violence that is identified by evolutionary accounts and lived by most of us, even followers of Jesus Christ, in our daily lives,
- But the trust in God, who is Life and who lives by giving and receiving, so that the battle is located properly: do we trust in God even to death or do we grasp our own lives and seek to save and sustain them by taking and keeping?

It turns out, then, that survival of the fittest makes sense of the story line of the fallen world but leaves us within the prison of sin and death. That story line is absorbed and redeemed by the faithfulness of Jesus Christ,

> Who, being in very nature God,
>   did not consider equality with God something to be used to his own
>   advantage;
> rather, he made himself nothing
>   by taking the very nature of a servant,
>   being made in human likeness.
> And being found in appearance as a man,
>   he humbled himself
>   by becoming obedient to death—
>   even death on a cross!

> Therefore God exalted him to the highest place
>   and gave him the name that is above every name,
> that at the name of Jesus every knee should bow,
>   in heaven and on earth and under the earth,
> and every tongue acknowledge that Jesus Christ is Lord,
>   to the glory of God the Father.
>
> Philippians 2:6–11

When we come to know that survival of the fittest means life lined up, "fit," for the kingdom of God, then a whole new way follows from it, the way of Christian discipleship that follows the grain of the universe and leads to the new creation in which human life will flourish forever.

The way to this life, however, is not ours to accomplish. Only one person has lived perfectly with the grain of the universe, and thus only one is fit to survive: Jesus Christ. Now we are confronted once again with the same question that confronts the first humans in Genesis 2–3: will we trust in God for blessing, gift, and life? In Christ, creation is once again being given back to us as God's blessing, gift, and life. Only through believing in him and thus trusting God in him do we enter into the resurrected life of his own faithfulness to the way of creation. Only in him do we become "the fit who survive" by receiving the Holy Spirit as the guarantor of our own resurrection to perfect life in the new creation. This is the good news of the survival of the fittest in the kingdom of God: Jesus Christ, from, through, and to whom are all things.

Natural Selection

Along with survival of the fittest, natural selection is one of the most widely known descriptions of the world. As we have moved from a clockwork universe and the blind watchmaker to the selfish gene and survival of the fittest, we have moved toward the human scale of the way of the world. Of course, these descriptions seek to capture the life not just of humans but of all animate beings. As with the other descriptions, natural selection powerfully describes the process that rules the development and extinction of forms of life due to genetic traits that give them a competitive advantage over the generations. But like other descriptions, it operates within the limits of this world as the only world that ever has been and ever will be against the horizon of death.

The redemption of creation in Jesus Christ describes the world in a different way and thus invites us into another story: not the story of natural selection but the story of gracious election. This story has been told in many ways. It is often told in such a way that it falls short of being good news. It simply exchanges one necessity, natural selection, for another necessity, God's election. I will not attempt to sort out the history of the doctrine of election here—a gargantuan task that has no clearly helpful aim. Instead, I will simply articulate an account of God's gracious election that is good news for the fallen world.

"God's gracious election" construes the world according to the dialectic of the kingdom.[19] Although some Christians today may want to avoid the language of election or eradicate it from Christian vocabulary because it is sometimes misused, abused, or used abusively, the term is deeply biblical and pervades the biblical witness to God's grace. The proper response to misuse and abuse is the reclamation of its proper use. The world may be ruled by natural selection; creation is ruled by gracious election.

As a description of God's work of creation, "election" teaches us that God created not out of necessity but in freedom. The trinitarian grammar of creation teaches us that God creates freely from the depths of God's character as one who lives by giving. Thus, God's living and God's loving are one. Since God creates freely, God is bound by nothing in creation; God is "bound" only by God's character because there is no gap between God's action and God's character. God does not "intend" to do one thing and then fail to do it. There is no gap between God's intention, God's character, and God's action. These three are one, as are any other ways that we might try to divide God.

So "natural selection" may be a perfectly accurate description of the way of the fallen world that binds us to an apparently blind, random story that is describable in retrospect but indescribable in prospect because it seems lacking in direction and design. "Natural selection," however, is not the last word. The one God—Father, Son, and Spirit—is not bound by the fallen world. God is bound only by God's intention, character, and action. God intentionally (not accidentally) and graciously (not from necessity) creates life other than God. God fulfills this intention fully in character with God's life in the dynamic of giving and receiving in the mutuality of love as Father, Son, and Spirit. This same dynamic provides the power in which God acts to create all things.

Having created in the freedom of God's own life, God is not bound to any necessity by the free acts of God's creation. When God's work of creation freely turns away from the telos for which God creates, this turning toward death does not affect God's freedom. Natural selection may tell the story of an ironclad necessity by which the fallen world seems to be sustained, but it does not tell the story of creation.

19. In the Reformed tradition, where election is a special focus, Karl Barth brings election, creation, and redemption together in creative ways to declare the good news of Jesus Christ. Barth, *Church Dogmatics* III/I §41.

The God who freely creates also freely redeems. God's election of the creation of life other than God is fully consonant with God's redemption of life that is other than God. The fall of creation from its telos into a dysteleology of death binds creation to death as its fate—except that God is not bound by the fall of creation, by the dysteleology of the world, or by death.

In popular culture, natural selection is an account of the fate of the fallen world. Gracious election is a construal of the destiny of the redeemed creation. In this account, election should be a cause for rejoicing and thanksgiving. In the world, we may be bound to a fate described by natural selection, but in creation we are freed for the destiny described by gracious election: on the one hand, survival unto death; on the other hand, life unto the new creation.

At this point, we must also recover the connection between creation and church that engaged us in our study of Colossians, Romans, and other New Testament passages. The New Testament recognizes a certain status to the claims of "natural selection" in its acknowledgment of Jew and Greek, slave and free, male and female (Gal. 3:28).[20] This list and others similar to it name the identity of the Christian disciples according to one measure of their "natural" status and in doing so acknowledges their place in the story of the fallen world. Paul goes even further down the road of natural selection when he describes the disciple community in Corinth: "Not many of you were wise by human standards; not many were influential; not many were of noble birth" (1 Cor. 1:26). Natural selection would not be looking to these for the formation of a new community and for giving leadership to it. God's gracious election works differently: "But God chose the foolish things of the world to shame the wise; God chose the weak things of the world to shame the strong. God chose the lowly things of this world and the despised things—and the things that are not—to nullify the things that are, so that no one may boast before him" (1 Cor. 1:27–29).

We have all but forgotten that it is the weakness of the church (by "human standards"—that is, according to the world's accounting practices) that constitutes its life and testimony to God's redemption of creation. In God's creation, one does not have to be strong and privileged by natural selection to live. In God's creation, life is freely given by God to all who will receive it. In a culture that is increasingly global in its ideological capitulation to the story of natural selection, the bondage of fate narrated by natural selection blinds

20. I am using the term "natural selection" anachronistically and applying it to a time when people lacked the material theory to help them articulate this reality. But the cultures of the NT nevertheless had an account of "natural selection" that they articulated in their own ways.

us to the grace of God, which offers life to all regardless of their classification on the scale of natural selection.[21]

The good news of Jesus Christ is that God's gracious election is grounded in God's intention, character, and action. Nature pretends to determine our fate. God transforms our fate into destiny in Jesus Christ: the new creation. This is the good news of Jesus Christ.[22]

Virtuality

We often mistake the sciences as the means to analyze, understand, and describe the universe so that we might gain enough knowledge to defeat fate and control our own destinies. But the sciences operate within the limits of what is, even as we look to them to give us the ability to transform what is. They can analyze, understand, describe, and to some extent control the fallen world. They cannot transcend the dysteleology of death, which is the consequence of our turning away from and rebelling against the relationship between Creator and creation that realizes the telos of creation in the new creation.

These assertions are not "scientific" claims but theological convictions. This recognition puts the sciences in their proper place and allows us to celebrate and give thanks for what they do to ameliorate our lives, conquer and treat diseases, postpone our deaths, and delight in the order of the world even in its fallen state. As we realize the limits of the sciences, we may also engage properly with the universe, recognizing that the burdens, suffering, and death that mark the world are signs of its fallenness, but that within this same world are signs of the redemption of the world as creation in such realities as the continuation of life, the disciple community, and the resurrection of Jesus Christ.

What happens if we realize the limits of the sciences, their failure to transform our fate, and their inability to conquer death, but do not have theological resources to place the sciences properly in the fallen world? What happens when we discover the inability of the sciences to fulfill our expectations that they will deliver us from evil and death, but do not then see or believe the signs of redemption? One response to this failure of the sciences is the rise of *techne*, the culture of technology.

21. I use *global* here to refer to the attempt to erase differences and local identity in the treacherous pursuit of hegemony. Against this "globalization" stands the catholicity of the people of God. Such a claim would be laughable were not the Holy Spirit with us.

22. One of the disturbing ironies today is that many Christians who vigorously teach and defend a particular account of "creation" live according to the world's account of "survival of the fittest" and "natural selection."

There is a long-standing difficulty in the choice of words that we use to describe the power that I call *techne*.[23] By my choice I intend to signal that the reality that I am addressing is not sufficiently characterized by "technology" or "the technological." These terms may be rightly used to describe something as basic as a wheel or the ability to make a fire when and where one chooses. These terms may also be used to describe the more complex realities today in our machines that we call computers as well as the larger reality of systems and networks. None of these is quite what I mean by *techne*, though all are implicated in this reality.

By *techne*, I mean the development of technology as our savior. Simply put, *techne* is the promise and claim that since the sciences have failed to provide us with the knowledge and power to transform our fate and control our destiny, we will develop technology that enables us to escape this world and thus avoid our fate and our destiny.[24]

Techne promises to create a virtuality: an alternative reality in which the fate of the universe and of humans is different from this universe. This virtuality is not a transformation of this world or its redemption but rather a new creation of humankind that competes with the story of the new creation in Christ. We must be careful to recognize that few users of technology have heard and publicly confessed belief in *techne*'s promise. At the same time, *techne* has become one of the powers of this age that masquerades as a way to life and a means of salvation. *Techne* is pervasive in a way that most previous idols have not been. Its increasingly global reach has the potential of being the most powerful viceroy of death in the fallen world that we have ever seen.

Such language is meant not to create a fear of *techne* but to expose its lure, its illusion, and its impotence so that we may turn away from *techne* to the good news of Jesus Christ. The lure of *techne* is strong; it appeals to our deepest fears and is especially alluring as we see with increasing clarity the failure of the expectations that we mistakenly placed on the sciences and as the plausibility of modernity collapses around and upon us. Since these "saviors"—modernity and the sciences—have failed us, we are now incredibly vulnerable to a new messianic claim.

As the plausibility of modernity collapses and we experience dislocation, dissonance, and culture shock, we are open, even desperate for something to believe in and guide our lives. The allure of *techne* is increased by the way that it appears to be a correction and extension of the sciences. We are now harnessing much of the knowledge and power of the sciences for the production

23. See the controversy over the translation of Ellul's work and the use of terms in other more recent works, esp. Borgmann, *Technology and the Character of Contemporary Life*. In the context of ecology and creation, see Wirzba, *Paradise of God*, 77–85.

24. In an earlier age, alchemy made this same promise.

of technology necessary for the rise of *techne*. In this case, *techne* has the advantage of assuring us that the previous culture was not entirely mistaken and that we have not wasted the enormous amounts of money, time, and energy that developed the sciences. All we need to do is reconceive their uses and reconfigure their artifacts.

Interestingly, some of the best critique of *techne* is found in science fiction novels and popular movies. *Techne* then turns around and co-opts these critiques for entertainment both in their novel and cinematic forms, but even more powerfully in casual internet usage and the more consuming forms of computer gaming. In all of this, *techne* offers the illusion of a new identity. Nerds may become warriors; couch potatoes become US Navy Seals; someone in a recliner drives fast and furious; the impotent or sexually frustrated choose from an almost endless array of partners and scenarios. We can "escape" the limitations of our bodies, our circumstances, and our relationships.[25] At a deeper and more haunting level, future thinking in service to *techne* imagines a never-ending life for one's "identity" that survives in the virtual world of computers and beyond.[26]

In light of this present reality and power of *techne* and its imagined future, we might paraphrase the good news of *techne*: "If anyone is online, there is a whole new creation: the old is escaped, the new is entered" (cf. 2 Cor. 5:17). This "story" of escape through *techne* is still in an early stage of development. It would not do for an idolatrous power to show itself too quickly. We must first be cultivated at an apparently innocuous level. Our appetite has to be developed slowly; our desire has to be drawn along carefully; habits must be inculcated patiently. Step-by-step we are drawn into the web of seduction until we are so far in that we are ensnared and escape is impossible apart from God-with-us.[27] The "we" in this story is the human person, but it is also a society and a culture, even potentially a global culture.

The story of *techne* and its allure is not the good news of the redemption of creation. It is not an alternative gospel. Instead, the story is bad news. It is a new opiate of and for the masses that enchants us with false hope and ensnares us with lies so that we go quietly and blithely to our death.[28] *Techne* does not

---

25. Postman's *Amusing Ourselves to Death* and *Technopoly* are still illuminating.

26. I know that the power and reality of *techne* go much deeper than these mundane examples. But this is where most of us live. Therefore, it is also where we have the greatest possibility of uncovering and resisting its allure. At the same time, I have found that identifying the deeper dynamic of *techne* helps free people from its everyday domination of their lives.

27. I take many of my cues here from the book of Proverbs and its description of how a naïf becomes a fool and then a mocker. See esp. the sardonic observations of Proverbs 5–7. For my account of this in relation to pornography, see "Simpletons, Fools, and Mockers."

28. Once again I am thinking of Proverbs and esp. its portrayal of Folly and her victims in Prov. 9:13–18.

promise the redemption of creation and the telos of a fulfilled, flourishing, and forever human life; rather, it promises us escape from the universe and from our bodies into the (counterfeit) life of machines.[29] *Techne* is another manifestation of the enemies of God and creation.

This does not make technology an enemy of God and creation.[30] This situation is the reality of "principalities and powers" that are created by God for good but have become weapons of the enemies of God and creation in the fallenness of the world. The doctrine of creation guided by trinitarian grammar and the dialectic of the kingdom teaches us that these powers, which destroy life, may by the rule of Jesus Christ once again become gifts that enhance and enable life. In his crucifixion, Christ humiliated these powers and triumphed over them. They are now his servants, and they become ours when we construe them according to God's redemption of creation.

The good news of Jesus Christ is that the way of life through the redemption of creation remains steadfast and sure even in the midst of the collapse of the plausibility of modernity and the failure of the sciences to meet our expectations. One of the first steps toward exposing and out-narrating virtuality is to explain the collapse of the predecessor culture and the plausibility of the sciences. In the midst of the rise of *techne*, we Christians must offer our persuasive account of why the sciences do not meet our expectations and why we should nevertheless celebrate and give thanks for them.

A large part of the allure of *techne* is its own testimony to provide a more advanced story of "salvation" than did modernity. In the midst of this allure of virtuality, the good news of Jesus Christ is nearly impotent if we do not have a mature, robust doctrine of creation grounded in trinitarian grammar and the dialectic of the kingdom. Without this doctrine of creation, all we may offer is a more tepid version of the claims of virtuality. That is, apart from trinitarian grammar and the dialectic of the kingdom, all that we have to offer is another version of escape from the universe and the abandonment of our bodies.

29. My favorite among C. S. Lewis's fiction is *That Hideous Strength*, which, although perhaps a bit overwritten and fanciful, portrays *techne* in its servility to death and inhumanity with bone-chilling, stomach-churning clarity.

30. For a thorough, insightful, and nuanced account of technology and Christian faithfulness, see Brock, *Christian Ethics in a Technological Age*. Although I have learned a lot from Brock, his work suffers from the absence of a full doctrine of creation, such that he can write, "As the power to manipulate *creation* grows, so too does the temptation of technology" (235, emphasis added). I agree with the point that he makes about technology, but his use of the term "creation" confuses the situation. We cannot manipulate God's work; what we seek to manipulate is *the world* (as I use it here). This distinction is critical to perceiving God's redemption of creation, participating in it, and witnessing to it.

The good news of creation redeemed in Jesus Christ construes this universe as the place by which the one God—Father, Son, and Spirit—enters into loving relationship with us and creates loving relationships in all creation. Salvation does not consist in a putative escape from this world through the power of *techne*. Salvation and redemption for all creation is declared in the good news that we are given eternal, perfected life forever through the power of Christ's resurrection in the new creation. This is more than we could ever dream of and hope for. All other gods are idols, and their promises not only empty but death dealing.

I Hold the Keys of Death and Hades

> I am the First and the Last. I am the Living One; I was dead, and now look, I am alive for ever and ever! And I hold the keys of death and Hades. (Rev. 1:17–18)

In this final section, we turn from other putative claims of describing the world to the one true claim that is the hope of redemption and the power of the new creation: the resurrection of Jesus Christ. Apart from the resurrection of Jesus Christ, we would not know the "world" in its fallenness and impotence. The keys to death and hades held by the risen Jesus Christ signify not only that he rules these realities but also that he is the key to their meaning.

In John's vision, the resurrected (and therefore also crucified) Jesus Christ is the key to the entire meaning of the entire cosmos. In the resurrection of Jesus, the entire reality of creation and redemption crescendo in never-ending life in the new creation that will praise the Father, the Son, and the Spirit for eternity through the just shalom of the universe in life with God.

By the sin-bearing of the Risen One, we and all creation are justified. All that we are by being born into the land of sin cannot derail or destroy God's intention for creation. This world is made for the glory of God as blessing, gift, and life. Sin is contrary to the telos of creation, but it is real and cannot be ignored or denied or magically erased. By bearing the sin of the world, Jesus Christ makes possible our justification. Each of us is subject to condemnation and death for all that we have done and all that we are that is out of alignment with the telos of creation. God's wrath falls on all that is contrary to life and servant of death. We escape condemnation and wrath only because Jesus has borne that condemnation and wrath for us. The resurrection of the One who bears our condemnation demonstrates the depth of God's love, which cannot be exhausted by our turning away from and rebelling against Life. "I hold the keys of death and Hades" declares the power by which all that stands against

God's work of creation is defeated, so that this world, ruled by death and destined for hades, is redeemed as creation.

The resurrection of the Crucified One reveals his conquest of death. We must be very careful here and allow our thinking and lives to be guided by the biblical witness and the gospel story. In the biblical passages that trumpet Jesus's defeat of death and the power of death, that defeat is located not in his resurrection but in his crucifixion:

> When you were dead in your sins and in the uncircumcision of your flesh, God made you alive with Christ. He forgave us all our sins, having canceled the charge of our legal indebtedness, which stood against us and condemned us; he has taken it away, nailing it to the cross. And having disarmed the powers and authorities, he made a public spectacle of them, triumphing over them by the cross. (Col. 2:13–15)

> Since the children have flesh and blood, he too shared in their humanity so that by his death he might break the power of him who holds the power of death—that is, the devil—and free those who all their lives were held in slavery by their fear of death. (Heb. 2:14–15)

These passages emphasize the defeat of death by the death of Christ.[31] Colossians says that Christ disarmed the principalities and powers and triumphed over them *by the cross*. Hebrews tells us that he broke the power of death *by his death*. This biblical witness may surprise us; it is difficult for us to imagine death defeated by death.

We may be helped to understand the defeat of death by Christ's death by recognizing that the world into which we are born is ruled by death. The world studied by the sciences is bounded by death. The world from which we seek to escape through *techne* is the world that ends in death. In each of these worlds, death is the ruler and the last word. Death is the power to be feared, to be avoided, or to be mastered. Jesus's death exposes each of these as a lie built on illusion guarded by phantoms. Only God is to be feared because only God has the power of life. Death is not to be avoided; it is the inevitable telos of the fallen world. But the fallen world is not the final and most real world. Creation redeemed is the most real world: the new creation. We enter it by trusting in God, not by avoiding death.

The last lie—that death is to be mastered—is the most difficult to expose and resist. If we believe that death is the ruler of the world, then we also believe that death is the most powerful force in the universe. Thus, we end up with a

31. I explore this imagery in more detail in Wilson, *God So Loved the World*, 83–97. This will be expanded in my forthcoming new Christology tentatively titled *Jesus Christ: Lord of Life and Light of the World*.

conflict that we cannot win. The only way to "defeat" death is by mastering the power of death—that is, by being more skilled in dealing out death than anyone else.[32] But as soon as we think that we have mastered death, death has mastered us by convincing us that there is no greater power than death. In seeking to master death, we perversely become enslaved to death. Jesus exposes that lie and the illusions that sustain it by refusing to take up the weapons of death in a doomed attempt to defeat death. In the face of death, he simply entrusts his life to the God who is Life. And so he triumphs over death and over the phantoms that sustain the illusion of death's final power.

Death has power; it is the power of the fallen world. Christ undergoes a real death, not a phantom death. He exposes the lie that death is the final and greatest power in the world by submitting to the limited power of death. The resurrection of the Crucified One is the vindication of his trust in God, the revelation of the power of life, the confirmation of Jesus's way as the way of life destined for the new creation and the justification of the universe.

This account provides us with a tentative construal of "deaths" according to this doctrine of creation. Is it possible that prior to our fall away from our telos as creation, death was the self-giving of creatures and creation that sustained life because it was grounded, sustained, and guaranteed by God's self-giving, which cannot be exhausted or overcome? In this (counterfactual) case, God the Son would have become incarnate to die, not for our sins, but to take death into the life of God so that death would be no more.[33] Death becomes the enemy of life when we turn from God as the ground and telos of life, so that death is no longer the self-giving that leads to life beyond death. Since we sinned in turning from God and from our telos, God the Son becomes incarnate to die for our sin, in order to redeem creation for the new creation.

"I hold the keys of death and Hades." When this world appears to us to be ruled by death; when death seems to be the key to the meaning of this world; when this world seems like hell; when this world seems to live on violence; when this world seems bound by fate—it is then that this triumphant shout of the glorious, crucified, and risen Jesus Christ reverberates throughout the cosmos as the good news of the redemption of creation for the telos of the new creation. He gave his life; he became servant of all; he trusted his life to its destiny in the God who is Life. He himself is the telos of the redemption of creation. This is the story of the most real world.

---

32. This is one way that technology is taken over by the principalities and powers in the fallen world and becomes a tool of *techne*, which is then manifested in the awe-inspiring, death-dealing weapons of the postmodern military.

33. I take the declaration of Rev. 21:4, "There will be no more death," to require an account of the telos of creation that does not include death.

9

Whatever Happened to Worldliness?

The Christian tradition in which I came to faith in Christ gave me a very strong and clear consciousness of "the world" as a reality that opposed Christ and posed a danger to my faith and my faithfulness. Bible verses such as the following still come easily to mind:

> Love not the world, neither the things that are in the world. If any man love the world, the love of the Father is not in him. (1 John 2:15 KJV)

> And be not conformed to this world: but be ye transformed by the renewing of your mind, that ye may prove what is that good, and acceptable, and perfect, will of God. (Rom. 12:2 KJV)

Of course, we also knew

> For God so loved the world, that he gave his only begotten Son, that whosoever believeth in him should not perish, but have everlasting life. (John 3:16 KJV)

We brought these two dispositions toward the world together in a strong account of the world and worldliness and in a passionate commitment to evangelism. As important and long-lasting as these commitments have been in my life and should be throughout the disciple community, it took quite some time for me to sort through the mistaken ways that these were taught, practiced, and imposed. It is very easy to see only the mistakes and throw out

199

the central and essential insights of this teaching. It has been commonplace for those who grew up in fundamentalism and even conservative evangelicalism to slip free of the "chains" and prejudices and limitations of the ways that those traditions identified the world and worldliness.

In reaction to those mistakes, we have often allowed the pendulum to swing to the opposite extreme, where we have no conception of a world that is opposed to Christ and that poses a danger to Christian faithfulness. Whereas a conception of "world" and "worldliness" shaped the lives, ministry, and mission of previous generations of Christians, today we are concerned with engaging culture, making culture, and shaping culture. Without a clear and well-established doctrine of the world derived from a robust doctrine of creation, our engaging, making, and shaping culture makes us profoundly vulnerable to ideologies, to principalities and powers eager to exploit religious communities for alien purposes.

To provide some impetus for beginning a recovery of a more mature doctrine of the world and worldliness grounded in a doctrine of creation, I will first acknowledge the limitations and mistaken identifications of worldliness in some of the earlier traditions; then I will argue for a recovery of a proper and robust understanding of worldliness rooted in the trinitarian grammar of creation and the dialectic of the kingdom.

In the denomination in which I was born and raised, Free Will Baptist, I remember a very clear delineation of worldliness that was mostly focused on behavior and appearance.[1] For instance, when hippies and rock stars began wearing wire-rim glasses as a signifier of their subculture, we denounced the wearing of wire-rim glasses as worldly and approved the wearing of horn-rim glasses. All of us knew, of course, that the pictures of the early founders of the denomination portrayed them in wire-rim glasses. But fashions changed, and keeping apart from the world required some changing rules. Likewise, when bell-bottom pants became fashionable, they were proscribed at our denominational Bible college. Dancing and consuming alcohol were hardly worth mentioning as worldly since they were so obviously worldly.

But when the smoke rises, the picture begins to blur. In the northern United States, Free Will Baptists regarded smoking as worldly and sinful. In the southern states, however, the porches of Free Will Baptist churches might be filled with smokers, including deacons, in between Sunday school and the worship service. But mixed swimming (that is, men and women swimming together)?

1. I have elsewhere written about my gratitude for my Free Will Baptist heritage. Here is another side to my memory of that heritage. For my gratitude, see Wilson, *Gospel Virtues*, 137–38; *God So Loved the World*, 183–86. These brief passages reflect only a part of my gratitude for the formation that I received from Free Will Baptists.

In the North acceptable; in the South worldly and sinful. The denomination lived well with these and other tensions. For me, the differences in judgment led not to indifference on my part but rather to a deep sense that something called "the world" mattered a lot.

At the same time, the particular way that the world was identified made less and less sense. I was born in 1951, and until I was twenty-four most of my years were spent in Arkansas and Tennessee. I became quite sensitive to the pervasive racism of society. I worried about the Vietnam war and unquestioned support for it in my denomination. While I was a student at the denominational Bible college, I was simultaneously visiting recruiters for the various branches of the armed forces and writing and performing an antiwar poetry program for my Bible college speech class. I became quite cynical about the behavioral standards that protected us from worldliness; I dropped out of the Bible college in the middle of my junior year. After God reclaimed me when I was twenty-one, I returned to the Bible college and was untroubled by the behavioral and appearance standards. However, I was deeply troubled by the church's silence on racism, nationalism, and as I would now put it, sexism. To me, it seemed that these things were not about political correctness but about gospel faithfulness. They were ways of the world that deeply infected a church that was completely unaware of its disease. I was also quite troubled by the way that church politics was conducted, with the chief characteristics being plotting, gossip, innuendo, and power-mongering.

These things, it seemed to me, were signs of a worldliness more profound and dangerous than dress, music, hairstyle, and other markers. Many others of my generation from similar traditions came to the same conviction. As a result, we simply dispensed with the categories "world" and "worldliness." Many of us stayed in the church and were careful not to pass on to our children any concerns about "the world." Instead of the world, we now concern ourselves with something called "culture." And who wants to be against culture?

This left later generations of Christians, such as the undergraduate students whom I taught for many years, with no theological category called "world" to help guide them through life. They had categories like "culture" and "culture wars," as well as political and economic markers to help them distinguish friends and foes. Although they used "Christian" words for these purposes, they had nothing theological, nothing grounded in the gospel, and certainly nothing grounded in a doctrine of creation.

Even among evangelical scholars, I am amazed by the seductive power of "culture" as a more dominant category than "world." Surely the basic theological question about cultures and cultural artifacts is the extent to which they are captive to the "world" and captivate us in "worldliness." But that assertion begs for an explication of the world and worldliness that is grounded in the doctrine of creation and the recovery of the telos of the redemption of creation in the new creation.

As I have been arguing, one consequence of a shallow, immature doctrine of the world and account of worldliness is capitulation to the world. Another consequence is retreat from the world. Christians often retreat from "the world" when they begin to recognize or fear that their doctrine of the world and their account of worldliness cannot compete with the allure of the world and its power to describe "reality."[2] In some ways, this describes the history of fundamentalism in North America from roughly 1925 to 1950. This retreat did give them some protection and provided them with room to develop their own networks and strengthen their ministries.[3] But it took a variety of forces—Youth for Christ, Billy Graham, a few scholars, and Carl Henry's *Uneasy Conscience of Modern Fundamentalism*—to bring some of them back into the mainstreams of society. Other fundamentalists did not return to the mainstream but remained in their retreats where they could sustain an account of the world and worldliness that perpetuated their identity but no longer pertained to the world and worldliness that had grown and taken new shape in American culture.[4]

This history, however, should not distract us from the main concern here: to understand the dynamics that underlay previous accounts of the world and worldliness and the reasons for the absence of concern about the world and worldliness today. Due to a shallow theology of the world and worldliness, some who were formed in that tradition abandoned any concern with a doctrine of the world and worldliness. Many of them replaced "the world" with a concern for "culture." Others who were formed by earlier, shallow conceptions of the world and worldliness retreated from "the world" and have maintained a strong account of the world that has little significance for understanding "the world" today.

In the previous chapter, I interpreted "the world" according to various claims that have been made about the world and sought to bring those claims and the world that they describe under the rule of God through the work of the redemption of creation. The "world," then, as I am using it here, is all

---

2. See Borgmann, *Holding On to Reality*, for an illuminating study of the "nature" of reality.

3. It is important to note that they were separating from "the world." They were not "against culture." Indeed, in their separation from "the world," fundamentalists created a vibrant culture of institutions, practices, arts, and more.

4. Today, the best accounts of the world and worldliness do not come from fundamentalists, who have mostly capitulated to one version of American culture that ensnares them in the world. The best accounts come from Stanley Hauerwas.

things in creation, visible and invisible, that has not recognized and submitted to God's work of redeeming creation, which we may also describe as "the lordship of Jesus Christ."

This description of the world does not require us to have equivocal definitions of the world to account for the variety of New Testament statements about it:

"God so loved the world . . ." (John 3:16).

"In the world you face persecution. But take courage; I have conquered the world" (John 16:33 NRSV).

"Do not love the world or the things in the world" (1 John 2:15 NRSV).

"Do not be conformed to this world . . ." (Rom. 12:2 NRSV).

"In Christ God was reconciling the world to himself" (2 Cor. 5:19 NRSV).

"Adulterers! Do you not know that friendship with the world is enmity with God?" (James 4:4 NRSV).

These passages may create an apparent conflict for some that leads to real confusion, but the conflict is only apparent. If we know that "the world" describes powers and creatures that have their being and life by the gift of God, then we may also describe them as enemies of God because they have turned from their God-created telos. And we may also know that they are simultaneously loved by God and servants of God because they have been reconciled—aligned rightly in relationship—to God.[5]

In light of a trinitarian doctrine of creation and the dialectic of the kingdom, we may say then that worldliness is living as if the claims of the world and the rule of death have not been publicly humiliated and defeated by Christ. This description does not give us tidy, concrete examples of worldliness. But that is precisely its strength. We must always be discerning the claims and allure of the world in our particular circumstances globally, nationally, societally, communally, and personally. (This list is not meant to be exhaustive but rather to indicate that "the world" operates on many levels.) This discernment of the world requires a continual process located in communities of disciples and grounded in a robust doctrine of creation.

Differing circumstances require differing accounts of the way that the world is at work as the servant of death. I am well aware that my construal of the world in the previous chapter is almost entirely directed toward European cultures. If I were writing my account in the context of village life in northern

5. Readers should recall that in one sense—the sense that I am using here—reconciled means the enactment of judgment about their proper relationship to God: do they serve death or life?

India, it would be very different. But the same is true of change within a particular culture or society. We must give concrete accounts of how the world is manifest in North America today and on various levels of life in North America. But we must never think that one particular account is good for all times and places, no matter how perceptive and persuasive it is. The work of giving concrete descriptions of the world and worldliness is the responsibility of sermons, the practices of the church, and work that is done under the rubric of "critique of culture."[6]

Although my accounts of the world and worldliness are broadly drawn in this context, I can identify some of the traps that we must avoid while we recover an account of the world and worldliness. Some may rebel against the claim that this world is the way that things are supposed to be and always will be because they cannot accept the suffering, injustice, and oppression of this world. But in their rebellion, they may unintentionally capitulate to this world by allowing it to circumscribe their strategies, tactics, and weapons. In other words, if we try to change this world by working within the limits set by this world and with the powers offered by the world, then we have in fact capitulated to the world.

There is no way out of this conundrum except through a robust doctrine of creation that leads to a robust understanding of the world as an enemy of God and thus also of life. This does not mean that we should be cynical or passive in the face of suffering, injustice, and oppression. It means rather that the one ground of hopeful action is belief in the Father, the Son, and the Spirit, whose purposes are for life.

To provide a full account of this world and our proper response to its suffering, injustice, and oppression, we must also understand that a robust doctrine of creation always understands that creation is reconciled to God and redeemed through Jesus Christ. Thus, a proper account of the world testifies to the reality that Jesus Christ has overcome the world through the strategies, tactics, and weapons of the kingdom of God—that is, love, obedience, forgiveness, sacrifice. The "world" has already been decisively changed for all eternity. With a robust doctrine of creation redeemed and reconciled, we are called to participate in that reality and bear witness to it through Christian love, obedience, forgiveness, and sacrifice. We betray this belief and calling when we "love" the world by fighting with its weapons, when we allow the imperatives of the world to set the boundaries for our actions, when we believe

6. Although I am critical of the ways that "culture" has replaced "world," much good is still done by a theological critique of culture. I particularly recommend the work of Julian Hartt, Stanley Hauerwas, and Wendell Berry. See also McClendon and Murphy, *Systematic Theology*, vol. 3: *Witness*.

that the weakness of forgiveness leads to death, and when we think that we save our lives by gaining the world.

Without an account of the world in rebellion against God, the way things are today becomes "natural." In this development, *nature* simply tells us the way things are and the limits on our actions. We may be able to modify nature for good or for ill, but those modifications take place within the horizons set by nature itself. So diseases, famines, floods, and the like are "natural disasters" that are simply the processes of life. In this way of thinking and living, "life" is simply subject to death.[7]

In this way of thinking, we also come to believe and act as if the only way to overcome these death-dealing aspects of life were to discover the mechanisms of nature that we can take over and control. In the history of this development, we moved from (1) creation, in which we looked to the Creator and Redeemer to heal a rebellious and fallen creation and save us from that fate, to (2) nature, in which we looked to science to explain the mechanisms of the world and save us from death, to (3) virtuality, in which we look to technology to create an alternative reality to the one ruled by death.

The great, pending tragedy for our society is that we Christians should have a lively, disruptive, alternative account of reality created not by our technology but given by the Triune Creator and Redeemer. We should be able to identify "the world" as the place where rebellion against God and the idolatry of the human has led to meaninglessness, anxiety, and death. But we do not have such a witness. We squander time and energy with petty concerns and fight with the weapons of the world. So our life and witness are defeated even as they begin because our own life and testimony are circumscribed by the boundaries of "the world." We are not grounded in a robust doctrine of creation that helps us understand the world as the world.[8]

In addition to these practices that reveal our worldliness, our captivity to the world may also be revealed in our character. Paul's many catalogs of Christian character and behavior describe this for us in some detail. The fruit of *pneuma* that grows with our participation in the redemption of creation contrasts with the acts of *sarx* that mark our subjugation to the world (Gal. 5:13–26). The character of the old self, captive to the lies of the world, must be shed, and we

---

7. In this paragraph I use *nature* in a carefully defined way to identify the error that takes the way things are today as the way things are meant to be—this situation is just "natural." I am not referring to the theological discussions of nature and grace. Those discussions use *nature* to refer to something altogether different from what I have in mind in this chapter.

8. In chap. 8, I pursued this task of knowing the world as the world and bearing witness to the world that it is the world: in rebellion against God and thus subject to death, loved by God and thus reconciled to God in Christ.

must put on a new self formed by the telos of the kingdom (Eph. 4:17–5:20, especially 5:5). And the life that we now live as "new creation" and in "new creation" is still grounded in earthly realities, but completely taken over by the story of the redemption of creation in contrast to the story of the world and its powers (Col. 3:1–17). These are familiar passages in which we often miss the dynamic that drives these contrasting ways of life. On the one hand are those who believe the lies of this world: its claims to power and lordship. These live according to *sarx*. On the other hand are those who believe the truth of Jesus Christ: in him the one God—Father, Son, and Spirit—acts to redeem creation for the new creation. These live according to *pneuma*. One is the way of the world that leads to death; the other is the way of the kingdom that leads to life.

Worldliness is not a trivial matter that concerns human rules: "Do not handle! Do not taste! Do not touch!" (Col. 2:21). Rather, worldliness is foolish, indulgent captivity to the claim that the way things are is the way they always have been and always will be. Therefore, you should submit your life to the way of the world so that you may enjoy life while you can. Little do the worldly know that they are dead, already in the depths of the grave (Prov. 9).

10

Consuming Desire

I n my own life, I find the power and habits of a society of consumption so deeply ingrained in me that I am often enslaved to a desire for "stuff."[1] I need a radical change in the way I look at the world in order to break free from the chains of consumption and become a more faithful disciple. In other words, I need God's grace to empower me to repent—to change the way I think and live. I need this personally as a disciple of Jesus Christ, and we need it corporately as a community of disciples. To understand fully the repentance that God's grace works in us, we must first understand our circumstances.

We are consumers. Aren't we used to hearing this in North America and around the world? In fact, isn't it so familiar that we barely pause to notice it anymore? The accusation that we consume a disproportionate share of the world's resources is so much a part of our mental landscape that we simply absorb it and move on. It is like the old billboard advertisement that you don't even notice on your morning commute—until a new, visually shocking ad replaces the old.

Let's move beyond the familiar, ineffective "we are consumers" and "we consume a disproportionate share of resources." Here is a deeper and more deadly truth: *we are being consumed.*

Our lives are becoming thinner, shallower, and less abundant as a result of the deeper truth that the things that we think we are consuming are actually consuming us. We are becoming less human, even as we consume more and

---

1. Portions of this chapter were previously published in *Mosaic* (Fall 2008): 6–9. For a profound exploration of these themes, see Cavanaugh, *Being Consumed.*

more. And part of this deadly dynamic of consumption is that as we become less human, our anxiety rises and we frantically consume more. This sends us into a whirlpool of ever-deepening despair and anxiety.

The Old Testament prophet Joel describes in powerful, imaginative detail how waves of locusts strip the land bare of life.

> Hear this, you elders;
>   listen, all who live in the land.
> Has anything like this ever happened in your days
>   or in the days of your ancestors?
> Tell it to your children,
>   and let your children tell it to their children,
>   and their children to the next generation.
> What the locust swarm has left
>   the great locusts have eaten;
> what the great locusts have left
>   the young locusts have eaten;
> what the young locusts have left
>   other locusts have eaten.
>
> Joel 1:2–4

Joel's chilling recitation of the varieties of locusts describe lives stripped bare by successive waves of consumption. Those who sink into spiraling consumer debt know that same cycle of being stripped bare of life. So do those of us who can pay our bills and even give to the church, but whose lives are consumed by advertisements, sales flyers, internet shopping, and the desire for things.

This dynamic is the reason that things never satisfy—and why we still pursue them even when we have experienced that disappointment.

So:

We are consumers.
We are being consumed.

Here is an even deeper and deadlier truth:

We are consuming others.

The message of Deuteronomy, the prophets, Jesus, and Paul is that when we participate in unjust patterns of consumption, we are devouring others. We are consuming their lives in the way that we live ours. To express it in a shocking image, we are cannibalistic.

This disturbing image and its truth are reality for us today in the midst of a world marked by increasing insecurity about food and water. This is true in many of the ways that we in the West both produce (grow?) food and distribute it.[2] It is also true in our use of water in manufacturing and our attempts to recapture it.

The message of Deuteronomy, the prophets, Jesus, and Paul is also that God will not tolerate injustice because it is contrary to life. Injustice destroys our lives; it destroys others' lives. Justice is not an arbitrary rule dictated by a capricious God; justice is the order of things that leads to human flourishing and, indeed, the flourishing of all creation. Justice aligns us with God and the life that God has created.

At this point you may be thinking about and expecting an account of "just consumption." That is, you may be looking for me to give an account of how we can participate in a "Society of Consumption" as disciples of Jesus Christ in a way that is just and promotes a just order.

But it is wrong for followers of Jesus Christ to think that we can simply make our way within a society of consumption and make the best of it given what we have. To think this way is to accept the fallen order of things; it is the opposite of "repent and believe the good news: the kingdom is at hand."

To repent—change our way of thinking and living—and begin to serve and witness to the kingdom of God, we must turn from an "economy of consumption" to an "economy of communion." As long as our vision, our thinking, our longing, and our acting is framed by an economy of consumption and a view of ourselves as consumers, we cannot break free from our enslavement to our present, consumptive way of "life"—which is in reality a way of death.

The phrase "economy of communion" is not common. I hope that it shocks us out of our complacent consumptive lifestyle. What a strange notion, "economy of communion." What could it mean?

To repent—to change our view of ourselves from consumer to communer—we must begin where the economy of communion is memorialized and entered into today: the Lord's Supper. Here we learn that life is sustained not by competition and consumption but by gift and communion.

That's right: every breath I take, every beat of my heart, the continuing knitting together of the molecules in my body, all of this depends on God's grace climactically enacted in the gift of Jesus Christ for the redemption of creation. Jesus Christ exposes the taking and keeping practices of the world that lead to death. He humiliates them and defeats them. In doing so, he reveals the overflowing giving and receiving that is life: the LIFE of the one God—Father, Son, and Spirit—and the life of creation redeemed.

2. See Pollan, *Omnivore's Dilemma*; Wirzba, *Food and Faith*.

"Bottled"

Jesus Christ is God the Son communing with humankind fully—even to the point of bearing our sin, including our injustice and our consumptive lives. In that economy of communion we are forgiven, redeemed, reconciled, adopted, and given abundant, eternal life.

An economy of communion begins with the recognition that my life is a gift from God not a human achievement. Life is sustained by God's grace not by human effort. Life is not a zero-sum game in which I am competing for limited resources. True life is abundant and eternal.

As we have seen, that economy of communion is the reality of God's own eternal life. Without beginning or end, God lives by communing as Father, Son, and Holy Spirit. The Father is "father" because of his relationship with the Son—that's what makes him Father. And the Son is "son" because of his relationship with the Father. And Father and Son are united by the power of the Holy Spirit, whose relationship with the Father and Son is the manifestation of their love for each other. In other words, God lives eternally by the giving of the Father, Son, and Holy Spirit in communion.

Therefore, when followers of Jesus Christ move from an economy of consumption to an economy of communion, we move more deeply into an understanding of the work of Christ and the life of the Triune God. Jesus's prayer in John 17 describes this deepening and, after praying for the disciples present with him, Jesus concludes:

> My prayer is not for them alone. I pray also for those who will believe in me through their message, that all of them may be one, Father, just as you are in me and I am in you. May they also be in us so that the world may believe that you have sent me. I have given them the glory that you gave me, that they may be one as we are one—I in them and you in me—so that they may be brought to complete unity. Then the world will know that you sent me and have loved them even as you have loved me.
>
> Father, I want those you have given me to be with me where I am, and to see my glory, the glory you have given me because you loved me before the creation of the world.
>
> Righteous Father, though the world does not know you, I know you, and they know that you have sent me. I have made you known to them, and will continue to make you known in order that the love you have for me may be in them and that I myself may be in them. (John 17:20–26)

This is the life and love that overcomes the world and participates in creation redeemed (John 1:5; 16:33; Rom. 12:21).

What I have described as the economy of consumption—consuming, being consumed, and consuming others—is what was happening on a local level in the church at Corinth almost two thousand years ago. As I have done, Paul addressed the Corinthian disciples on the basis of their celebration of the Lord's Supper (1 Cor. 10:14–22; 11:17–34). Admittedly, Christians bound by consumption take communion every day in various places around the world. What we need is a renewed understanding and practice of the Eucharist that recognizes and embodies our conviction that as we eat and drink we are receiving the gift and life of creation through Christ's work of redemption.[3]

We must refuse to let the world press us into the mold of an economy of consumption. Instead, we must be transformed by God's economy of communion. When this happens, we will grow in our recognition that God is life, and we will learn to confess with the psalmist, "Whom have I in heaven but you? / And earth has nothing I desire besides you. / My flesh and my heart may fail, / but God is the strength of my heart and my portion forever" (Ps. 73:25–26).

God's economy of communion means that we will seek to live ever more deeply in communion with the life of the Triune God. The consumptive desires that have ruled our lives will fade away. The energy that we have misdirected toward illusions and counterfeit pleasures will be redirected toward the good life for which God has created and redeemed us and has shown us in the way of Jesus Christ.

As our desires are purified and as we participate more fully in Christ (1 Cor. 10:16), we will grow in knowing that our life is guaranteed for eternity by the life, death, and resurrection of Jesus Christ. The presence of the Holy Spirit in us is the sign, seal, and down payment on that promise.

God's economy of communion means that we who are guaranteed eternal life can joyfully give our lives in generosity and hospitality to others. In an economy of consumption, such generosity would be either a manipulative act from which I expect to receive more in return or else an act in which I ultimately extinguish or destroy myself. But in God's economy of communion, such self-giving is an act of communion in which my true life in Christ flourishes.

Finally, if God's economy of communion transforms my vision, my attitude, and my way of living, then I will always live in communion with other disciples of Jesus Christ. I will be conscious of their presence with me when I shop, when I eat, when I plan my vacation, my professional travel, my giving to the church. If I am truly being transformed, this consciousness will not be merely a dialogue that goes on in my head; it will be a reality practiced in my everyday relationships when I invite others to participate with me and examine me as I seek to be transformed.

3. For further reflection, see Schmemann, *For the Life of the World*; Cavanaugh, *Torture and Eucharist*; Wilson, *Why Church Matters*, 109–12.

But our circumstances are even more tragic than those I have just described. Today, we no longer live solely or perhaps even primarily in a culture of consumption. Today, we live in a culture of desire. What we know as "the consumer society" was characterized by the abundance of goods in which our business was sought and our purchasing power flourished. Now as a society we have more than we need, even when that more is shrinking. Therefore, it is no longer our business that is sought; now our desire is cultivated. To cultivate our desire for things that we don't need, the market (that is, advertisers, shops, catalogs, newspapers, magazines, and television) has developed skills and practices to an exquisite precision.

In *Merchants of Cool*, a *Frontline* documentary, the filmmakers chronicle the work of "cool hunters."[4] These "cool hunters" are market researchers who seek out the trendsetters among young people and study their choices in music, food, and clothing. Then they develop marketing programs to sell these images of cool to other young people. The techniques used to capture and market "cool" are astonishing in their sophistication. The amount of money devoted to the process is even more astonishing.

Of course, it is not just youth who are the victims of the marketing of desire. All of us are targets in the new global market. Our desires are continually being formed by television commercials, magazine covers, newspaper ads, email spam, internet pop-ups, and more. But it is not just these obvious means that cultivate and nourish desire. That same counterfeiting of true desire takes place insidiously in movies, television shows, novels, and music.

The first time I saw *Merchants of Cool*, I was depressed and discouraged. I thought, "There's no way for the church to counter the skills and money of these marketers." They are the modern equivalent of wizards and witches, weaving their spells to ensnare us. I concluded that a generation of young people all over the globe was lost to the gospel.

Then I remembered the power of the Holy Spirit to convict us and bring us to faith. And in discussions with pastors, especially youth pastors, I learned of the continued longing for something more than "cool." Teenagers (and the rest of us) want real friendships that do not take life from us but rather give life to us.

But it is not enough simply to repeat, "The Holy Spirit will help us" and "People long for something that only God can provide." We must not simply denounce consumerism and desire. We do not encourage discipleship by saying, "Don't consume, don't desire." Our consuming and desiring will not come to an end by simple command, primarily because our needs and desires are

4. *Merchants of Cool*, WGBH Educational Foundation, 2001.

rooted in our God-created nature. Yes, we usually mistake what it is that we desire, but the Christian answer is not the suppression of our longings but their fulfillment. As C. S. Lewis reminds us,

> If we consider the unblushing promises of reward and the staggering nature of the rewards promised us in the Gospels, it would seem that our Lord finds our desires not too strong but too weak. We are half-hearted creatures, fooling about with money and sex and ambition when infinite joy is offered us, like an ignorant child who wants to go on making mud pies in a slum because he cannot imagine what is meant by the offer of a holiday at the sea. We are far too easily pleased.[5]

We have been given many resources—education, health, money, technology. We are going to do something with them. We will settle for the wonders of the false desires and the illusory needs of the market unless we find something greater, something more marvelous and glorious to command our resources.

That is what the church has been given in the gospel of Jesus Christ. This good news of God's redemption of creation through the sending of his Son is our joy and our desiring. This gospel is the true longing of all creation. As Jesus declares in the parables of the hidden treasure and the pearl of great price (Matt. 13:44–45), this kingdom is worth all that we have.

Stewardship, then, is not simply a matter of some adjustments in our spending habits. Rather, stewardship begins with a radical transformation in our vision and our hearts. In the midst of "the marketplace of desire," what can we do as the church to transform our vision and "counter-cultivate" our hearts?

Some simple suggestions: reduce your exposure to the marketing of desire by avoiding mail-order catalogs unless you have a specific need. Don't browse in shops—even if you purchase nothing, you are cultivating desire. Don't browse on the internet; don't bookmark online retailers; don't subscribe to RSS feeds for retailers. Limit or reduce television viewing. Mute the commercials—or better mock them and turn product placement in TV shows and movies into another source of laughter. Don't read the sale flyers that appear in your mailbox or newspaper. Don't talk about your recent purchases with friends; or, alternately, commit to talking about them so that your friends can hold you accountable.[6]

But even more important, establish habits that transform your vision and cultivate other desires. Instead of going to a mall, regularly volunteer at a homeless shelter or other service agency. Learn about the persecution of Christians and others through websites. Gather a group of friends or family who will

5. Lewis, *Weight of Glory*, 26.
6. For more help, read Kenneson, *Life on the Vine*.

join with you in resisting the counterfeit and second-rate needs and desires offered by our society. Discuss with them what resources you have (tangible and intangible), then discern together how those resources may be directed toward God-given longings. Bookmark alternative internet news sites; connect with news about Christians around the world; follow sites that cultivate a communion vision of the world.

Begin to think carefully about how the various activities of the church are meant to reorient the desires of our hearts. Then become explicit in directing those practices toward the cultivation of lives that desire God and his kingdom above all else. Read regularly through the psalms and learn from them what we should desire. (Psalm 73 is a personal favorite.) Consider the blessings of the beatitudes (Matt. 5). Write "advertising copy" that promotes those desires and promises, not the blessing of a new car or a fine meal or fancy clothes, but the blessing that comes from a longing for the kingdom.[7] As our vision and our hearts are transformed radically, lives of faithful stewardship will follow.

7. See my practice of this in Wilson, *Gospel Virtues*, 88–95.

11

Stories, Practices, Prayers

I f the work of the Father, the Son, and the Spirit is the work of redeeming creation for its telos in the new creation, in the midst of a world that has fallen away from its telos, turning from life to death, then we who believe that the Father, the Son, and the Spirit redeem creation for the new creation live with tensions and difficulties.[1] One of the most significant is what is traditionally called the problem of evil. Another way to state the challenge to Christian convictions is to call it the problem of suffering. There are many complications when we look closely at these "problems": the problems of natural and moral evils, the problems of just and unjust suffering. The challenges are also diverse.[2]

Humankind has wrestled with these issues for ages, so I am certainly not going to resolve the problems and the disagreements here. My modest aim is to propose and develop a way of thinking and living in the midst of evil and suffering in a way that is congruent with the trinitarian grammar of creation

1. Although I do not often note it in the text, this chapter is largely a meditation on what I learned from my wife, Marti, who suffered from Gaucher disease, a lifelong, hereditary, degenerative disease that disabled her in 1999 while she was serving as Assistant Registrar at Westmont College. Marti died on September 16, 2010, at age sixty-two. We learned so much in our life together. I am grateful, sorrowful, and living in hope.

2. Because I take a different approach, I will note four books that look at somewhat more traditional ways of considering the problem of evil, though each is also creative. Tilley, *Evils of Theodicy*; Surin, *Theology and the Problem of Evil*; Stackhouse, *Can God Be Trusted?*; Plantinga, *God, Freedom, and Evil*.

and the dialectic of the kingdom that I have presented here. My proposal is not unique; it is rooted in belief that God's work of creation is nourished by a robust account of the dialectic of the kingdom and fluent trinitarian grammar. When we bring these two together, we recognize that a Christian doctrine of creation must be christological and eschatological. That is, since any Christian account of creation must include the redemption of creation, any account of creation must also be grounded in the source and power of its redemption: the work of the Triune God in Jesus Christ. Also grounded in this conviction of the redemption of creation, any understanding of creation must be teleological, eschatological, and apocalyptical.[3] Each of these points is a different way to the completion of the redemption of creation in the new creation.

Taking these markers as our guide, we may now begin to approach an account of Christian thinking and living in the midst of evil and suffering. In light of my account of creation, we may say that Christian faithfulness in the midst of evil comprises two stories, two practices, and two prayers. The stories are those of the fallen world and of creation. The practices are presence and patience. The prayers are "How long?" and "Maranatha." None of these constitutes an answer to the problems of the various evils. They are not grounded in the philosophical challenges to which we must respond, nor do they correlate with questions of the world. Rather, they call the disciple community into the story of the redemption of creation so that we may enter more fully into life and bear witness to the good news of life in the God who creates and redeems.

Two Stories

I have been telling these two stories throughout this book: (1) the story of the fallen world, turned away from the telos of creation that is life, and (2) the story of creation, redeemed for the telos of life in the new creation. One of the large obstacles to Christian faithfulness in the midst of evil is that we have not often distinguished these two stories. Instead, we have tried to make sense of the world and of the call to Christian discipleship on the basis of one or the other of these stories.

If we focus on the story of the fallen world, as if some account of the fall, its origin, and its logic can explain the presence of evil and guide our thinking and living, then we will be trapped in the logic and the story of the fallen world. In this case, the fallen world sets the terms of the argument and the

---

3. I use the rare form "apocalyptical" rather than "apocalyptic" in part to parallel the forms of the other descriptions, but mostly to jar readers out of the usual connotations of the word "apocalyptic."

limits of explanation and of life in the midst of evil. When we follow this story as an explanation for evil, then evil makes sense of the world. We are offered the world of the *Enuma Elish* as the way things always have been and always will be. We may try to turn this story into another story or make it come out differently, but as long as we think that the fallen world is the primary or exclusive setting for our account of evil, then the fallen world wins. It is the most real world, and any other "world" becomes subordinate to the fallen world.

If we focus on the story of the redemption of creation to the exclusion of the fallen world, which has not occurred often in the history of Christianity, then we end up with an account of evil that separates it from creation and sequesters the redemption of creation in its own transcendent realm that transports us away from the fallen world. Such an account may be pursued by limiting "the redemption of creation" to one part of creation, such as the inner life of humans. Evil, then, is transformed when believers' hearts are changed. Or we may limit "the redemption of creation" to a separate slice of history—the "history of salvation"—that leaves most of history untouched. In effect, we reduce the "redemption of creation" to a reality that is smaller than the world, often because we do not think that the gospel of Jesus Christ is big enough to account for the redemption of all creation, let alone bigger than all creation.

If we tell these two stories well, we may give an account of Christian faithfulness to the redemption of creation that reflects the cosmic significance of the incarnation, crucifixion, and resurrection of Jesus Christ, which brings into being the church and guarantees and empowers the new creation. This account acknowledges the reality and power of evil and the logic of the fallen world. We can make a certain sense of the world as it is, ruled by death. But we also know through the Spirit, by whom we believe in Christ, that this story of death is part of a larger story. The reality of the redemption of creation for the new creation is the larger story. The story of the fallen world and death is the smaller story; it is the story that is limited and constrained. Instead of an explanation for evil, we have the story in which evil is revealed to be finally a weak, defeated power, a power whose wounds and devastation will one day be undone. Again, evil makes sense in the fallen world, and any explanation that makes sense of evil leaves the fallen world in place and in control. Only the story of the redemption of creation reveals the truth about evil and its defeat.

Two Practices

If we bring these two stories together in our thinking and living in the midst of evil, then we will be called to two practices: presence and patience. These practices are possible as Christian practices only by the grace of God—that is, by our participation in the redemption of creation that comes by faith in Jesus Christ.

To be present in the midst of evil is to follow Christ, the Word made flesh, who promised that he would never leave us, that he would be present with us to the end of this age. The incarnation is not some new turn in God's disposition toward humankind and the fallen world. The incarnation *is* a new way of God's being present, but it is a coherent continuation of the story of the God who seeks out the first humans in the garden after their sin (Gen. 3), who comes to Abram and calls him (Gen. 12), who appears to Moses and comes down to deliver the Israelites from Egypt (Exod. 3). This same "condescension" climaxes in the Messiah, Jesus of Nazareth, and will be consummated in God's condescension to dwell with redeemed humankind in the new creation (Rev. 21). God is present with us in the midst of evil but in that very presence transforms the reality of evil, humiliating it, and triumphing over it in the crucifixion of Jesus.

If we locate our practice of presence in the redemption of creation, then we place ourselves in Christ and know that we are already participating in the conquest of evil and the victory of life over death. But if we locate our practice of presence in the story of the fallen world, then we effectively remove ourselves from Christ. In this case, we are an anxious presence in the world and look for ways to overcome the world by the power and logic of that world. We may make some things better, but we will always live with a sense of defeat and failure that will drive us to greater anxiety and more frantic activity that deepens our quest for control of this world.

As a counter to this anxiety and frenzy, our participation in the redemption of creation forms a second practice: patience. The practice of patience also forms in us the virtue—that is, the godly character of patience. Patience is a primary mark of God's work in the world, as God took time to form a people through whom the Savior Messiah comes to us. And following the coming of the Messiah, God continues to work patiently. In the midst of the continuation of evil and the seeming lack of consequences for evildoers, we must remember Peter's words of instruction and encouragement:

> Above all, you must understand that in the last days scoffers will come, scoffing and following their own evil desires. They will say, "Where is this 'coming' he promised? Ever since our ancestors died, everything goes on as it has since the beginning of creation." But they deliberately forget that long ago by God's word the heavens came into being and the earth was formed out of water and by water. By these waters also the world of that time was deluged and destroyed.

By the same word the present heavens and earth are reserved for fire, being kept for the day of judgment and destruction of the ungodly.

But do not forget this one thing, dear friends: With the Lord a day is like a thousand years, and a thousand years are like a day. The Lord is not slow in keeping his promise, as some understand slowness. Instead he is patient with you, not wanting anyone to perish, but everyone to come to repentance. (2 Pet. 3:3–9)

If patience is the key to understanding God's own response to evil, then it must be the key to ours as well.[4]

But we must not understand patience as passivity or an excuse for inaction, denial, fatalism, or withdrawal. The same God who is patient is the one who became incarnate and dwelled with us, the one who proclaims healing and liberation, the one who denounces injustice. The key to the practice of presence and patience is locating ourselves within the story of God's redemption of creation, not within the rule of the fallen world. These practices and the virtues that they form and that in turn sustain faithful witness are formed in us over a long period of time.

Presence and patience are key elements of Christian faithfulness in any part of life when we are guided by a Christian doctrine of creation. The trinitarian grammar of creation teaches us that God is continually present to, with, and for creation without being consumed by creation. The dialectic of the kingdom tells us that redemption does not deliver us from creation but rather realigns the world with its proper telos, thus making it once again creation. So our participation in God's work of creation and redemption does not remove us from the world but thrusts us into the world with renewed life grounded in hope. Properly grounded in our participation in the redemption of creation, presence and patience do not deflect us from works of justice and mercy but orient the works properly to God's work and the promise of the new creation.

At the same time, because the power of our presence is our participation in the redemption of creation, we also seek to be patient in our presence, as Christ is formed in us and forms us into the disciple community by the presence and patience of the Holy Spirit. This may seem like an impossible dream, but let us remember that it is the exhortation and expectation of the New Testament:

Be joyful in hope, patient in affliction, faithful in prayer. (Rom. 12:12)

4. Those who are present in the midst of great, inexplicable suffering and horrors to care for victims are engaged in this practice and bearing witness by their presence even when the limitation of resources and circumstances allows them only to be present.

For this reason, since the day we heard about you, we have not stopped praying for you. We continually ask God to fill you with the knowledge of his will
through all the wisdom and understanding that the Spirit gives, so that you
may live a life worthy of the Lord and please him in every way: bearing fruit in
every good work, growing in the knowledge of God, being strengthened with all
power according to his glorious might so that you may have great endurance and
patience, and giving joyful thanks to the Father, who has qualified you to share
in the inheritance of his holy people in the kingdom of light. For he has rescued
us from the dominion of darkness and brought us into the kingdom of the Son
he loves, in whom we have redemption, the forgiveness of sins. (Col. 1:9–14)

Paul describes the dynamic of this practice and the process by which patience
is formed in us. The word (Gr., *hypomonēn*) translated "perseverance" here,
and "endurance" in the NRSV, is translated "patience" in the KJV. It is part
of the family of words that refers to the ability of believers to stay the course
of discipleship to Christ in a world that is in rebellion:

And we boast in the hope of the glory of God. Not only so, but we also glory
in our sufferings, because we know that suffering produces perseverance; perseverance, character; and character, hope. And hope does not put us to shame,
because God's love has been poured out into our hearts through the Holy Spirit,
who has been given to us. (Rom. 5:2–5)

This account by Paul acknowledges the reality of the fallen world but places
the life of believers in the story of the redemption of creation for the new
creation. This is what enables faithful presence and patience.[5]

Two Prayers

> How long, I AM? Will you forget me forever?
>   How long will you hide your face from me?
> How long must I wrestle with my thoughts
>   and day after day have sorrow in my heart?
> How long will my enemy triumph over me?
>   Psalm 13:1–2 (NIV slightly altered)

> He who testifies to these things says, "Yes, I am coming soon."
>   Amen. Come, Lord Jesus.
>   Revelation 22:20

---

5. In *Green Witness,* 153–60, Laura Yordy perceives and describes the relevance of patience
to Christian care for creation. See my complementary account below in chap. 12, "Blessed Are
the Meek."

These two passages represent the two prayers that Christians pray in the midst of the fallen world and in the face of evil as we learn to live in the redemption of creation. As representative, they sum up the way that we pray so that we may be further formed in presence and patience, but most of all so that we may bear witness to God.

"How long?" is the prayer of lament that reminds us that we live in the midst of a fallen world. It forces us to direct our doubts, struggles, anxieties, frenzy, and failure to God. When we ascribe to God the responsibility to act, we take the question of evil and suffering away from the story of the fallen world and the rule of death. We place evil and suffering within the story of the redemption of creation. Our lament is no longer centered in this world, on humankind, or on ourselves: When will we ever learn? What can we do in the midst of so much suffering and so few resources? What lies within our power? How can we change the world? When we pray, "How long?" our lament is properly centered on God, who alone brings life in the midst of death, who alone brings evil to account without doing evil, who alone changes the world not just for the better but for the new creation in Christ. Job's lament may be simply summed up in "How long, I AM?" His friends, however, remained steadfastly bound by the limits of this world. God condemns the friends and affirms Job, who has spoken rightly of God (Job 42:7–9).

"Come, Lord Jesus" (Aram., *Maranatha*) is the prayer of hope that reminds us that in the midst of the fallen world and the rule of death we are caught up into a greater story of the most real world: the redemption of creation for the new creation. This prayer orients us to the promise, the telos, of creation: life. In the midst of evil and suffering, we do not receive an explanation for their existence, nor can we discern progress toward their end or their defeat. Instead, when we pray, "Come, Lord Jesus," we are praying in other words, "Your kingdom come, your will be done, on earth as it is in heaven" (Matt. 6:10). This is an apocalyptic prayer. It teaches us that the redemption of creation does not arise from within any power or process native to creation. Creation is "apocalyptic" in its dependence on God, who is not any part of creation. The redemption of creation is also apocalyptic. The apocalypse of the redemption of creation is Jesus Christ. This work is apocalyptic, but it is not alien. We have seen already that all things are made by him, all things are sustained by his word, and all things are for his glory, even as this is the work of the Father, the Son, and the Spirit.

When we pray, "Come, Lord Jesus," we learn that we cannot read the redemption of creation from signs within the limits of the (fallen) world. To know God's work of creation and its redemption, we must be trained by the practices of the disciple community to see God present in Christ. We must pray this prayer even to begin to participate in the disciple community and to learn the discipline of Christ so that we may see the redemption of creation that rules over the fallen world and will one day bring it to its proper end. We pray, "Come, Lord Jesus" as a prayer for the realization of the telos of creation in new creation, but we also pray it in the midst of suffering and in the face of evil because we may enter into life today only by God answering this prayer, sending us the Spirit, and bringing us to life in Christ.

Maranatha. Come, Lord Jesus.

12

Blessed Are the Meek

Blessed are the meek,
    for they will inherit the earth.
                        Matthew 5:5

Refrain from anger and turn from wrath;
    do not fret—it leads only to evil.
For those who are evil will be destroyed,
    but those who hope in I AM will inherit the land.

A little while, and the wicked will be no more;
    though you look for them, they will not be found.
But the meek will inherit the land
    and enjoy peace and prosperity.
                    Psalm 37:8–11 (NIV altered slightly)

When we are considering the doctrine of creation in our present context, caring for creation is high on our agenda. Indeed, many of the books and articles about creation today focus primarily on this concern under such descriptions as eco-theology, environmental concerns, stewardship, and so forth. There are many issues to untangle and address in this discussion. Do we really want to refer to creation as "the environment"? Doesn't that term—"the environment"—remove God from our consideration of the things that we have in mind? That is, doesn't "the environment" place control of these things in our hands without reference to God? If we recognize that the cosmos is sustained by the work of Christ and that we live only because we are held within the life of the one Creator—Father, Son, and Spirit—who redeems this world as creation, then *environment* is a laughably weak description of our circumstances.

When we recognize that we live not in "the environment" but in creation-being-redeemed, we are beginning to become people who can receive and live the proclamation of the psalmist and of Jesus: "Blessed are the meek for they will inherit the earth." It is astonishing how little is written on this proclamation in our current literature on the "ecological crisis," even by Christians.[1] We are so caught in the web of the fallen world, the apparent explanatory power and control of the sciences, and the promises and imperatives of technology that we do not often pause to reflect on this proclamation.

The meek will inherit the earth. What would it take for us to understand and joyfully receive this as good news? It requires that we articulate, criticize, strengthen, and live a more robust doctrine of creation than we have for several centuries.

Before we consider the connection between meekness and inheriting the world, we must first give some attention to *meekness*. Against the misrepresentation of "gentle Jesus, meek and mild" and the easy equation of meekness with "Casper Milquetoast," the recovery of a proper understanding of meekness requires some work. Briefly, meekness is power under control. It is not an absence of power, nor is it an inability to act on the basis of one's power. Rather, meekness is the disposition of one who has power and who could act on the basis of that power but restrains or directs that power in such a way that the act of power is properly proportioned to the circumstance and the proper telos. Jesus himself is the one who teaches us the meekness that marks his disciples: "Come to me, all you who are weary and burdened, and I will give you rest. Take my yoke upon you and learn from me, for I am [meek] and humble in heart, and you will find rest for your souls. For my yoke is easy and my burden is light" (Matt. 11:28–30; the NIV translates the Greek *praus* as "meek" in Matt. 5:5 and "gentle" in Matt. 11:29; see also Matt. 21:5). In light of Jesus as our teacher of meekness, we know that meekness is not simply weakness or powerlessness. The Hebrew word *'ani*, translated meekness in Psalm 37, does refer to the poor or weak in the land. But when Jesus comes and identifies himself with those who appear poor and weak, he takes them

---

1. Bessenecker, *How to Inherit the Earth*, is helpful but focuses on interpersonal relationships more than on our relationship with the earth and other creatures. More helpful is McMinn and Neff, *Walking Gently on the Earth*.

out of the story of the world, in which they are indeed poor and weak, and places them in the kingdom of God, in which they are made strong by their participation in the telos of the new creation.

This meekness of Jesus teaches us that when we become participants in the story of the redemption of creation, we become "poor" and "weak" according to the story of the fallen world. By that story, we are fools to lay down our lives for our friends. We are crazy to direct our energies and abilities to the flourishing of others in Christ. We are deluded when we give up our comfort and security to be present and patient in the midst of suffering and the face of evil. According to the story of the fallen world, we should take all our power and serve ourselves and those who most closely share our lives.

In its everyday expression, meekness characterizes the person who could dominate a committee by his knowledge, human insight, and rhetorical skills, but holds back so that a community is formed and the committee becomes not an extension of one person's ego, but a place where all people and their gifts have room to flourish, and human communing becomes a reality. Meekness is the gifted vocalist who could soar above all the other voices in the choir and thrill us with the timbre, range, and versatility of her voice restraining herself to blend in with the other voices so that the choir may be heard as the uniting of diversity in pursuit of musical excellence. In neither of these cases is meekness a substitute for or an obstacle to excellence. Rather, meekness in all circumstances depends on discernment of the proper setting and its telos and orients power according to the discernment of the proper telos. This is the excellence of life in creation-being-redeemed.

To accept that meekness is the key to the future of creation requires us to think with discipline and depth about the life of the world. If the life of this world is the life that can be fully understood and explained from within the world and whose telos is circumscribed by death, then we might reasonably regard meekness as a vice rather than a virtue. We could think of meekness as a ploy used by clever people to convince us to restrain our power so that there is more space for their exercise of power. If we were to fall into the "trap" of meekness, we might discover our loss of power too late to reclaim it in society. Then we would be vulnerable politically, economically, militarily, and in every other way.[2] In this case, meekness fatally misreads our condition and

---

2. I take this to be in large part the target of Friedrich Nietzsche's scorn for Christianity as a religion for the weak. Of course, there's a paradox in this interpretation of Nietzsche: if on the one hand he truly believed that this world was only and entirely about power, then perhaps he should have kept silent about Christianity. On the other hand, if his own community was being made vulnerable by its capitulation to Christianity, then Nietzsche would have passionately sought to disabuse that community of its error and weakness.

"Sowing Seeds"

our context by teaching us to restrain our power rather than using it fully for our own survival and flourishing.

However, there is another way to respond to the conviction that this world is all that there is and ever will be, one that embraces the call to meekness. In this response, people recognize that the best way to survive and flourish is to join together the powers of many. Thus, the various powers of many are joined together for the collective good, which also enables the constituents to survive and flourish as part of the group more than each could on his or her own. This collectivism, the subordination of one's power to the interests of the group, might be described as a form of weakness. But in this scenario, the story of the fallen world remains in place and determines our actions. One of the tragedies today is that the church is so often captive to this story.[3]

In light of this reality, it is crucial to recognize that the declaration of Jesus that the meek will inherit the earth must be located within Jesus's story—that is, within the redemption of creation for the new creation. Jesus's declaration is not a promise to any putative form of meekness but is particular to the way of creation that leads to life. Meekness, then, is not simply the disposition to restrain one's power in order to conform to any telos. Rather, throughout Scripture and especially in the life and on the lips of Jesus, meekness is the disposition to restrain one's power so that it aligns with the redemption of creation for the new creation.

In the context of our circumstances, where we are rapidly losing many forms of life and much that is necessary to life and salutary for its flourishing, the tendency, indeed the obvious and seemingly essential thing to do, is to act as quickly and powerfully as we can to bring the situation under control. To put it baldly, we frantically seek to develop new scientific insights and technologies to rescue us from the consequences of our sciences and technologies.

Our situation, however, is a bit more complex than I have just described. It is not exactly our sciences and technologies that have led to our crises. Rather, it is our submission to this fallen world and its horizon, as well as our own complicity in the dysteleology of this world, that have led us to direct the sciences and technology along the path ruled by death while expecting them to save us. What we face is not fundamentally an environmental crisis that will yield to a scientific and technological solution. Rather it is a moral-spiritual-theological crisis that is resolved in the redemption of creation for the new creation.

That may sound like a call to inaction, to simply go on with our lives as they are and trust God to solve things and rescue us from the consequences of our—let's call it what it is—sin. Isn't that what God's grace is really all

---

3. See Wilson, *Living Faithfully*, 2nd ed., "Resisting the Nietzschean Temptation," 38–45.

about? For those who know Scripture, this should immediately call to mind Paul's dialogue with an imagined (or real) interlocutor in Romans 5–6. After describing the superabundance of grace over sin and of Christ's righteousness over human unrighteousness, Paul imagines a question: "Shall we go on sinning so that grace may increase? By no means! We are those who have died to sin; how can we live in it any longer?" (Rom. 6:1–2).[4] In this context, we may imagine someone reading my account of the superabundance of creation and of life rooted in the Father, the Son, and the Spirit. Given this assurance, shall we simply go on using life for our own purposes so that God's superabundant life may be all the more evident to the world? By no means! (Clarence Jordan/ Jonathan Wilson: "Hell, no!" To live that way really is to submit ourselves to hell.) Don't you know that in Christ we have died to the way of the fallen world, where it is thought that life consists in taking and keeping instead of receiving and giving? If we have died to that way, let us now live in the way of the new creation through the redemption of creation.

This story is the story of Jesus Christ, in whom we become participants through the work of the Holy Spirit. When we become participants in this story, we begin to learn what meekness means. We do not become powerless; our skills and abilities are not suddenly and irrecoverably obliterated. Rather, we begin the long discipline of becoming free from the enslavement of our powers, skills, and abilities to the story of the fallen world. At the same time, we are freed for the use of our powers, skills, and abilities for life in and witness to the already arriving new creation.

In Psalm 37, we receive more instruction in meekness. The declarations of the psalm and its promises regarding the prosperity of the righteous and the punishment of the evil only make sense from an eschatological perspective to which the psalmist points but does not develop. Meekness may be sustained by the grace of God only in those who have been captured by the vision of the new creation in Christ, so that they can resist the temptations to power that the fallen world regards as necessary, natural, and even unavoidable. Those who are meek are the ones who are so captivated by the telos of creation in the new creation and so sustained by life in the disciple community that they may be numbered with those in John's Revelation who follow the Lion of the tribe of Judah, who turns out to be the Lamb that was slain (Rev. 5). There may be no more powerful image of meekness than this: the lion is the lamb.

---

4. As I noted in chap. 2, Paul's rejoinder "By no means!" is a very strong construction in the Greek. In Clarence Jordan's Cotton Patch version of the letters, he puts it this way: "So what are we advocating? 'Let's wallow in sin, so more grace may pour forth'? Hell, no! How can we who died in sin still live in it?" (Rom. 6:1–2; Cotton Patch version of Romans, http://rockhay .tripod.com/cottonpatch/romans.htm#chapter06; accessed July 15, 2011).

Even as I write these words, it is difficult for me to believe that such a practice of meekness is possible or even desirable in the context of the many threats to the flourishing of life in this world. Such doubt is in large part the measure of how well formed I am (we are) in the ways of the modern and postmodern world. But meekness is not passivity or weakness. Rather, in Christian terms it is the discipline of our power and action by Christ, who is the telos of this world in the new creation. In the process of learning meekness, we must enter more fully into the conviction that creation is redeemed in Christ so that we do not act in a frantic and fearful way to postpone or overcome the fate of earth. Rather, as we are schooled in meekness, we learn that fate has become destiny in Christ, who is the life of the world. Knowing that our destiny is sure from before the foundation of the world, we gladly and joyfully submit our fear and frenzy to the transforming power of the Spirit.

Meekness, then, becomes another way in which Paul's exhortation is made real in us: "Do not conform to the pattern of this world, but be transformed by the renewing of your mind" (Rom. 12:2; just after he has described our bodies as a "living sacrifice"). When we are conformed to the pattern of this world, we seek to solve the problems of this world by using its tools within the limits of this world by the power that we are granted by it. Such action simply ensnares us in this world and its fate. When we are transformed by the renewing of our minds—by thinking differently on the basis of the mercies of God that Paul has declared in the previous chapters in Romans—we are no longer enslaved by the allure of the illusion of power in this world. Contrary to what we might expect, our submission to the discipline of learning meekness actually frees us to participate in the redemption of creation and to direct our powers to receiving and giving life.

One more aspect of meekness must be explored. Earlier I set aside the conception of meekness as weakness or poverty (the poor of the land) to explore the notion of meekness as power properly oriented to the telos of creation. But the Hebrew and the Greek words that we translate as *meek* may also be used to refer to those who have no power, not just those who submit their power to Christ. There are those who are without power in this world on many levels and in many dimensions: political, economic, social, sexual, educational, intellectual, military, and so on. The testimony of Scripture is that these weak and poor are included among those who inherit the earth. Prosperity, power, and influence are not necessarily signs that one is living in line with the telos of creation. They are more often—if we believe Scripture—signs that one has to some degree mastered the story and reality of the fallen world (see Ps. 73, for example). The warning throughout Scripture, and especially in the prophets

(Hosea 4; Amos 5), is that such mastery is actually our enslavement to a story and reality that ends in death.[5]

When we bring our "mastery" into alignment with the story of the redemption of creation, our prosperity may be exposed as our capitulation to the fallen world and an impediment to our participation in the redemption of creation. Consider, for example, this testimony from Mary's "Magnificat":

> My soul glorifies the Lord
>   and my spirit rejoices in God my Savior,
> for he has been mindful
>   of the humble state of his servant.
> From now on all generations will call me blessed,
>   for the Mighty One has done great things for me—
>   holy is his name.
> His mercy extends to those who fear him,
>   from generation to generation.
> He has performed mighty deeds with his arm;
>   he has scattered those who are proud in their inmost thoughts.
> He has brought down rulers from their thrones
>   but has lifted up the humble.
> He has filled the hungry with good things
>   but has sent the rich away empty.
> He has helped his servant Israel,
>   remembering to be merciful
> to Abraham and his descendants forever,
>   just as he promised our ancestors.
>
>   Luke 1:46–55

This declaration, placed at the beginning of Jesus's life in this world, is celebrated as the story of his life in the hymn that Paul records in Philippians 2, which narrates the meekness of Christ and his exaltation and inheritance of all things. Those who are in Christ are caught up in this same story. He became poor so that he could make the poor rich in him. He became weak so that the weak could be made strong in him. We who know our poverty and weakness may know and live with hope and contentment even in the midst of crises because we know that the meek will inherit the earth. That meekness, however, sets such Christians apart both from those who think that we must act without God to save our planet and ourselves and from those who think that the superabundance of life from God gives us license to drain the resources of life in this world.

---

5. See Marlow, *Biblical Prophets and Contemporary Environmental Ethics*, esp. 146–57, 182–94.

Today, we hear many voices promising us that their way is the way to "inherit the earth" through advances in sciences, the wonders of technology, a previously undiscovered formula or program for prosperity. In Christ, we are told that "the meek will inherit the earth." This blessing, this promise, makes sense if we believe that in Christ we see the way to life in and through the redemption of creation for the new creation. In the midst of death and the destruction of the things of this world, the way to life is not to gain better control of this world but to look to God and conform our lives to Christ. Here is the promise:

> The desert and the parched land will be glad;
>   the wilderness will rejoice and blossom.
> Like the crocus, it will burst into bloom;
>   it will rejoice greatly and shout for joy.
> The glory of Lebanon will be given to it,
>   the splendor of Carmel and Sharon;
> they will see the glory of the LORD,
>   the splendor of our God.
>
> Strengthen the feeble hands,
>   steady the knees that give way;
> say to those with fearful hearts,
>   "Be strong, do not fear;
> your God will come,
>   he will come with vengeance;
> with divine retribution
>   he will come to save you."
>
> Then will the eyes of the blind be opened
>   and the ears of the deaf unstopped.
> Then will the lame leap like a deer,
>   and the mute tongue shout for joy.
> Water will gush forth in the wilderness
>   and streams in the desert.
> The burning sand will become a pool,
>   the thirsty ground bubbling springs.
> In the haunts where jackals once lay,
>   grass and reeds and papyrus will grow.
>
> And a highway will be there;
>   it will be called the Way of Holiness;
>   it will be for those who walk on that Way.
> The unclean will not journey on it;
>   wicked fools will not go about on it.

No lion will be there,
    nor any ravenous beast;
    they will not be found there.
But only the redeemed will walk there,
    and those the LORD has rescued will return.
They will enter Zion with singing;
    everlasting joy will crown their heads.
Gladness and joy will overtake them,
    and sorrow and sighing will flee away.
                        Isaiah 35[6]

This vision does not call us to quietude and passivity in the face of earth's devastations, nor does it call us to complacent exploitation of the earth on the basis of God's promised renewal. Rather, this vision calls us to the meekness to live on earth in this time by bearing witness to the gentle, careful, and simple way of living that Jesus Christ himself calls us to. If we do not live in that way, we should examine whether we are in Christ and Christ in us. Christ's declaration of blessing for the meek is also a declaration of curse for those who are not meek. May God give us the grace to live as part of God's creation knowing that life is abundant and eternal in Christ, not in our own power.

6. Ibid., 234–38.

13

Being and Becoming Persons

In the introduction I warned that I would not offer a large-scale account of humankind—theological anthropology—as part of this work for three reasons. One reason is that I wanted to counterbalance the frequent imbalance in other accounts of the doctrine of creation, where theological anthropology comprises a disproportionate amount of text. Another reason is the recent publication of David Kelsey's *Eccentric Existence*. We need some time to explore, understand, and map this magnum opus before much more is written about humankind. In this context, I do not want simply to provide a digest of Kelsey's work. Most important, I was determined to disperse the doctrine of humankind throughout this text in order to exemplify my conviction that theological anthropology does not actually constitute a separate locus for doctrine but rather depends on other doctrines. So within the doctrine of creation, we may all along the way discover teaching about humankind. The incarnation of the Word is the act that most clearly reveals to us what it means to be human. Therefore, Christology is the doctrinal locus where theological anthropology should receive its most comprehensive treatment. If our account of humankind is located in Christology, then theological anthropology will also most appropriately be located within the story of the redemption of creation.

To exemplify this conviction I will here give an account of one part of what it means to be human: being and becoming persons.[1] This is not the whole account of what it means to be human; it traces only one trajectory in the human story. In particular, the account that I give here makes a fairly large presumption of human circumstance: it presumes that we have access to the resources necessary to being persons in the way described here. *In the world*, many do not have access to the resources conducive to being persons because their own bodies or their circumstances do not provide access to those circumstances due to natural or social constraints. That is, some people are limited physically by disease or disablement; others are limited by the absence of the necessities of life, the effort required to obtain those necessities in their place, or by social impediments (for example, race, gender, class). *In creation-being-redeemed*, all are given access by God's grace to being and becoming persons. As I develop my account of "being and becoming persons," I will seek to clarify how this account includes everyone by locating our being persons within the story of God's redemption of creation for the new creation.

What does it mean to be human? Among many things, to be human is to be a person. But the very language of "personhood" requires unpacking for it to have meaning for the way of life. Being and becoming a person is possible only by God's work of the redemption of creation. That is, being and becoming a person begins with our dependence on God. We do not achieve personhood; we receive it and participate in it. That is why we can speak of being a person and also of becoming a person. Why do we have to speak of "becoming" if we are already persons? The answer to that question lies in the story of the redemption of creation.

When God redeems the world for its telos as creation, the telos of humans is also redeemed. The telos of humans is the telos of all creation: life in the new creation. But the telos of life for humans in the new creation is particular to the form of life that makes us human. One way to specify that form of life as human is to say "person." But then we must go on to describe the proper way to use *person* to refer to the life of humans. As we do so, we locate humans in the dialectic of the kingdom. When humans are taken from the story of the fallen world into the story of the new creation and thus also taken from death to Life, we are then simply persons. Through the work of Christ, we

---

1. See Rolnick, *Person, Grace, and God*, for an excellent recent account of personhood that engages many more issues than I consider here. My account is congruent with Rolnick's, though we differ in details. See esp. Rolnick's account of gift (145–85) and the human person (208–56). Rolnick addresses issues raised by the sciences more than I do. Also, his confidence in progress, usually carefully set within the context of sanctification, contrasts with my more apocalyptic vision of the fulfillment of human persons.

are made to *be* persons by this dying to death and rising to life.[2] This aligns us with God's intention for humans in the context of all creation. Using older theological language, we may say that we are now "justified."[3] But now that we are, by God's grace, in the life-giving story, we must begin to live in it. Again, using older theological language, we may say that as we live into the story we become "sanctified." That is, once we are in the right story, we are both declared righteous and made righteous, where "righteousness" is understood as proper alignment with God's redemption of creation.

This work is also being and becoming persons. In his "Manifesto: The Mad Farmer Liberation Front," Wendell Berry's gaze pierces our habits and "the way things are" to reveal to us our captivity to the fallen world and the rule of death. Then he celebrates the presence of God's work in and for creation to call us to the way of Life. In these two visions, he sets before us the path to being and becoming persons. Berry does not write his poem in stanzas, but I will work through it in stages to show how his poem calls us to be and become persons in the dialectic of the kingdom.[4]

> Love the quick profit, the annual raise, . . . Be afraid to know your neighbor and to die.

The first four lines expose our captivity to the way things are. Indeed for most people, the circumstances that Berry describes are the very things we desire and count as success and achievement in our lives: money obtained quickly and without effort; the assurance of a "bullet-proof career," where the trajectory

2. I am trying to prescribe not who counts as a person but only how one becomes a person. Becoming a person can only come to be through what God does in Jesus Christ. Some Christian traditions have set out rigid and precise guidelines for determining who qualifies as a person in Christ. I make no such claim and offer no comfort for those who make such claims. I am certain that we become persons only in Christ. Who is in Christ is only for God to know and reveal in the new creation. Our task is to bear witness to this good news.

3. At present there is considerable debate, disagreement, and at times rancor over the meaning of *justification* in relation to humans. See Piper, *Future of Justification*; N. T. Wright, *Justification*; among many others. See also the recent tome by Campbell, *Deliverance of God*, which argues an alternative to justification and salvation-history accounts. On a quick first reading, Campbell seems to offer considerable support for and guidance to my account of the redemption of creation in his "apocalyptic" reading of the gospel and in his larger description of "participatory-pneumatological-martyrological-eschatology." Campbell does not abandon the language of "justified" and "justification," for that language indeed comes from the NT. Instead he sets that language and reconceives its meaning and testimony in an apocalyptic story, as I would say, the redemption of creation for the new creation.

4. "Manifesto: The Mad Farmer Liberation Front" was first published in Wendell Berry, *The Country of Marriage*. It is included most recently in Berry, *New Collected Poems* and is available on the internet with copyright permission at http://www.context.org/iclib/ic30/berry/.

is clear and guaranteed. Both of these ways are valued because they "free" us for the important things in life: ready-made goods, an independent life, and the means to postpone death and even, we hope, choose the time of our deaths so that we may bring our fear of death under control.

This description of life is, at base, simply a description of the marketing and self-help that we turn to so often and that appears constantly on television, in computer games, in our newspapers, on the web, and in the TV commercials that are punctuated by TV shows, which also teach us the rule of death and the limits of "life." This is how we "live" and what we "live," that is, *die* for. Even when our words deny this, our lives reveal it.

And you will have a window in your head. . . .

Then Berry stings us with the reality behind the way things are and the way that we aspire to live. When we aspire to these things, we open ourselves up to the forces that serve the rule of death in this fallen world. We accept the way things are, we look for ways to go ahead with the way things are, we accept the messages of those servants of the way things are, and we give our desiring and consuming, our time and our energy, to those things. We are like the guests at Folly's party in Proverbs 9 who are so captivated by the goodies they consume and the desires they indulge that they do not know that they are already in Sheol.

If "the way things are" is all that there is, if there is nothing more than this fallen world, then the way that Berry describes in these first four lines is about as good as we can expect. But even then, we should see clear-eyed what we are giving ourselves to. We are enslaving ourselves to consumption and profit. For these things we are willing to die. This is our fate. For Berry, this fate is tied to our technology: he draws on early computing to portray to us the form that our deaths will take. ("Your mind will be punched in a card. . . ." reflects the way data were originally put into computers.)

So, friends, every day do something that won't compute. Love the Lord. Love the world.

But the way of folly is not the only way in the world. Berry spends the rest of his "Manifesto" proclaiming that other way. He does so with wit, insight, and vivid images that simultaneously unveil how upside-down our fallen world is and call us to life in the right-side-up world of the redemption of creation. He acknowledges the power of "the way things are" and subverts them. In doing so, he also calls us to enter into a new story with a new telos: "Be joyful though you have considered all the facts." There is nothing commonplace in his vision, and yet he returns ordinary things to us so that we see them entirely new as God's creation. What he proclaims here are vivid representations of much that I have described less vividly: the two stories, life and death, and habits such as hope, patience, humility, and meekness.

These are the things that make us persons. To be a person is to be and become a participant in God's redemption of creation. In that participation we leave behind the rule of death and enter into the rule of life. As we do so, we begin to reflect the life of the Father, the Son, and the Spirit in ways appropriate to our being human persons. We become persons as we grow in the belief that life is from, for, and to God. As this conviction grows, we learn that we do not need to fear death, save our own lives, or protect ourselves from all other things. All things have been reconciled to God through the blood of Christ's cross. We need not fear even the principalities and powers, since they have been publicly humiliated and defeated by the crucifixion.

Being and becoming a person in the world today seems to mean being and becoming independent, self-sufficient, powerful, and protected. Even if we deny the individualism that has often and for so long been a part of this story, we are still trapped within the way things are in a fallen world whose telos is death. Berry exposes that deep error and calls us to life in this world as creation, redeemed for the new creation. In that story, being and becoming a person are about learning the receiving and giving that sustain life even beyond death and knit us together in the never-ending exchange of life.

In that exchange of life between persons, all of us are sustained only by the sustaining of all of us. In the same way that the Father, the Son, and the Spirit live perfectly and eternally in their mutual relations, so humankind lives perfectly and without end as we are brought by God's grace to our telos as persons. As this is happening, it is possible for us to affirm the present lives of those who are disabled, diseased, or marginal to the way of the world and to look forward to their healing. Their disablement simply makes more evident in them what is equally true of us but usually deeply hidden or denied: humankind is made new as the people of God only in our full and continual dependence on others for our lives. We must not depreciate the suffering that comes with disablement, disease, and marginalization; we who are able bodied and healthy do not suffer from disability or disease or exclusion. But all humans live in the same way: in dependence on God and in mutual relations with one another. There is no alternative; there is no other way to life. The alternative to living in dependence on God and in mutual relations with others is . . . death.

We become persons—that is, humans who are alive—as we know this mystery of life. Those who are diseased, disabled, or marginalized may know it before others do. Neither disease nor disablement, neither oppression nor marginalization, is an impediment to becoming a person in creation-being-redeemed. However, we also must not romanticize these circumstances and suffering. Those who suffer from them may long wrongly for "independence" and self-sufficiency in the same way that those who are poor may be just as enslaved by money and the desire for wealth as those whose possession of wealth enslaves them. If we see clearly our telos as persons in the new creation, then we can see through our longings for independence and self-sufficiency to the ecstatic fulfillment of our telos. But we do not have to wait for the healing and wholeness of the new creation. The reality of being and becoming a person begins already in Christ. We are not made persons by healing and wholeness; we are made persons in Christ. In the new creation, all will be healed and made whole. In Christ, we will be fully the persons that we are created to be. In that time and for eternity, our full beauty and goodness will shine in the glorious splendor of life.

14

Bodies

T he theological neglect of the doctrine of creation has led to many weaknesses and pathologies in church, academy, and society. We may identify one resultant pathology in some understandings of human bodies. Traditionally, theology and biblical studies have carried on a lively, unresolved debate between dichotomist and trichotomist views of humans. Dichotomists argue that we are a combination of body and soul. Trichotomists argue that we are body and soul and spirit.[1] In recent years, this traditional debate has been reframed, partly in response to developments in the sciences, especially the neurosciences. Now we theologians and biblical scholars debate the significance of our bodies and various proposals that follow from the interaction between theology, biblical studies, and the sciences.[2]

1. One influential variation on trichotomy is taught by Watchman Nee, who argues that before we come to faith in Christ we are body-soul. Faith in Christ makes us body-soul-spirit. Among his many works, see Nee, *Spiritual Man*; *Sit, Walk, Stand*; and *Normal Christian Life*.

2. Among others, see John Paul II, *Man and Woman He Created Them*; Paulsell, *Honoring the Body*; Kelsey, *Eccentric Existence* (throughout, but esp. in discussions of "personal bodies"). We still await a seminal text for today on a theology of the body. The lively discussion about "souls" and "bodies" may be a precursor to such work. On that debate, see the older work by Gundry, *Soma in Biblical Theology*, and more recent works by Cooper, *Body, Soul, and Life Everlasting*; Machuga, *In Defense of the Soul*; Brown, Malony, and Murphy, *Whatever Happened to the Soul?*; Murphy, *Bodies and Souls, or Spirited Bodies?*; Green, *Body, Soul, and Human Life*. One concern I have with this last debate is that it still seems engaged in Christian intramural issues, which, though important, do not directly engage the larger question today of the very existence of human *nature*, where "nature" assumes a stable entity whose essence may

This debate is ongoing, complex, and in my judgment will have no satisfactory resolution. As with many of these kinds of debates, I want to ask about the practical effect they may have on Christian thinking and living. That is, I want to know what follows for Christian discipleship from any position that is taken. I enjoy the intellectual challenges and puzzles that these questions pose for us, but in the end I want to ask, "What difference does it make?" I ask that question not to dismiss the arguments but to push to the place where they are important for life.[3]

Many of us who teach courses in doctrine in Christian colleges have learned from our students that they have no theology of the human body grounded in the good news of Jesus Christ. They think of salvation as a "spiritual" process that only involves some immaterial part of their being human, whether they describe that part as "soul" or "spirit." They imagine eternal life in "heaven," which is an immaterial realm where our spirits will "live" in bliss after having escaped material creation, including our bodies. They have a "liberation theology" that teaches them that salvation is freedom from this world. They have no doctrine of creation to teach them that "this world," even in its brokenness and sin and suffering and death, belongs to God, whose work of creation and redemption will be completed in the new creation.

They come to Christian colleges with these views because the theological neglect of the doctrine of creation has left our churches without the resources to teach a proper doctrine of creation and a theology of the human body that testifies to the joyful promise of the redemption of our bodies. It is in these issues that we confront so clearly the critical need for a robust, maturing conversation and argument about the doctrine of creation. We fall into a very subtle enemy trap if we think that we have such a doctrine of creation when we argue about the age of the earth, the time that it took God to create, and the conflict with "evolution." If this is all that we have as a doctrine of creation, then we are profoundly vulnerable to other ideological claims about how we are to live in this world and especially what we are to do with our bodies. Without a theology of the body rooted in a trinitarian grammar of creation and the dialectic of the kingdom, we place

---

be contested but whose existence is assumed. In today's context, we need a more teleological—that is, narratival—account of what it means to be human. My call for such an account is not a capitulation to cultural or a correlational strategy but rather recognition that the questioning of "human *nature*" actually opens up the biblical teaching in new ways. On this entire debate, see the critical and illuminating discussion, which contrasts with my account in many places, in Rolnick, *Person, Grace, and God*, 239–56.

3. David Blumenthal makes this same point about the doctrine of creation. See D. Blumenthal, "Creation: 'What Difference Does It Make?,'" in Burrell and McGinn, *God and Creation*, 154–72.

our bodies in service to political, economic, and many other ideological claims. Remember Wendell Berry:

> When they want you to buy something
> they will call you. When they want you
> to die for profit they will let you know.

In order to subvert these powers over our bodies, rather than consider the various theologies of the body that are being proposed and debated, I will simply lay out an exposition of what must be said about human bodies on the basis of my exposition and argument in this book.

It should be clear by now that the doctrine of creation presented here leads to the confession that our bodies are part of God's creation and thus also are part of God's redemption of creation for its telos in the new creation. From this it follows that we believe and teach that our bodies are even now in this world being made to participate in God's work of redemption and that life in the new creation will be an embodied life. We may perhaps capture this by noting that we have "dirty bodies"—that is, bodies made of the stuff of creation, the dust of the earth—and for that very reason are also related to God and participants in God's redemption of creation.[4]

To believe that our bodies even now participate in redemption runs contrary to a widespread popular belief that in this world, redemption, or more commonly, salvation, is a spiritual matter that involves only some immaterial part of our being human and excludes our bodies. But this commonly held belief runs contrary to the central episodes in the story of creation and its redemption.

In the beginning, God makes humans who are embodied. In Genesis 2, we are told that God fashions the human from earth and breathes into the human. In this text, there are two acts of God—the fashioning and the breathing—but there is no distinction made between body and spirit. That is, the text does not say that God fashioned a body and then inserted a spirit; the text says simply that God made "a human" by means of this two-part act. The grammatical structure of the Hebrew indicates clearly that this is not a two-stage process or two separate acts, but one act performed in two movements. Moreover, as is regularly written in the notes of study Bibles and commentaries, the description used for the result of this two-part act, "living being" (Gen. 2:7; Heb., *nephesh hayim*), is the same term used for other creatures (Gen. 1:20, 24).

---

4. I was provoked to think about our "dirty" bodies by my reading of an early draft of a book by my son-in-law. See Wilson-Hartgrove, *Awakening of Hope*.

From this it is important to note, first, that human embodiment is God's handiwork. Our bodies are part of the gift and blessing of God's creation. When we experience our bodies as burden and curse, that experience is part of the story of the fallen world. Second, humans have bodies from their beginning as humans.[5] Therefore, there is no other way of being human apart from our bodies.[6] If the salvation that Christ brings to us does not include our bodies, then our salvation is the process of becoming something other than fully human. In this case, we are not "redeemed"—that is, Christ does not make it possible for us to come to our telos as humans in the new creation. Rather, in this heretical scheme Christ makes it possible for us to realize some other telos. If this were the case, then creation and salvation would be separate stories. And the "good news" would not be the good news to which the Old and the New Testaments bear witness, but another version of "good news" that is not good news at all.[7]

The reality of our bodies in relation to God does not come to an end with our fall into sin and our turn from our God-created telos. Bodies are also part of the continuing story of Israel. In that story, God trains the people of Israel in how their bodies and their bodily actions belong to God and to God's ordering of creation in conflict with their habitual submission of their bodies and bodily actions to the fallen world. This training is deeply embedded in the entire Tanak. We miss the overwhelming presence of this bodily training because we do not read the Tanak faithfully and because our theological prejudices are so well formed by the separation of "spiritual" and "material" matters.

This bodily story continues in the coming of Israel's Messiah, Jesus of Nazareth, the Word made flesh. This embodied life—whom John declares they saw, heard, and touched (1 John 1:1–4)—brings God's creation to redemption

---

5. This text leaves open and perhaps even invites speculation on the origin of humans. It is clear from this text that the human is made from preexisting matter. The change in the way that God's actions are described here combined with God's deliberation in Gen. 1:26 make it quite possible to imagine that this preexisting matter took the form of a prehuman. At the same time, however, the testimony that God breathed into what God had formed requires us to affirm that humans came into being by some direct action of God. Moreover, "fashioning" is a "hands-on" image.

6. This raises the question of our continuing existence from the time of death to the return of Christ and our resurrection. Our theological heritage offers several answers to this question; all of them recognize that we will not be fully human until we are raised to life in bodies that are imperishable and incorruptible (1 Cor. 15).

7. This is why any alternative scheme of salvation, such as gnosticism, must dispense with the Old Testament, eviscerate the New Testament, and write different stories of Jesus, such as the Gospel of Thomas. I am amazed by the silliness in our culture that can draw people to a revival of creation-denying gnosticism and at the same time anguish over the abuse of the earth. This tells us something about the effect of our neglect of the doctrine of creation.

and opens the way to life. It is in his incarnation that he is conceived in Mary's womb and born bodily. It is the crucifixion of this person in the flesh, the one who thirsted, whose side was pierced, whose legs were left intact, that reconciles all things to God (Col. 1:20). It is the bodily resurrection of this person that reveals Christ's victory over sin, death, and the devil and vindicates the good news that he proclaimed: creation is redeemed for its telos in the new creation. It is the ascension and return of the incarnate, crucified, buried, and raised, *embodied* Messiah that promises and consummates the telos of the redemption of creation in the new creation.[8]

In the reality of Jesus Christ, there are no gaps between spirit and body; or soul and body; or spirit, soul, and body. The redemption that he brings is whole from beginning to end, however anyone may wish to apportion human life among various descriptions. We have trouble thinking of this bodily redemption as our possession and experience because we are captive to one story in this world. We typically have only the story of the fallen world to guide our lives. And because our bodies so clearly participate in this fallen world, we think that our bodies belong only to this world. Therefore, salvation, in which we belong to God, must be a "spiritual" matter that separates us from this world and our bodies.

If we learn the good news of Jesus Christ rightly, then the trinitarian grammar of creation and the dialectic of the kingdom tell us that we cannot separate the work of Christ from the Father and the Spirit. Nor can we separate the work of the Spirit from the Father and the Son. If Christ is bodily incarnate, crucified, and raised for our salvation, then the work of the Father and the Spirit for our salvation cannot be separated from the redemption of our bodies. Likewise, if we give an account of the Spirit as the one who brings us into the redemption of creation by bringing us to faith in Christ and empowering us in the life of the new creation, then our bodies must also participate in that redemption.

Here we encounter an apparent obstacle to developing a theology of bodies caught up in the redemption of creation: the pervasive talk about the Spirit in the New Testament. Does not the very work of the Spirit that I just described mean that salvation is a spiritual work and not a bodily work? There is partial truth implied in the question. Our salvation—and more fully, the redemption of creation—is a "spiritual work." That is, the Spirit is at work, as we have seen in many previous chapters, especially chapter 5. But this affirmation does

---

8. I have only begun to see the significance of Christ's *burial*, in which his body is returned to the earth from which our bodies are made. But earth cannot hold Christ's body. If we take this "earthiness" of his body seriously, then even more theological insight may be forthcoming.

not mean that the Spirit is at work in only one part of a human, that part being "spiritual" in separation from body or from body and soul. Rather, the work of the Spirit makes us holy in every way.

If this is difficult to imagine or accept, think about this challenge: once you are in Christ and the Spirit begins to make you holy, name one thing "holy" that the Spirit enables you to do apart from your body. When I ask live audiences this question, I see a long, thoughtful pause and then the dawn of recognition that begins to ripple through the audience. Occasionally I have someone thrust his hand in the air and respond, "I can pray!" Oh, really? Then, of course, a sheepish look follows from deeper thought and recognition that the process of redemption that we think of as "spiritual," separated from bodies, is actually dependent on our bodies. Even if we try to press the fruit of the Spirit into this separation, careful reflection and faithful living teach us that love, joy, peace, patience, kindness, goodness, faithfulness, gentleness, and self-control depend on bodies for their formation and practice.[9]

Even after these insights, we have difficulty changing our way of thinking and living for two reasons. One reason is simply our experience of our bodies. We often find them a burden and a curse. They are the source of limitations, pain, and suffering. To put it briefly and bluntly: our bodies die.

My wife, Marti, suffered from a hereditary disease called Gaucher disease. Gaucher is a nasty, insidious disease, though there are many worse. Marti suffered limitations, immobility, and pain from the disease. It shortened her life. She died at age sixty-two from complications due to an occurrence of severe pancreatitis. She lived most days with unavoidable reminders of the limitations of her body. But she also lived with immense joy. At Marti's memorial service, our daughter Leah said this:

> I'd like to take a few minutes to say what it felt like to be loved by my mom. As I've thought about her this past week, and especially as I've thought about the gifts she gave me, I'm most grateful for the way she loved me. If it didn't sound so cliché, I'd almost want to say that she showed me what unconditional love looks like. I know she loved me completely. But "unconditional love" sounds far too idealistic a description for the reality that was my mom. It seems that her love needs an unconventional adjective to describe it. I think I want to call it *a fierce love*.
>
> As most of you here today probably know, my mom did nothing gently. She drove a car with force; she moved around quickly (even with pained legs); she threw things into the dishwasher. Even the way she brushed her teeth was quick and forceful. When I was with my mom in the hospital a few weeks ago, she

9. See Kenneson, *Life on the Vine*.

was frail. Her voice had been reduced to a whisper, and she needed someone to help her put the ice chips in her mouth most of the time. But I remember sitting by her bed one day as she was holding a tissue. When she was done with it, she threw it down. I laughed out loud. "Jonathan says I'm always throwing things instead of placing them," I said. "I guess I got that from you."

My mom didn't "hold back." Even with a cane, she plunged ahead, determined to get where she was going despite whatever got in her way. She loved like that too. She didn't hold back. She threw her love at you like she threw a glass of water in my face when I was a teenager who didn't want to get up and go to school. Fierce love, I learned from her, can be angry and faithful at the same time. When I was a selfish teenager, she called me out and even called me things on a few occasions that I shouldn't repeat here. But during those same years, when the police brought me home at 3:00 a.m. one night, she insisted that I was not the one at fault. I was, after all, the object of her fierce love. Nothing I did could reduce its force.

Marti was also an immensely passionate woman. She enjoyed life with as much gusto as anyone I have known. She could embarrass me with her vocal expressions of pleasure. I have said that she taught me the difference between being lusty and being lustful.

I learned from her how we can live our lives in two stories. The story of her disease, disability, and death belongs to the story of the fallen world. It is real, and it is inescapable. But that story is caught up in a bigger story—the biggest story possible, the story of the redemption of creation for the new creation. Marti knew that she was made by God for life with God and for pleasures of life now and for pleasures future that we cannot bear in this world and these bodies. We must not let the story of the fallen world determine the story of the burdens and curses of our bodies. When we do, we are wide open to the powers of the world that are fallen and ruled by death. Bodily pleasures then become ways of denying death or distracting us from burdens and sorrows. We frantically seek out ways of postponing death. We exercise and care for our bodies simply for the purpose of extending the years of our lives. In these things we give no thought to what we are made for or what "life" really is. Our bodies are burdens and curses that end in death.

In addition to all the talk about the Spirit in the New Testament, another similar obstacle to living by the good news of Jesus Christ in our bodies is a shallow and mistaken grasp of some of the language of the New Testament. At numerous points, "spirit" and "flesh" are set against each other. But when these two are contrasted and when *flesh* clearly references sinful actions and dispositions, *flesh* is not referring to our bodies simply as bodies. Rather, *flesh* is here being used to refer to our bodies under the rule of this fallen world.

Some contemporary translations try to clear up the confusion by translating the Greek word (*sarx*) as "sinful nature" rather than "flesh." But this translation misses the very concrete claim that Paul makes. When Paul says that we must not live according to *sarx*, he really is referring to our bodies. But he is making an assertion about our bodies *under the rule of death rather than under the rule of the Spirit*. So he writes:

> For what the law was powerless to do because it was weakened by *sarx*, God did by sending his own Son in the likeness of *sarx* to be a sin offering. And so he condemned sin in *sarx*, in order that the righteous requirement of the law might be fully met in us, who do not live according to *sarx* but according to the Spirit.
>
> Those who live according to *sarx* have their minds set on what *sarx* desires; but those who live in accordance with the Spirit have their minds set on what the Spirit desires. The mind governed by *sarx* is death, but the mind governed by the Spirit is life and peace. The mind governed by *sarx* is hostile to God; it does not submit to God's law, nor can it do so. Those who are in the realm of *sarx* cannot please God.
>
> You, however, are not in the realm of *sarx* but are in the realm of the Spirit, if indeed the Spirit of God lives in you. And if anyone does not have the Spirit of Christ, they do not belong to Christ. But if Christ is in you, then even though your body is subject to death because of sin, the Spirit gives life because of righteousness. And if the Spirit of him who raised Jesus from the dead is living in you, he who raised Christ from the dead will also give life to your mortal bodies because of his Spirit who lives in you. (Rom. 8:3–11, with *sarx* inserted for "flesh")

As I noted in chapter 1, perhaps the best way to grasp this and live it is to think in terms of two kingdoms or realms (see Rom. 8:8–9). These two realms are the worlds of *Sarx* and *Pneuma*. *Sarx* is this fallen world whose telos is death. When we live by and in *Sarx*, we live in a world in rebellion against God and alienated from God's love and life. This determines how we think of our bodies and what we do with them. Because we have been born into this world, we must die.

But there is another story, the story of the redemption of creation for the new creation. This is the realm of *Pneuma* because it is by the Spirit that we are brought into this story. The story of *Pneuma* is the story of resurrection. *Pneuma* does not deny or circumvent the story of *Sarx*. Rather, *Pneuma* redeems those who are born into and captive to *Sarx*. *Pneuma* overcomes the alienation of *Sarx* so that in the Spirit (to revert now to familiar language) we know God's love and life.

In light of this, we must bring our bodies into the good news of the redemption of creation for the new creation. Our bodies are subject to wasting away and to death because we are born into a fallen world that has turned away from the telos of creation. We may call this the country of *Sarx*. This reality rules our bodies until we hear and believe the good news of the redemption of creation for the new creation. The Spirit then brings us into Christ so that our citizenship is no longer in the country of *Sarx*. We now live in the country of *Pneuma*. In this country, bodies are raised from the dead. Knowing this, we follow the way of Christ so that our bodies are no longer subject to death-dealing ideologies that control our thinking and acting in the country of *Sarx*. In the country of *Pneuma*, we may properly enjoy and celebrate the pleasures of embodiment and the fullness of physical life. *Pneuma* is the country where Marti lived more and more deeply.

Having been born in the country of *Sarx* and now having our citizenship transferred to the country of *Pneuma*, we can understand and live with the burdens and curses that attend our bodies that are born into a country ruled by death. But we are free of the fear and selfishness created by the rule of death because in the Spirit we know that death has been defeated and will one day be destroyed. Our bodies in the country of *Pneuma* are given life that bears fruit: love, joy, peace, patience, kindness, goodness, faithfulness, gentleness, and self-control (see Gal. 5:22–23). This is the work of the redemption of creation for the telos of the new creation.

15

Worship

The most significant thing that the disciple community could do to begin to recover a robust and maturing doctrine of creation is to recover the practice of worship that praises the Father, the Son, and the Spirit and participates in the dialectic of the kingdom. To bring these two together—worship and the doctrine of creation—would be a quest with little expectation of success, except that it is always by grace that God judges and renews God's people. When we have "services of celebration" and Sunday-morning gatherings that are largely evangelistically focused, to recover the practice of worship requires a change of mind (repentance) in many parts of the church.

Often our "worship" has no clear trinitarian grammar and thus fails to bring us into the presence of the one God—Father, Son, and Spirit.[1] Likewise, our worship receives little guidance from theological convictions and thus is shaped not by the praise of God but by congregational politics and preferences. Along with these failings, we often think of "worship" as a means of getting us through the next week in this fallen world rather than as participation in the redemption of creation and anticipation of the telos of the new creation. Too often we simply accept the way things are and look to "worship" to help us manage with the way things are. Worship of the Father, the Son, and the

---

1. I have addressed the practice of worship in Wilson, *Why Church Matters*, chaps. 2–5. See esp. chap. 4 for an account of the trinitarian grammar of worship.

Spirit should bring us into that most real world of God's redemption of creation so that our lives are continually transformed. This aspiration may be realized only by the gracious work of God. To know God and to be known by God in transformative ways are what gathers us to be the disciple community from first to last.

As we gather to praise the Father, the Son, and the Spirit and give thanks for creation and its redemption

- we submit our lives in the fallen world to the story of God's redemption of creation,
- we focus our lives as a community in God's presence,
- we encourage one another to patience, and
- we lament, and we pray, "Come, Lord Jesus."

In these practices we may be

- renewed in Sabbath rest,
- restored by the hope of resurrection,
- recaptured by the story of the redemption of creation that worship recapitulates,
- reoriented by the vision of the new creation as God's temple and God as the temple of the new creation, and
- transformed by these practices that reclaim us for life with God and bring us into the life of the new creation that is coming.

Sabbath

When we gather to worship, we continue the keeping of Sabbath that reflects the Genesis story of creation and the two versions of the Decalogue, the "ten words" that describe the life of God's people. In Genesis, the story of creation climaxes with the seventh day, on which God rests. Some recent work on Genesis has opened up new insights into the cosmos as the temple of God. With this understanding, to say that God "rests" is to say that God takes up God's dwelling in God's creation, the universe that God has made.[2] Like a carpenter who has built a home for his family, when that work is completed he invites his family and friends to sit down with him in the new space and enjoy it together.

2. Walton, *Lost World of Genesis One*; Howard-Brook, *Come Out, My People!*; Barker, *Creation*. See below for further exploration of these proposals.

The call to Sabbath rest is located in both creation and redemption. In Exodus 20:8–11, we are called to Sabbath because after creating, God rests on that seventh day.[3] In Deuteronomy 5:12–15, the call to Sabbath is rooted in God's deliverance of Israel from Egypt, where the people of God were enslaved and toiled for others.[4] This change from the Exodus call for Sabbath to the Deuteronomy call beautifully reflects the dialectic of the kingdom. We cannot simply root Sabbath in the Genesis story of God's work of creation. We must also situate it in God's work of redeeming creation. This second story is essential to both a commitment to keep Sabbath faithfully and a full understanding of Sabbath. That is, Sabbath not only grounds us in the recognition of God's work of creation as gift and blessing; it also resists, subverts, and overthrows the claims of other powers in our lives.

If we have only the call to Sabbath from Exodus, then we may very well find ourselves thinking, "That's well and good for the original state of creation, but now we live in a world of competition and survival of the fittest. We can't afford to take a day off."[5] But the call of Deuteronomy teaches us that even in the midst of possible enslavement to other powers and the toil of a fallen world, we are called to rest in God. This very call to Sabbath, if we hear and practice it well, will call to mind and teach us the patience and meekness that we have earlier explored as part of our doctrine of creation.

The Eighth Day of Creation

Followers of Christ "keep Sabbath" and worship on the first day of the week as our participation in the resurrection of Jesus Christ, which is the telos of creation in the new creation. In the wonderful witness of Eastern Orthodoxy, the day of Christ's resurrection is "the eighth day of creation."

"The eighth day of creation" bears witness to the reality of Christ's resurrection in the work of creation. Christ's resurrection is not something that occurred in some other place and time. It took place in this world, and it makes this world God's creation. At the same time, the resurrection of Christ is not something that takes place within the matrix of the fallen world. The

3. There are numerous recent studies of the practice of Sabbath. See Dawn, *Keeping the Sabbath Wholly*; Wirzba, *Living the Sabbath*; Buchanan, *Rest of God*.

4. For a helpful study of this command, see Miller, *Ten Commandments*, 117–66. Miller extends his study beyond exegesis into a number of doctrinal and moral reflections.

5. In this regard, I have always been amused and saddened by the story of a Christian business person who faithfully maintained a lifelong strict observance of the Sabbath and always went without sleep overnight Monday to Tuesday in order to make up the time lost to Sabbath observance.

telos of the fallen world is death. The resurrection of Christ reveals that this fallen world is not all that there ever has been and ever will be. His resurrection proclaims throughout the entire universe and to all things that God is the Creator of all and the Redeemer of all. Christ's resurrection reveals the defeat of death and thus the eternality of God's life and of created life with God.

"The eighth day of creation" teaches us that by the act of God in Christ, our worship catches up our lives in this time and place and brings us into the telos of creation in the new creation. In worship on the eighth day of creation, we gather around the throne of God envisioned by John in Revelation, and proclaim

> You are worthy, our Lord and God,
>   to receive glory and honor and power,
> for you created all things,
>   and by your will they were created
>   and have their being.
>   Revelation 4:11

And

> "Worthy is the Lamb, who was slain,
>   to receive power and wealth and wisdom and strength
>   and honor and glory and praise!"

Then I heard every creature in heaven and on earth and under the earth and on the sea, and all that is in them, saying:

> "To him who sits on the throne and to the Lamb
>   be praise and honor and glory and power,
>   for ever and ever!"
>   Revelation 5:12–13

This vision—set within the context of John's first vision of the risen Christ who is Alpha and Omega, who was dead and is now alive forevermore and holds the keys of death and Hades—is of the eighth day of creation. Our worship is not bound by the time and space and realities of the fallen world but is caught up in the time and space created by the everlasting life of the Father, the Son, and the Spirit, and in the dialectic of creation and redemption accomplished by the crucified and risen Christ. In our worship, we declare that all things are made by him, through him, and for him.

The Ethos of Worship

This engagement in worship on the eighth day draws us into life in the new creation and forms us in that life so that as we live in the midst of the fallen world marked by death, we begin to perceive the ways in which the fallen world shapes and controls our life—or at the very least the way the fallen world seeks to do so.[6] As this resistance to conformity to the world and participation in the transformation of our life takes place in Christ, a new ethos arises around the disciple community. This new ethos is lived out in an ethics that displays the practical import of Christian belief in the redemption of creation in Christ. The practices of worship incorporate us into the reality of the good news, teach us how we are to live as the disciple community, and make us into a people whose life together bears witness to the way of life whose telos is the new creation.

This formation begins as we are called to worship by God. Life begins with God, not with us. The reality of worshiping the Father, the Son, and the Spirit is the work of these three among us. It is not the work of human hands and will; it is not energized by human initiative. Life with God is a gift from God, not an achievement of humans. So also worship.

As we come to recognize God's gift in our gathering to worship, we come before God in praise. The central act of praise is the vision and confession, "Holy, holy, holy is I AM, the Almighty." This confession recognizes that nothing in creation teaches us who God is and how God acts apart from its dependence on God for its life. At the same time, this confession teaches us that when we recognize the dependence of all things on God, everything then teaches us about God.

When we bring ourselves before God to see and confess God's holiness, we immediately also confront our unholiness. We are people who are unclean. Apart from Christ, we are citizens of the fallen world and slaves to death and the fear of death. We treat things as if they were the source of life. Captive to this lie, we follow and trust created things that cannot give life. This is the practice of idolatry from which all other sin springs. Therefore, immediately upon confessing God's holiness, we confess our unholiness. In this confession, we acknowledge that we have followed the way of the fallen world and been enslaved to death. We confess that we have lived as citizens of the country of *Sarx*. When we make this confession we are beginning to learn what it means to be citizens of the country of *Pneuma*.

6. One wonderful resource for the church is the series Christian Reflection, ed. R. Kruschwitz. For guidance in worship and the doctrine of creation, see no. 2, *Moral Landscape of Creation*, esp. the worship resources, 42–51, and no. 4, *Sabbath*.

In the country of *Pneuma*, we know ourselves to have been freed from life according to *Sarx*. We are forgiven and united with the one God—Father, Son, and Spirit—who is Life and who gives life to creation. When we lived in *Sarx*, we simply conformed to "the way things are." In *Pneuma*, we begin to learn how things are meant to be and simply are, by the work of creation and redemption. The confession of our sin that follows from our vision and confession of the holiness of God is not a recital merely of how things used to be in our lives; it is also an exposure of the way of the fallen world. In this confession, we publicly expose and humiliate the principalities and powers that serve death and begin to learn how to live in this world as God's creation redeemed in Christ. This way of the redeemed in Christ aligned with God's intention for creation is, in biblical terms, righteousness: living in right relationship with the Father, the Son, and the Spirit, who create and redeem.

Following this confession of the way of sin and declaration of the way of righteousness, we give thanks to God because we realize that if we are aligned with God, and if we are living in this world as creation redeemed for the new creation, then God has given us every good gift and all that we need for abundant, everlasting life. Prior to this confession, death forms the last horizon and the telos of this world. When we "lived" enslaved to the rule of death, everything was dark and there seemed to be no provision for life. Even those things that seemed perhaps to be good fell under the rule of death. And many more things that seemed to be good in the dark shadow of death are revealed to be bad in the light of the resurrection of Jesus Christ.

Having given thanks for all good gifts, most of all for the gift of life, we are now prepared to hear and receive the declaration of the good news of Jesus Christ. We need the work that precedes hearing the gospel in order to be prepared for the gospel. Without the earlier work, we simply assimilate the words that we hear into the story of the fallen world. In this assimilation, we receive any testimony to the gospel, even if it is faithful and true, as merely a tool or a program for managing our way through another week in this fallen world. But when we properly prepare ourselves to hear the gospel in the midst of worship that brings us into the life of creation redeemed, then we hear God's word, which gives us life by

- bringing us into the presence of the Father, the Son, and the Spirit,
- showing us God's holiness, which cannot be overcome by sin and death,
- revealing to us our enslavement to things that have no life in them,
- freeing us from our enslavement and forgiving our disobedience,
- reciting God's acts of goodness and mercy that bring life to us,

- empowering our thanksgiving for God's good gifts of creation redeemed,
- equipping us for right living in this world,
- forming us as God's people, and
- sending us into the world with a renewed conviction that this is God's creation, which God redeems for the telos of the new creation in which we already participate.

When we celebrate Eucharist (or communion, or the Lord's Supper), we recapitulate all of this with the material reality of creation-being-redeemed before us and taken in by us.

Each time that I have taught the doctrine of creation in an academic setting, I have ended the course with water, bread, and wine before us. We do not perform a baptism or celebrate Eucharist in that setting, but this "stuff of life" reminds us forcefully in that setting and in others that the very matter of creation is the means of the redemption of creation and new life, through the Word made flesh, whose body and blood enable us to pass from death to life in the waters of baptism. This "stuff of creation" that sustains life and redeems life should send us into the world no longer to be captive to this world but to be free to live forever in the new creation.

Temple

The place of worship in Israel's history was the temple. This was the place of God's dwelling, filled with God's glory. But the temple in Jerusalem came to represent a political and national ideology that became the focal point of control. It became a place of exclusion, where those who controlled the temple determined who could enter to worship. This entry to worship also signified those who had access to God's blessing in their lives. This became, in Wes Howard-Brook's terms, the religion of empire and the denial of creation.[7] This religion was rooted in a passion to control the way of this world and exercise power within the horizon of the fallen world and the rule of death. It became a religion that served death and did not bear witness to the life that God gives creation.

This ideology of the temple betrayed the teaching of the Tanak that through Abraham all the nations of the earth would be blessed (Gen. 12:1–3) and that the nations of the earth would come to the temple (Isa. 40–66). When Jesus came, he challenged temple religion and contested the rule of death. The status

7. Howard-Brook, *"Come Out, My People!"*

"Gathered 'Round"

and power of the temple was at the center of many of his conflicts with the representatives of the religion of empire circumscribed by this world. This context comes to a climax when Jesus stands in front of the temple, which had come to represent the best that religion can offer under the rule of death. He says, "Destroy this temple, and I will raise it again in three days" (John 2:19). This declaration brings the two stories into direct conflict. Here the denial of creation represented by the temple ideology of empire is exposed and defeated by the resurrection of Christ's body, the redemption of creation for the new creation. The temple religion that had developed is a religion of this fallen world. The good news that Christ proclaims is the coming of the kingdom, the story of the redemption of creation in which life, not death, rules, in which the telos is the new creation, not the rearrangement of power in the fallen world.

Those who are enslaved to the fallen world and the rule of death hear the good news of Jesus Christ as blasphemy against the order of the world and the false gods who rule by lies and illusions. They cry, "Crucify him!" Neither they nor the false gods they serve know that the crucifixion of God the Son made human is the means of the redemption of creation. In this act, all things are reconciled to God. In the temple of creation as God's dwelling place, atonement for the sin of the world takes place. In this atonement the whole of creation is caught up into the life of the one God—Father, Son, and Spirit. This one God then becomes the "temple," the place where God and creation, including humans, dwell together (Rev. 21:22–27). Our worship in the midst of the fallen world is a death-defying practice that bears witness to God's creation-being-redeemed and joins us with all who trust and follow the Lamb who was slain.

All glory be to God the Father, the Son, and the Holy Spirit, who redeem creation for the new creation. Let us enter in with joy.

Come, Lord Jesus.

Bibliography

Alison, James. *The Joy of Being Wrong: Original Sin through Easter Eyes*. New York: Crossroad, 1998.

———. *Raising Abel*. London: SPCK, 2010.

Allison, C. FitzSimons. *The Cruelty of Heresy*. Harrisburg, PA: Moorehouse, 1994.

Anselm. *The Major Works*. Edited by G. R. Evans and Brian Davies. Oxford: Oxford University Press, 2008.

Athanasius. *On the Incarnation*. Translated by Penelope Lawson. Crestwood, NY: St. Vladimir's Seminary Press, 1998.

Augustine. *The Trinity*. Edited by John E. Rotelle. Translated by Edmund Hill. Vol. 1/13 of Works of Saint Augustine. Brooklyn, NY: New City Press, 2002.

Bailie, Gil. *Violence Unveiled*. New York: Crossroad, 1995.

Barker, Margaret. *Creation: A Biblical Vision for the Environment*. London: T&T Clark, 2010.

Barnett, Paul. *Romans: The Revelation of God's Righteousness*. Fearn, Scotland: Christian Focus, 2007.

Barth, Karl. *Church Dogmatics III: The Doctrine of Creation*. Edinburgh: T&T Clark, 1958–61.

Bauckham, Richard. *Jesus and the God of Israel*. Grand Rapids: Eerdmans, 2008.

———. *Living with Other Creatures*. Waco: Baylor University Press, 2011.

Bergmann, Sigurd. *Creation Set Free: The Spirit as Liberator of Nature*. Translated by Douglas Stott. Grand Rapids: Eerdmans, 2005.

Berkhof, Hendrikus. *Christ and the Powers*. Translated by John Howard Yoder. Scottdale, PA: Herald Press, 1977.

Berry, Wendell. *The Country of Marriage*. New York: Harcourt Brace Jovanovich, 1971. Reprint, San Francisco: Counterpoint, 2013.

———. *New Collected Poems*. San Francisco: Counterpoint, 2012.

———. *Sex, Economy, Freedom & Community: Eight Essays*. New York: Pantheon, 1993.

Bessenecker, Scott. *How to Inherit the Earth: Submitting Ourselves to a Servant Savior*. Downers Grove, IL: IVP Books, 2009.

Blenkinsopp, Joseph. *Isaiah 56–66*. New York: Doubleday, 2003.

Blumenberg, Hans. *The Legitimacy of the Modern Age*. Translated by Robert M. Wallace. Cambridge, MA: MIT Press, 1985.

Bockmuehl, Markus N. A. *Seeing the Word: Refocusing New Testament Study*. Grand Rapids: Baker Academic, 2006.

Boersma, Hans. *Heavenly Participation: The Weaving of a Sacramental Tapestry*. Grand Rapids: Eerdmans, 2011.

Bonhoeffer, Dietrich. *Ethics*. Edited by Clifford J. Green. Translated by Reinhard Krauss and Charles C. West, with Douglas W. Stott. Vol. 6 of *Dietrich Bonhoeffer Works*. Minneapolis: Fortress, 2009.

———. *Letters and Papers from Prison*. Edited by John W. De Gruchy. Translated by Isabel Best, Lisa E. Dahill, Reinhard Krauss, and Nancy Lukens, with Barbara and Martin Rumscheidt and Douglas W. Stott. Vol. 8 of *Dietrich Bonhoeffer Works*. Minneapolis: Fortress, 2010.

Borgmann, Albert. *Holding On to Reality: The Nature of Information at the Turn of the Millennium*. Chicago: University of Chicago Press, 2000.

———. *Technology and the Character of Contemporary Life: A Philosophical Inquiry*. Chicago: University of Chicago Press, 1984.

Bouma-Prediger, Steven. *For the Beauty of the Earth: A Christian Vision for Creation Care*. Grand Rapids: Baker Academic, 2001.

Brock, Brian. *Christian Ethics in a Technological Age*. Grand Rapids: Eerdmans, 2010.

Brown, Warren S., H. Newton Malony, and Nancey C. Murphy, eds. *Whatever Happened to the Soul? Scientific and Theological Portraits of Human Nature*. Minneapolis: Fortress, 1998.

Brown, William P. *The Seven Pillars of Creation*. Oxford: Oxford University Press, 2010.

Buchanan, Mark. *The Rest of God: Restoring Your Soul by Restoring Sabbath*. Nashville: W Publishing Group, 2006.

Buckley, Michael J. *At the Origins of Modern Atheism*. New Haven: Yale University Press, 1987.

Bulgakov, Sergeĭ Nikolaevich. *The Lamb of God*. Grand Rapids: Eerdmans, 2008.

Burrell, David B. *Freedom and Creation in Three Traditions*. Notre Dame, IN: University of Notre Dame Press, 1993.

———. *Deconstructing Theodicy: Why Job Has Nothing to Say to the Puzzle of Suffering*. Grand Rapids: Brazos, 2008.

Burrell, David B., and Bernard McGinn, eds. *God and Creation: Ecumenical Symposium in Comparative Religious Thought*. Notre Dame, IN: University of Notre Dame Press, 1990.

Caird, G. B. *Principalities and Powers*. Oxford: Clarendon Press, 1956.

———. *The Revelation of St. John the Divine*. New York: Harper & Row, 1988.

Campbell, Douglas Atchison. *The Deliverance of God: An Apocalyptic Re-reading of Justification in Paul*. Grand Rapids: Eerdmans, 2009.

Carroll, John T. "Creation and Apocalypse." In *God Who Creates*, edited by W. Sibley Towner, William P. Brown, and S. Dean McBride, 251–60. Grand Rapids: Eerdmans, 2000.

Cashdollar, Charles D. *The Transformation of Theology, 1830–1890*. Princeton: Princeton University Press, 1989.

Cavanaugh, William T. *Being Consumed*. Grand Rapids: Eerdmans, 2008.

———. *Theopolitical Imagination*. London: T&T Clark, 2002.

———. *Torture and Eucharist: Theology, Politics, and the Body of Christ*. Oxford: Blackwell, 1998.

Charry, Ellen T. *By the Renewing of Your Minds*. New York: Oxford University Press, 1997.

———. *God and the Art of Happiness*. Grand Rapids: Eerdmans, 2010.

Childs, Brevard S. *Isaiah*. Louisville: Westminster John Knox, 2001.

———. *The Struggle to Understand Isaiah as Christian Scripture*. Grand Rapids: Eerdmans, 2004.

Clapp, Rodney. *A Peculiar People*. Downers Grove, IL: InterVarsity, 1996.

Cooper, John W. *Body, Soul, and Life Everlasting: Biblical Anthropology and the Monism-Dualism Debate*. Grand Rapids: Eerdmans, 2000.

Cranfield, C. E. B. *A Critical and Exegetical Commentary on the Epistle to the Romans*. 2 vols. London: T&T Clark, 2004.

Cunningham, Conor. *Darwin's Pious Idea: Why the Ultra-Darwinists and Creationists Both Get It Wrong*. Grand Rapids: Eerdmans, 2010.

Davis, Ellen F. *Scripture, Culture, and Agriculture: An Agrarian Reading of the Bible*. New York: Cambridge University Press, 2009.

Dawkins, Richard. *The Blind Watchmaker*. London: Penguin, 1991.

———. *The Selfish Gene*. Oxford: Oxford University Press, 1989.

Dawn, Marva J. *Keeping the Sabbath Wholly*. Grand Rapids: Eerdmans, 1989.

———. *Powers, Weakness, and the Tabernacling of God*. Grand Rapids: Eerdmans, 2001.

———. *Unfettered Hope: A Call to Faithful Living in an Affluent Society*. Louisville: Westminster John Knox, 2003.

Dawson, Gerrit Scott. *Jesus Ascended*. Phillipsburg, NJ: P&R, 2004.

Donovan, Vincent J. *The Church in the Midst of Creation*. Maryknoll, NY: Orbis Books, 1989.

Ehrman, Bart D. *The Orthodox Corruption of Scripture*. New York: Oxford University Press, 2011.

Ellul, Jacques. *The Presence of the Kingdom*. Translated by Olive Wyon. Colorado Springs: Helmers & Howard, 1989.

———. *The Technological Society*. Translated by John Wilkinson. With introduction by Robert K. Merton. New York: Alfred A. Knopf, 1964. Originally published as *La Technique ou l'enjeu du siècle*. Paris: Max Leclerc et Cie, 1954.

Evans, Craig A. *Fabricating Jesus*. Downers Grove, IL: IVP Books, 2006.

Farrer, Austin. *Faith and Speculation*. Edinburgh: T&T Clark, 1988.

———. *Finite and Infinite*. New York: Seabury Press, 1979.

———. *God Is Not Dead*. New York: Morehouse-Barlow, 1966.

Farrow, Douglas. *Ascension and Ecclesia*. Grand Rapids: Eerdmans, 1999.

———. *Ascension Theology*. London: T&T Clark, 2011.

Fee, Gordon D. *God's Empowering Presence: The Holy Spirit in the Letters of Paul*. Peabody, MA: Hendrickson, 1994.

Ford, David, and Graham Stanton. *Reading Texts, Seeking Wisdom: Scripture and Theology*. Grand Rapids: Eerdmans, 2004.

Fowl, Stephen E. *Engaging Scripture*. Malden, MA: Blackwell, 1998.

Fretheim, Terence E. *God and World in the Old Testament: A Relational Theology of Creation*. Nashville: Abingdon, 2005.

Funk, Robert Walter, and Roy W. Hoover, eds. *The Five Gospels: The Search for the Authentic Words of Jesus; New Translation and Commentary.* New York: Macmillan, 1993.

Funkenstein, Amos. *Theology and the Scientific Imagination from the Middle Ages to the Seventeenth Century.* Princeton: Princeton University Press, 1986.

Gillespie, Michael Allen. *The Theological Origins of Modernity.* Chicago: University of Chicago Press, 2008.

Girard, René. *I See Satan Fall Like Lightning.* Translated by James G. Williams. Maryknoll, NY: Orbis Books, 2001.

———. *The Scapegoat.* Translated by Yvonne Freccero. Baltimore: Johns Hopkins University Press, 1986.

———. *Things Hidden Since the Foundation of the World.* Translated by Stephen Bann and Michael Metteer. Stanford, CA: Stanford University Press, 1987.

Goldingay, John. *Israel's Faith.* Vol. 2 of *Old Testament Theology.* Downers Grove, IL: InterVarsity, 2006.

———. *Israel's Gospel.* Vol. 1 of *Old Testament Theology.* Downers Grove, IL: InterVarsity, 2003.

Gorman, Michael J. *Reading Revelation Responsibly: Uncivil Worship and Witness; Following the Lamb into the New Creation.* Eugene, OR: Cascade Books, 2011.

Gorringe, Timothy. *God's Theatre: A Theology of Providence.* London: SCM, 1991.

———. "The Principalities and Powers: A Framework for Thinking about Globalization." In *Globalization and the Good,* edited by Peter Somers Heslam, 79–91. Grand Rapids: Eerdmans, 2004.

———. *A Theology of the Built Environment.* Cambridge: Cambridge University Press, 2002.

Green, Joel B. *Body, Soul, and Human Life: The Nature of Humanity in the Bible.* Grand Rapids: Baker Academic, 2008.

Green, Joel B., and Max Turner. *Between Two Horizons: Spanning New Testament Studies and Systematic Theology.* Grand Rapids: Eerdmans, 2000.

Grenz, Stanley J. *The Millennial Maze: Sorting Out Evangelical Options.* Downers Grove, IL: InterVarsity, 1992.

———. *Rediscovering the Triune God: The Trinity in Contemporary Theology.* Minneapolis: Fortress, 2004.

Gundry, Robert Horton. *Soma in Biblical Theology: With Emphasis on Pauline Anthropology*. Cambridge: Cambridge University Press, 2005.

Gunton, Colin E. *The Actuality of Atonement: A Study of Metaphor, Rationality, and the Christian Tradition*. New York: T&T Clark, 2003.

———. *Christ and Creation*. 2nd ed. Eugene, OR: Wipf & Stock, 2005.

———. *The One, the Three, and the Many: God, Creation, and the Culture of Modernity*. Cambridge: Cambridge University Press, 1993.

———. "The Spirit Moved over the Face of the Waters: The Holy Spirit and the Created Order." *International Journal of Systematic Theology* 4, no. 2 (2002).

———. *The Triune Creator: A Historical and Systematic Study*. Grand Rapids: Eerdmans, 1998.

Gustafson, James M. *Ethics from a Theocentric Perspective*. 2 vols. Chicago: University of Chicago Press, 1981.

———. "Response to Hartt." *Soundings* 73, no. 4 (1990): 689–99.

———. *A Sense of the Divine*. Cleveland: Pilgrim Press, 1994.

Hall, Amy Laura. *Conceiving Parenthood: American Protestantism and the Spirit of Reproduction*. Grand Rapids: Eerdmans, 2008.

Hanson, Paul D. *Isaiah 40–66*. Interpretation. Louisville: John Knox Press, 1995.

Hardy, Daniel W. *God's Ways with the World*. Edinburgh: T&T Clark, 1996.

Harink, Douglas. *1 & 2 Peter*. Brazos Theological Commentary on the Bible. Grand Rapids: Brazos, 2009.

Hartt, Julian Norris. *A Christian Critique of American Culture: An Essay in Practical Theology*. New York: Harper & Row, 1967.

———. "Concerning God and Man and His Well-Being: A Commentary, Inspired by Spinoza, on Gustafson's 'Ethics from a Theocentric Perspective.'" *Soundings* 73, no. 4 (1990): 667–700.

———. *The Restless Quest*. Philadelphia: United Church Press, 1975.

———. *Theological Method and Imagination*. New York: Seabury Press, 1977.

Harvey, Barry. *Can These Bones Live? A Catholic Baptist Engagement with Ecclesiology, Hermeneutics, and Social Theory*. Grand Rapids: Brazos, 2008.

Hauerwas, Stanley. *With the Grain of the Universe: The Church's Witness and Natural Theology*. Grand Rapids: Brazos, 2001.

Hays, Richard B. *The Moral Vision of the New Testament: Community, Cross, New Creation; A Contemporary Introduction to New Testament Ethics*. San Francisco: HarperSanFrancisco, 1996.

Hebblethwaite, Brian. *The Philosophical Theology of Austin Farrer.* Leuven, Belgium: Peeters, 2007.

Heidel, Alexander. *The Babylonian Genesis: The Story of Creation.* Chicago: University of Chicago Press, 1963.

Horrell, David G., Cherryl Hunt, and Christopher Southatge. *Greening Paul: Rereading the Apostle in a Time of Ecological Crisis.* Waco: Baylor University Press, 2010.

Houston, J. M. *The Creator.* Edited by J. M. Houston. 4th ed. of *I Believe in the Creator* (Grand Rapids: Eerdmans, 1980). Colorado Springs: David C. Cook, 2007.

Howard, Thomas. *Christ the Tiger.* San Francisco: Ignatius Press, 1990.

Howard-Brook, Wes. *"Come Out, My People!": God's Call Out of Empire in the Bible and Beyond.* Maryknoll, NY: Orbis Books, 2010.

Hurtado, Larry W. *How on Earth Did Jesus Become a God?* Grand Rapids: Eerdmans, 2005.

———. *Lord Jesus Christ.* Grand Rapids: Eerdmans, 2003.

Hütter, Reinhard. *Suffering Divine Things.* Translated by Doug Stott. Grand Rapids: Eerdmans, 2000.

Irenaeus. *Against the Heresies.* Book 1. Translated by Dominic J. Unger. Ancient Christian Writers 55. New York: Paulist Press, 1991.

———. *Against the Heresies.* Book 2. Translated by Dominic J. Unger. Ancient Christian Writers 64. New York: Paulist Press, 2012.

———. *Against the Heresies.* Book 3. Translated by Dominic J. Unger. Ancient Christian Writers 65. New York: Paulist Press, 2010.

Jenkins, Willis. *Ecologies of Grace: Environmental Ethics and Christian Theology.* Oxford: Oxford University Press, 2008.

Jennings, Willie James. *The Christian Imagination: Theology and the Origins of Race.* New Haven: Yale University Press, 2010.

Jenson, Robert W. *The Triune God.* Vol. 1 of *Systematic Theology.* New York: Oxford University Press, 1997.

———. *The Works of God.* Vol. 2 of *Systematic Theology.* New York: Oxford University Press, 1999.

John Paul II. *Man and Woman He Created Them: A Theology of the Body.* Translated by Michael Waldstein. Boston: Pauline Books & Media, 2006.

Jonas, Hans. *The Gnostic Religion.* Boston: Beacon Press, 2001.

Kass, Leon. *The Beginning of Wisdom: Reading Genesis.* New York: Free Press, 2003.

Kaufman, Gordon D. *In the Beginning—Creativity*. Minneapolis: Fortress, 2004.

Kavanagh, Aidan. *On Liturgical Theology*. New York: Pueblo, 1984.

Keller, Catherine. *Face of the Deep*. London: Routledge, 2003.

———. *God and Power: Counter-Apocalyptic Journeys*. Minneapolis: Fortress, 2005.

Kelsey, David H. *Eccentric Existence: A Theological Anthropology*. Louisville: Westminster John Knox Press, 2009.

Kenneson, Philip D. *Life on the Vine: Cultivating the Fruit of the Spirit in Christian Community*. Downers Grove, IL: InterVarsity, 1999.

Kerr, Nathan R. *Christ, History and Apocalyptic: The Politics of Christian Mission*. Eugene, OR: Cascade Books, 2009.

Kidner, Derek. *The Proverbs: An Introduction and Commentary*. Tyndale Old Testament Commentaries. London: Inter-Varsity Press, 1964.

Kierkegaard, Søren. *Either/Or: Part 1*. Edited by Howard V. Hong. Translated by Howard V. Hong. Princeton: Princeton University Press, 1987.

———. *Either/Or: Part 2*. Edited by Howard V. Hong. Translated by Howard V. Hong. Princeton: Princeton University Press, 1987.

Kirk, J. R. Daniel. *Unlocking Romans: Resurrection and the Justification of God*. Grand Rapids: Eerdmans, 2008.

Kreeft, Peter. *Heaven, the Heart's Deepest Longing*. San Francisco: Ignatius Press, 1989.

Kruschwitz, Robert B., ed. *Moral Landscape of Creation*. Christian Reflection: A Series in Faith and Christian Ethics. No. 2 (2001).

———. *Sabbath*. Christian Reflection: A Series in Faith and Christian Ethics. No. 4 (2002).

Laansma, Jon. "The Cosmology of Hebrews." In *Cosmology and New Testament Theology*, edited by Jonathan T. Pennington and Sean M. McDonough, 125–43. London: T&T Clark, 2008.

———. "Hidden Stories in Hebrews: Cosmology and Theology." In *A Cloud of Witnesses: The Theology of Hebrews in Its Ancient Contexts*, edited by Richard Bauckham, Trevor Hart, Nathan MacDonald, and Daniel Driver, 9–18. London: T&T Clark, 2008.

Langford, Thomas A. *Reflections on Grace*. Edited by Philip A. Rolnick and Jonathan R. Wilson. Eugene, OR: Cascade Books, 2007.

Lee, Philip J. *Against the Protestant Gnostics*. New York: Oxford University Press, 1993.

Levenson, Jon Douglas. *Creation and the Persistence of Evil*. Princeton: Princeton University Press, 1994.

Lewis, C. S. *That Hideous Strength: A Modern Fairy-Tale for Grown-Ups.* London: HarperCollins, 2005.

———. *The Weight of Glory and Other Addresses.* San Francisco: Harper-SanFrancisco, 2001.

Longman, Tremper. *Proverbs.* Grand Rapids: Baker Academic, 2006.

———. "What Genesis 1–2 Teaches (and What It Doesn't)" in S. Daryl Charles, ed. *Reading Genesis 1–2.* Peabody, MA: Hendrickson, forthcoming.

Löning, Karl. *To Begin With, God Created . . . : Biblical Theologies of Creation.* Edited by Erich Zenger. Translated by Omar Kaste. Collegeville, MN: Liturgical Press, a Michael Glazier Book, 2000.

Macchia, Frank D. *Justified in the Spirit: Creation, Redemption, and the Triune God.* Grand Rapids: Eerdmans, 2010.

Machuga, Ric. *In Defense of the Soul: What It Means to Be Human.* Grand Rapids: Brazos, 2002.

MacIntyre, Alasdair C. *After Virtue: A Study in Moral Theory.* 3rd ed. Notre Dame, IN: University of Notre Dame Press, 2007.

———. *Three Rival Versions of Moral Enquiry: Encyclopaedia, Genealogy, and Tradition: Being Gifford Lectures Delivered in the University of Edinburgh in 1988.* Notre Dame, IN: University of Notre Dame Press, 1990.

———. *Whose Justice? Which Rationality?* Notre Dame, IN: University of Notre Dame Press, 1988.

MacKay, Donald MacCrimmon. *The Clockwork Image: A Christian Perspective on Science.* Leicester, England: Inter-Varsity Press, 1997.

Mackintosh, H. R. *The Doctrine of the Person of Jesus Christ.* New York: C. Scribner's Sons, 1912.

Mangina, Joseph L. *Revelation.* Brazos Theological Commentary on the Bible. Grand Rapids: Brazos, 2010.

Marlow, Hilary. *Biblical Prophets and Contemporary Environmental Ethics: Re-reading Amos, Hosea and First Isaiah.* Edited by John Barton. Oxford: Oxford University Press, 2009.

Marsden, George M. *The Outrageous Idea of Christian Scholarship.* New York: Oxford University Press, 1997.

———. *The Soul of the American University.* New York: Oxford University Press, 1994.

———. *Understanding Fundamentalism and Evangelicalism.* Grand Rapids: Eerdmans, 1991.

Martyn, J. Louis, ed. and trans. *Galatians.* New York: Doubleday, 1997.

———. *Theological Issues in the Letters of Paul.* London: Continuum, 2005.

McClendon, James William, and Nancey C. Murphy. *Systematic Theology.* Nashville: Abingdon, 1986. Revised edition. Waco: Baylor University Press, 2012.

McDonough, Sean M. *Christ as Creator.* Oxford: Oxford University Press, 2009.

McFague, Sallie. *The Body of God.* Minneapolis: Fortress, 1993.

McGrath, Alister E. *Dawkins' God.* Oxford: Blackwell, 2007.

———. *The Order of Things: Explorations in Scientific Theology.* Malden, MA: Blackwell, 2006.

———. *Nature.* Vol. 1 of *A Scientific Theology.* Edinburgh: T&T Clark, 2006.

———. *Reality.* Vol. 2 of *A Scientific Theology.* Edinburgh: T&T Clark, 2001.

———. *Theory.* Vol. 3 of *A Scientific Theology.* Edinburgh: T&T Clark, 2001.

———. *Understanding Jesus.* Grand Rapids: Academie Books, 1990.

McGrath, Alister E., and Joanna McGrath. *The Dawkins Delusion? Atheist Fundamentalism and the Denial of the Divine.* London: SPCK, 2007.

McMinn, Lisa Graham, and Megan Anna Neff. *Walking Gently on the Earth: Making Faithful Choices about Food, Energy, Shelter and More.* Downers Grove, IL: IVP Books, 2010.

Merchants of Cool. WGBH Educational Foundation, 2001.

Milbank, John. *Being Reconciled: Ontology and Pardon.* Radical Orthodoxy series. London: Routledge, 2003.

———. "Can a Gift Be Given? Prolegomena to a Future Trinitarian Metaphysic." *Modern Theology* 11, no. 1 (1995). doi:10.1111/j.1468-0025.1995.tb00055.x.

———. *The Future of Love: Essays in Political Theology.* Eugene, OR: Cascade Books, 2009.

———. *Theology and Social Theory: Beyond Secular Reason.* 2nd ed. Oxford: Blackwell, 2006.

Miller, Patrick D. *The Ten Commandments.* Louisville: Westminster John Knox Press, 2009.

Minear, Paul Sevier. *Christians and the New Creation: Genesis Motifs in the New Testament.* Louisville: Westminster John Knox, 1994.

———. "The Cosmology of the Apocalypse." In *Current Issues in New Testament Interpretation: Essays in Honor of Otto A. Piper*, edited by William Klassen and Graydon F. Snyder, 23–37. New York: Harper, 1962.

———. *I Saw a New Earth: An Introduction to the Visions of the Apocalypse.* Eugene, OR: Wipf & Stock, 2003.

Moltmann, Jürgen. *The Coming of God: Christian Eschatology*. Minneapolis: Fortress, 1996.

———. *God in Creation: A New Theology of Creation and the Spirit of God*. San Francisco: Harper & Row, 1985.

———. *The Spirit of Life: A Universal Affirmation*. Minneapolis: Fortress, 1992.

———. *The Trinity and the Kingdom: The Doctrine of God*. San Francisco: Harper & Row, 1981.

———. *The Way of Jesus Christ: Christology in Messianic Dimensions*. HarperSanFrancisco, 1990.

Moo, Jonathan. "Continuity, Discontinuity, and Hope: The Contribution of a New Testament Eschatology to a Distinctively Christian Environmental Ethos." *Tyndale Bulletin* 61, no. 1 (2010): 21–44.

Morse, Christopher. *The Difference Heaven Makes*. London: T&T Clark, 2010.

Mouw, Richard J. *When the Kings Come Marching In: Isaiah and the New Jerusalem*. Grand Rapids: Eerdmans, 1983. Revised edition, 2002.

Murphy, Nancey C. *Bodies and Souls, or Spirited Bodies?* Cambridge: Cambridge University Press, 2006.

Nee, Watchman. *The Normal Christian Life*. Wheaton: Tyndale House, 1977, 1985.

———. *Sit, Walk, Stand: The Process of Christian Maturity*. Fort Washington, PA: CLC Publications, 2009.

———. *The Spiritual Man*. New York: Christian Fellowship Publishers, 1977.

Neville, R. C. "On the Architecture of No Man's Land: A Response to Hartt and Gustafson." *Soundings* 73, no. 4 (1990): 701–25.

Newbigin, Lesslie. *Foolishness to the Greeks: The Gospel and Western Culture*. Grand Rapids: Eerdmans, 1986.

———. *The Gospel in a Pluralist Society*. London: SPCK, 1989.

Nichols, Terence L. *The Sacred Cosmos: Christian Faith and the Challenge of Naturalism*. Grand Rapids: Brazos, 2003.

Noll, Mark A. *The Scandal of the Evangelical Mind*. Grand Rapids: Eerdmans, 1994.

Northcott, Michael S. *An Angel Directs the Storm: Apocalyptic Religion and American Empire*. London: I. B. Tauris, 2004.

———. *The Environment and Christian Ethics*. Cambridge: Cambridge University Press, 1996.

———. *Moral Climate: The Ethics of Global Warming*. Maryknoll, NY: Orbis Books, 2007.

Packer, J. I. "What Did the Cross Achieve? The Logic of Penal Substitution." *Tyndale Bulletin* 25 (1974): 3–45.

Pagels, Elaine H. *The Gnostic Gospels*. New York: Vintage Books, 1981.

Pannenberg, Wolfhart. *Systematic Theology*. Translated by Geoffrey W. Bromiley. 3 vols. Grand Rapids: Eerdmans, 1991, 1994, 1997.

Paulsell, Stephanie. *Honoring the Body: Meditations on a Christian Practice*. San Francisco: Jossey-Bass, 2003.

Percy, Walker. *Love in the Ruins*. New York: Picador USA, 1999.

———. *The Thanatos Syndrome*. New York: Picador USA/Farrar, Straus, Giroux, 1999.

Peterson, Eugene H. *Christ Plays in Ten Thousand Places*. Grand Rapids: Eerdmans, 2005.

———. *The Contemplative Pastor*. Grand Rapids: Eerdmans, 1993.

———. *Reversed Thunder*. San Francisco: HarperSanFrancisco, 1991.

Phillips, J. B. *The New Testament in Modern English for Schools*. Revised ed. London: Collins, 1972.

Pinnock, Clark H. *Flame of Love: A Theology of the Holy Spirit*. Downers Grove, IL: InterVarsity, 1996.

Piper, John. *The Future of Justification: A Response to N. T. Wright*. Wheaton: Crossway, 2007.

Plantinga, Alvin. *God and Other Minds*. Ithaca, NY: Cornell University Press, 1990.

———. *God, Freedom, and Evil*. Grand Rapids: Eerdmans, 1977.

Polkinghorne, J. C., and Michael Welker, eds. *The End of the World and the Ends of God*. Harrisburg, PA: Trinity Press International, 2000.

Pollan, Michael. *The Omnivore's Dilemma: A Natural History of Four Meals*. New York: Penguin Press, 2006.

Post, Stephen Garrard, et al., eds. *Altruism & Altruistic Love: Science, Philosophy, & Religion in Dialogue*. Oxford: Oxford University Press, 2002.

Postman, Neil. *Amusing Ourselves to Death*. Revised ed. New York: Penguin Books, 2006.

———. *Technopoly: The Surrender of Culture to Technology*. New York: Vintage Books, 1993.

Rolnick, Philip A. *Person, Grace, and God*. Grand Rapids: Eerdmans, 2007.

Rusch, William G., ed. *The Trinitarian Controversy*. Philadelphia: Fortress Press, 1980.

Rust, Eric Charles. *Science and Faith*. New York: Oxford University Press, 1967.

Schaeffer, Francis A. *Pollution and the Death of Man*. Wheaton: Tyndale House, 1970.

Scheffczyk, Leo. *Creation and Providence*. London: Burns & Oates, 1970.

Schenck, Kenneth. *Cosmology and Eschatology in Hebrews*. Cambridge: Cambridge University Press, 2007.

Schmemann, Alexander. *For the Life of the World: Sacraments and Orthodoxy*. Crestwood, NY: St. Vladimir's Seminary Press, 2004.

Schreiner, Susan E. *The Theater of His Glory: Nature and Natural Order in the Thought of John Calvin*. Grand Rapids: Baker Academic, 2001.

Schweizer, Eduard. *The Holy Spirit*. Translated by Reginald H. Fuller. Philadelphia: Fortress, 1980.

Snyder, Howard A. *Salvation Means Creation Healed*. Edited by Joel Scandrett. Eugene, OR: Cascade Books, 2011.

Stackhouse, John G. *Can God Be Trusted? Faith and the Challenge of Evil*. Oxford: Oxford University Press, 2000.

———. *Making the Best of It: Following Christ in the Real World*. New York: Oxford University Press, 2011.

———, ed. *What Does It Mean to Be Saved?* Grand Rapids: Baker Academic, 2002.

Stearns, Richard. *The Hole in Our Gospel*. Nashville: Thomas Nelson, 2009.

Steinmetz, David. "Uncovering a Second Narrative: Detective Fiction and the Construction of Historical Method." In *The Art of Reading Scripture*, edited by Ellen F. Davis and Richard B. Hays, 54–65. Grand Rapids: Eerdmans, 2003.

Surin, Kenneth. *Theology and the Problem of Evil*. Eugene, OR: Wipf & Stock, 2004.

Swartley, Willard M. *Covenant of Peace*. Grand Rapids: Eerdmans, 2006.

Taylor, Charles. *The Ethics of Authenticity*. Cambridge, MA: Harvard University Press, 1992.

———. *Philosophy and the Human Sciences*. Philosophical Papers 2. Cambridge: Cambridge University Press, 1985.

———. *A Secular Age*. Cambridge, MA: Belknap Press of Harvard University Press, 2007.

———. *Sources of the Self: The Making of the Modern Identity*. Cambridge, MA: Harvard University Press, 1989.

Thompson, Marianne Meye. *Colossians and Philemon*. Grand Rapids: Eerdmans, 2005.

Tilley, Terrence W. *The Evils of Theodicy*. Eugene, OR: Wipf & Stock, 2000.

Tolkien, J. R. R. *The Monsters and the Critics, and Other Essays*. Edited by Christopher Tolkien. London: Allen & Unwin, 1983.

Torrance, Thomas F. *Atonement*. Edited by Robert T. Walker. Milton Keynes, England: Paternoster, 2009.

———. *The Christian Doctrine of God, One Being Three Persons*. Edinburgh: T&T Clark, 2001.

———. *The Trinitarian Faith*. Edinburgh: T&T Clark, 1988.

Towner, W. Sibley. "Clones of God: Genesis 1:26–28 and the Image of God in the Hebrew Bible." *Interpretation* 59, no. 4 (2005): 341–56.

Tracy, Thomas F. *God, Action, and Embodiment*. Grand Rapids: Eerdmans, 1984.

Tran, Jonathan. *The Vietnam War and Theologies of Memory*. Chichester, England: Wiley-Blackwell, 2010.

Treier, Daniel J. *Introducing Theological Interpretation of Scripture: Recovering a Christian Practice*. Grand Rapids: Baker Academic, 2008.

———. *Proverbs & Ecclesiastes*. Brazos Theological Commentary on the Bible. Grand Rapids: Brazos, 2011.

Vanhoozer, Kevin J., Craig G. Bartholomew, Daniel J. Treier, and N. T. Wright, eds. *Dictionary for Theological Interpretation of the Bible*. Grand Rapids: Baker Academic, 2005.

Volf, Miroslav. "On Loving with Hope: Eschatology and Social Responsibility." *Transformation: An International Journal of Holistic Mission Studies* 7, no. 3. doi:10.1177/026537889000700314.

Wallace, Mark I. *Fragments of the Spirit: Nature, Violence, and the Renewal of Creation*. Harrisburg, PA: Trinity Press International, 2002.

Waltke, Bruce K. *The Book of Proverbs*. Grand Rapids: Eerdmans, 2004.

———. *An Old Testament Theology*. Edited by Charles Yu. Grand Rapids: Zondervan, 2007.

Waltke, Bruce K., and Cathi J. Fredricks. *Genesis: A Commentary*. Grand Rapids: Zondervan, 2001.

Waltke, Bruce K., J. M. Houston, and Erika Moore. *The Psalms as Christian Worship: A Historical Commentary*. Grand Rapids: Eerdmans, 2010.

Walton, John H. *The Lost World of Genesis One: Ancient Cosmology and the Origins Debate*. Downers Grove, IL: IVP Academic, 2009.

Webber, Robert. *Ancient-Future Faith: Rethinking Evangelicalism for a Post-modern World*. Grand Rapids: Baker Books, 1999.

Westermann, Claus. *Genesis 1–11: A Continental Commentary*. Minneapolis: Fortress, 1994.

Wilken, Robert Louis. *Isaiah*. Grand Rapids: Eerdmans, 2007.

———. *The Spirit of Early Christian Thought*. New Haven: Yale University Press, 2003.

Willard, Dallas. *The Divine Conspiracy*. San Francisco: HarperSanFrancisco, 1998.

Williams, Stephen. "The Partition of Love and Hope: Eschatology and Social Responsibility." *Transformation: An International Journal of Holistic Mission Studies* 7, no. 3 (1990). doi:10.1177/026537889000700313.

Williamson, H. G. M. *Holy, Holy, Holy: The Story of a Liturgical Formula*. Berlin: Walter de Gruyter, 2008.

Wilson, Edward O. *Biophilia*. Cambridge, MA: Harvard University Press, 1984.

———. *The Creation: An Appeal to Save Life on Earth*. New York: W. W. Norton, 2006.

Wilson, Jonathan R. "Do Pietists Need a Doctrine of Creation?" *Pacific Journal of Baptist Research* 6, no. 1 (2010): 65–78.

———. *God So Loved the World: A Christology for Disciples*. Grand Rapids: Baker Academic, 2001.

———. *Gospel Virtues: Practicing Faith, Hope & Love in Uncertain Times*. Downers Grove, IL: InterVarsity, 1998.

———. *Living Faithfully in a Fragmented World*. Eugene, OR: Cascade Books, 2010.

———. *A Primer for Christian Doctrine*. Grand Rapids: Eerdmans, 2005.

———. Review of *Divine Freedom and the Doctrine of the Immanent Trinity: In Dialogue with Karl Barth and Contemporary Theology*, by Paul D. Molnar. *Pro Ecclesia* 13, no. 1 (Winter 2004): 108–9.

———. Review of *The Trinity*, by Roger E. Olson and Christopher A. Hall. *Perspectives in Religious Studies* 31, no. 2 (Summer 2004): 242–47.

———. "Simpletons, Fools, and Mockers." *Christian Reflection: A Series in Faith and Ethics*, no. 5 (Winter 2002): 24–30.

———. *Theology as Cultural Critique*. Macon, GA: Mercer, 1996.

———. "Toward a New Evangelical Paradigm of Biblical Authority." In *The Nature of Confession: Postliberals and Evangelicals in Conversation*, edited by Dennis Okholm and Timothy Phillips, 151–61. Downers Grove, IL: InterVarsity, 1996.

———. *Why Church Matters*. Grand Rapids: Brazos, 2006.

Wilson-Hartgrove, Jonathan. *The Awakening of Hope: Why We Practice a Common Faith*. Grand Rapids: Zondervan, 2012.

Wink, Walter. *Engaging the Powers*. Minneapolis: Fortress, 1992.

———. *Naming the Powers*. Philadelphia: Fortress, 1984.

———. *Unmasking the Powers*. Philadelphia: Fortress, 1986.

Wirzba, Norman. *Food and Faith: A Theology of Eating*. New York: Cambridge University Press, 2011.

———. *Living the Sabbath: Discovering the Rhythms of Rest and Delight*. Grand Rapids: Brazos, 2006.

———. *The Paradise of God: Renewing Religion in an Ecological Age*. Oxford: Oxford University Press, 2007.

Wiseman, P. J. *Clues to Creation in Genesis*. London: Marshall, Morgan & Scott, 1977. Originally published in two volumes: *New Discoveries in Babylonia about Genesis* (1936) and *Creation Revealed in Six Days* (1948).

Wolterstorff, Nicholas. *Justice: Rights and Wrongs*. Princeton: Princeton University Press, 2008.

Work, Telford. *Deuteronomy*. Grand Rapids: Brazos, 2009.

Wright, Christopher J. H. *God's People in God's Land: Family, Land, and Property in the Old Testament*. Grand Rapids: Eerdmans; Exeter, England: Paternoster, 1990.

———. *Old Testament Ethics for the People of God*. Downers Grove, IL: InterVarsity, 2004.

Wright, N. T. *Justification*. Downers Grove, IL: IVP Academic, 2009.

———. *The Resurrection of the Son of God*. London: SPCK, 2003.

———. *Surprised by Hope*. New York: HarperOne, 2012.

Yoder, John Howard. "Armaments and Eschatology." *Studies in Christian Ethics* 1, no. 1 (1988): 43–61.

———. *The Politics of Jesus: Vicit Agnus Noster*. 2nd ed. Grand Rapids: Eerdmans, 1994.

———. *The Priestly Kingdom: Social Ethics as Gospel*. Notre Dame, IN: University of Notre Dame Press, 1984.

Yordy, Laura. *Green Witness: Ecology, Ethics, and the Kingdom of God*. Eugene, OR: Cascade Books, 2008.

Notes on the Artwork

Some thoughts from the artist Joy Banks and the author on the artwork found throughout the book.

"Waiting" page 2

Jonathan: This image, with an aesthetic different from the other prints in this book, powerfully portrays the effects of the absence of the doctrine of creation and the waiting—the longing—of all creation.

"Mustard Seed" page 48

Joy: This print was inspired by the parable of the mustard seed, in which the Kingdom of God is likened to a tiny seed that grows into a large tree where many creatures find home and rest.

Jonathan: The dialectic of creation and redemption is the kingdom of God.

"Behold" page 100

Jonathan: Not every image needs words.

"Growing Together" page 124

Jonathan: Joy created this image to guide a ministry in which she served. This portrays simply the call upon God's people to come together as witnesses to the disarming of the principalities and powers so that we may be liberated, united, healed, and thus flourish along with the rest of creation. This vision is described on pages 140–42 and elaborated in part 3.

"Psalm 46" page 130

Joy: This image was inspired by my friend, Peter La Grand's, musical rendition of Psalm 46. The line of the psalm, "There is a river whose streams make glad the city of God," made me think of the slums I had just visited in Asia, and I began to wonder what it would be like to read these slums as the city of God. What kind of river would make glad these humble dwelling places of God? I have put the image of the slum on the hem of Christ's garment, the place of healing, and from there Christ rises, releasing doves of peace to end war and other mechanisms of death.

"Bottled (Bird in a Bottle)" page 210

Joy: Part of a series of bird prints used for a friend's CD booklet, this image has several layers of possible meanings. On one level it is a bird in a bottle, a critique of the ways in which consumerism has bottled and destroyed wild life. As a tropical bird, a parrot, and a bottle of a North American multinational corporation, Coke, the image can also be read as a commentary on the ways in which multinational corporations of wealthy nations have exploited poorer nations. Finally it is also a metaphor for the ways in which we also allow ourselves to be bottled by consumerism. In many ways we too are like this parrot.

Jonathan: This offers a more powerful prophetic witness to consuming and being consumed than all my words.

"Sowing Seeds" page 228

Joy: This image was inspired by some lines in my friend, Tom Wuest's, CD, "Although I am weeping, Lord, help me keep sowing seeds for the day when your peace will arise with the dawn." I used icon references in this image as my tribute to the "saintliness" of all who sow seeds of peace in the midst of seemingly insurmountable odds. The farmer is blessing this seedling with the sign of Christ, the one who holds our hope that these seeds can grow.

Jonathan: This image beautifully teaches the fertility of meekness for the life of all creation.

"Gather 'Round" page 258

Joy: The rhythm that gathers us. The Spirit that stirs us. Many cultures. Many ages. One body broken. The center that holds us.

Subject Index

Scripture Index